Advance Praise for

Living As Learning

Both Dewey scholars and initiates to his work will be fascinated by the discussion of connections between his ideas and those of Tsunesaburo Makiguchi, the "value creator." The collegial relationship that both Dewey and Makiguchi described between mentor and disciple (teacher and student) is especially valuable in this age of dull, one-way, authoritarian pedagogy. Readers will be encouraged to renew efforts to establish genuine education in the United States and abroad.

—Nel Noddings, Lee L. Jacks Professor of Education, Emerita, at Stanford University, and author, *Caring: A Relational Approach to Ethics and Moral Education*

In this timely book, two outstanding philosophers—Jim Garrison and Larry Hickman—engage President Daisaku Ikeda of the Soka Gakkai International in a wide-ranging exchange about the enduring value of John Dewey's philosophy of life and of education. The book offers an intellectual and ethical richness that will provoke, inform, and inspire readers. Listen in on the dialogue, and learn.

—David T. Hansen, Weinberg Professor of Philosophy and Education, Teachers College, Columbia University

I urge you to read and ponder this book. I have studied John Dewey's work for over forty years. Less than a decade ago, I became acquainted with the educational contributions of Tsunesaburo Makiguchi, the great Japanese scholar-practitioner of education. Recognizing similarities in their humanistic pedagogies, I yearned to hear Dewey and Makiguchi in dialogue, but did not think it possible. Not until now!

In *Living As Learning*, Jim Garrison and Larry Hickman, two of the most astute students of Dewey's contributions, join Daisaku Ikeda, the premier student of Josei Toda (who was the foremost student of Makiguchi) to provide a beautifully expressed, intellectually stimulating, and compellingly hopeful seedbed for educational action. Reading this book makes me feel as if I am experiencing Dewey and Makiguchi in dialogue that grows through myriad ideas (past, present, and possible) and a mutual quest for peace and justice. This dialogue should inspire readers to do their best to envision and enact a more humane world.

—William H. Schubert, Professor Emeritus of Curriculum and Instruction at the University of Illinois at Chicago, and author, *Love, Justice, and Education: John Dewey and the Utopians*

In this invigorating and wide-ranging dialogue, scholars Jim Garrison and Larry Hickman and Buddhist leader Daisaku Ikeda come together to explore powerful ideas of great learning and flourishing living drawn from the legacies of John Dewey, Tsunesaburo Makiguchi, and other inspiring thinkers. These ideas help cultivate a philosophical and educational landscape that commits not only to the shared interests of diverse individuals and groups, but also to our shared potential for creative, harmonious, and joyful *living as learning* in an increasingly complex, complicated, and contested world.

—Ming Fang He, Professor of Curriculum Studies at Georgia Southern University

Living As Learning

Living As Learning

John Dewey in the 21st Century

JIM GARRISON
LARRY HICKMAN
DAISAKU IKEDA

Dialogue Path Press
Cambridge, Massachusetts
2014

Published by Dialogue Path Press
Ikeda Center for Peace, Learning, and Dialogue
396 Harvard Street
Cambridge, Massachusetts 02138

Printed in the United States of America

Cover design by Gopa & Ted2, Inc.
Interior design by Gopa & Ted2, Inc., and Eric Edstam

ISBN: 978-1-887917-12-4

Library of Congress Cataloging-in-Publication data
has been applied for.

10 9 8 7 6 5 4 3 2 1

About Dialogue Path Press

Dialogue Path Press is the publishing arm of the Ikeda Center for Peace, Learning, and Dialogue, and is dedicated to publishing titles that foster cross-cultural dialogue and greater human flourishing. Books published by the Center (including those produced in collaboration with other publishers) have been used in more than 800 college and university courses. Previous titles are:

The Art of True Relations: Conversations on the Poetic Heart of Human Possibility (2014)

America Will Be!: Conversations on Hope, Freedom, and Democracy (2013)

The Inner Philosopher: Conversations on Philosophy's Transformative Power (2012)

Into Full Flower: Making Peace Cultures Happen (2010)

Creating Waldens: An East-West Conversation on the American Renaissance (2009)

About the Ikeda Center

The Ikeda Center for Peace, Learning, and Dialogue is a not-for-profit institution founded by Buddhist thinker and leader Daisaku Ikeda in 1993. Located in Cambridge, Massachusetts, the Center engages diverse scholars, activists, and social innovators in the search for the ideas and solutions that will assist in the peaceful evolution of humanity. Ikeda Center programs include public forums and scholarly seminars that are organized collaboratively and offer a range of perspectives on key issues in global ethics. The Center was initially called the Boston Research Center for the 21st Century and became the Ikeda Center in 2009.

For more information, visit the Ikeda Center website:
www.ikedacenter.org

Table of Contents

Left to Right: Jim Garrison, Larry Hickman, Daisaku Ikeda

CONVERSATION ONE

What Dewey Stood For

IKEDA: "Democracy begins in conversation."[1] John Dewey made this assertion in a speech on his ninetieth birthday. These words epitomize the great American educator's philosophy. Conversation, dialogue, is indeed the essence of democracy.

Without openhearted dialogue, the human spirit stops growing and withers away. Without intellectual and spiritual exchange, society rigidifies and grinds to a halt. Dewey clearly pointed out the path to the unfettered development of humanity and society.

It gives me the greatest pleasure and is a sincere honor to begin this dialogue with Dr. Jim Garrison, past president of the John Dewey Society (2007–2009), and Dr. Larry Hickman, past president of the John Dewey Society (2005–2007) and current director of the Center for Dewey Studies (1993–). I deeply respect both of you for keeping Dewey's thought alive today.

GARRISON: I am honored. As I mentioned on the occasion of our first meeting, in Nagano, Japan, in August 2008, your eyes impressed me most at the time. On that day, you kindly answered each of our questions with eyes as bright as those with which you must have seen Josei Toda for the first time, when you were a nineteen-year-old youth.[2] Given how much I enjoyed our conversation then, I look forward to further energetic dialogue.

Ikeda: Thank you for your kind words. You said then that true value creation is achieved through dialogue. I completely agree with you. My hope is that our dialogue will be exhaustive, expansive, and sufficiently infused with the youthful breath of life to radiate the light of value creation and education—consistent with the highest human values—to those responsible for the twenty-first century, the youth.

Living in the Fullest Sense

Hickman: First, President Ikeda, let me say what an honor it is to begin this conversation with you and Dr. Garrison. I have long admired your many accomplishments, including those in the fields of peace, human rights, and education. The two great universities that you have founded in Japan and the United States are testimony to your commitment to a better human future.

Ikeda: Thank you for your profound understanding. Professor Hickman, you are kind enough to serve on the Board of Trustees of Soka University of America. I am grateful for the valuable advice you frequently give us and the way you warmly encourage our students on campus. Many of them have expressed their happiness at engaging in meaningful exchanges with you, too, Professor Garrison, when you visited SUA in January 2008. I am sure that Dewey would look with favor on the encouragement you give them. As founder, I am grateful to you both.

Garrison: As a Deweyan educator, I see SUA as a very good expression of student-centered, not student-indulgent, education.

Everywhere I went on the SUA campus, I found students in dialogue with faculty members and one another. It is significant that students and faculty engaged in dialogue with staff members. The lunchroom staff, the custodial service, and the groundskeepers all greeted and chatted with students and faculty in what was a very good learning community.

I have seen for myself how the student-centered system permeates Soka University in Tokyo, Soka Women's College, and the Soka schools[3] as well. All of the institutions I visited are clearly on the right path.

HICKMAN: From meeting many of them, I know that SUA students are encouraged to honor their university mottos[4] by becoming "philosophers of a renaissance of life," "world citizens in solidarity for peace," and "pioneers of a global civilization." We know that progress toward these goals is possible only when the administration, faculty, and staff work together to create an environment in which administrators support the cutting-edge research that overflows into great teaching, which, in turn, receives the sustained logistical support of staff members who view their efforts as central to the mission of the university.

IKEDA: Warm encouragement from two such outstanding teachers delights me more than I can say. Your remarks are a source of great pride for the faculties of our educational institutions.

Professor Garrison, you have spoken about the need for rich interchanges and a caring, inspiring atmosphere between students and faculty, and among students themselves, and have praised SUA for demonstrating the kind of right relationship that Dewey considered essential to the development of individual potential[5]—an assessment for which I express my gratitude and appreciation.

Professor Hickman, in a personal message you sent to the first SUA commencement exercises (May 2005), you said:

> I am confident that if the great educators Tsunesaburo Makiguchi[6] and John Dewey could be present on this occasion they would join me in celebrating the educational values of Soka University of America. . . . They shared the idea that education is not so much *preparation* for living, but rather living *in the fullest sense of the word.*

I believe that you have summed up here the educational philosophies of both Dr. Dewey and Mr. Makiguchi.

Garrison: When I read the Lotus Sutra, I was deeply moved by its reverence for life. I know that this reverence for life pervades the mission of the Soka Gakkai. *Living*, in the fullest sense of the word, is the highest form of reverence. It is universal wisdom. The same sense of reverence guides the educational philosophies of both Mr. Makiguchi and Dr. Dewey. In creative dialogue with others, students at SUA have wonderful opportunities to learn and grow.

To Continually Question

Ikeda: I am grateful to you for indicating an extremely important point in connection with the meaning of Soka, or value-creating, education.

During his long life, Dewey wrote many books and essays that had tremendous intellectual influence around the world. The Outlawry of War movement,[7] promoted by Dewey and others near the end of World War I, was a philosophical influence on Japan's Peace Constitution,[8] promulgated in 1947. His educational philosophy was important to the reformation and democratization of education in Japan after World War II. Subsequent calls for the reformation of education have repeatedly advocated a return to his educational philosophy. In this sense, he has had a profound influence on all Japanese, and the Japanese people are deeply beholden to him.

Tsunesaburo Makiguchi and Josei Toda founded the Soka Kyoiku Gakkai (Value-Creating Education Society), later renamed the Soka Gakkai (Value-Creating Society), in 1930. In 2010, we celebrated the eightieth anniversary of the founding of our organization. Both men had the greatest respect for John Dewey, which to me imparts even greater significance to our present dialogue.

It is interesting that the names *Dewey* and *Makiguchi* share a connection. *Dewey* derives from the Flemish name *de Wei*, which means "of the meadows." The first Chinese character in Makiguchi's name, *maki*, means "pasture," and the second, *guchi*, "entrance." The two thinkers both advocated harmony between human beings and nature—an idea that seems to be reflected in their names.

HICKMAN: You point out an interesting connection between the two surnames and the interface between nature and humanity that I had never considered. Long before environmentalism existed as a movement, Dewey was already contributing to what we today would call environmental philosophy.

In 1898, at the age of thirty-eight, he published a seminal essay on the subject.[9] Thomas Huxley, an ardent defender of the evolutionary theory of Charles Darwin, had argued that there are two opposing orders: an artificial, ethical, human order and a natural, amoral, cosmic order. Dewey rejected Huxley's model. He argued that we as human beings should not be in conflict with the natural order, since we are an important part of it. It is up to us to manage one part of our natural environment artfully with reference to other parts, to work for balance and harmony. Dewey's views were very close to those of the pioneering American environmentalist Aldo Leopold.

Garrison: As a young student, Dewey read a book on physiology by Huxley, *The Elements of Physiology and Hygiene*,[10] in which he found an expression of organic, living unity that was tremendously appealing to him. Now, of course, you are thinking what I am thinking, which is that what life means in your Buddhist tradition means a great deal to Dewey as well. It was that dynamic, homeostatic sense of unity—the organic unity of life—that he found in Huxley.

It must have been a great disappointment to him that Huxley later claimed that there was a dualism between human beings and the natural order, as Professor Hickman points out. Dewey had to respond to such a serious mistake.

Ikeda: Dewey wrote, "The processes of living are enacted by the environment as truly as the organism; for they *are* an integration."[11] His idea that all things are connected and interdependent, integrated with the environment, within which everything lives and develops, is closely related to Buddhist teachings, like the doctrines of dependent origination and the oneness of life and its environment, which I want to discuss in detail later on.

As is indicated by his attitude toward Huxley's view of life, Dewey always maintained his independence toward ideas, critically examining other scholars' thoughts, accepting some and rejecting others, regardless of their authors' fame or authority. In this, he demonstrated his experiential and pragmatic way of living and thinking.

Hickman: Dewey held the experimental sciences, including the social sciences, in high regard because of their independence from claims based on authority. He thought that our world—including the part we call *social*—reveals much to us, but that those revelations are just a start.

It is our responsibility as individuals and communities to build up from those beginnings to enrich the meanings of human experience. In order to do so, we must continually question received views to determine whether they are true, and we must challenge the opinions of even the most famous and powerful when they obstruct what he called "growth" and what Makiguchi called "value creation." One of the central ideas of the philosophical movement known as pragmatism, which Dewey founded together with Charles Sanders Peirce and William James, is that it is the conceivable consequence of an idea, and not its source, that constitutes meaning.

Growing Up Dewey

Ikeda: At this point, I think we should examine Dewey's childhood and the historical background that contributed to the development of his personality and thought. He was born on October 20, 1859—two years before the outbreak of the Civil War—in Burlington, Vermont, on the shores of Lake Champlain. His parents ran a grocery store and had four sons, of whom John was the third.

What were his mother and father like?

Garrison: Dewey's father, Archibald Sprague Dewey, was a man of action and a businessman. He would have been about fifty when the Civil War started. He volunteered and went off to war.

Dewey's mother, Lucina Artemisia Rich Dewey, was a reformed Congregationalist who believed that people get into heaven by undertaking socially responsible and moral action in the world. In addition to being good to her husband and children, she was involved in the community.

A child born before John, John Archibald Dewey, was accidentally scalded to death in the bathtub. Demonstrative of an interesting family dynamic, his parents considered John, born ten months later, a replacement child.

Dewey's mother constantly questioned the state of her sons' souls and whether John was "right with Jesus." This made Dewey strongly dislike excessive introspection. In his written works, he mentioned very little that was introspective.

However, she also wanted him to have a first-rate education and expected him to be engaged in the community and in social amelioration. Clearly this attitude remained with him throughout life, growing into great interest in the social reform actions that had been dear to his mother. Dewey developed a great concern with ameliorative action in real time in this world, which involved him in politics and public affairs, making him perhaps the most prominent intellectual writing in English in the twentieth century. Of course, this often made him quite controversial.

IKEDA: Dewey's strong social concern, it can then be said, was something he inherited from his mother. Thank you for so clearly identifying the origins of his preference for positive action as opposed to introspective thought—an extremely important point in understanding Dewey.

What kind of a place was the Burlington of his youth?

HICKMAN: It was a small town, and several of its aspects played an important role in the formation of his character. First, it was the home of the University of Vermont. Members of the university faculty were among the Dewey family's friends and neighbors, so he was introduced to the possibility of an academic career from early childhood.

Second, Burlington is surrounded by the natural beauty of lakes and mountains. Throughout his life, Dewey sought out such places of beauty—Long Island in New York, Nova Scotia in Canada, and Key West in Florida, among others—in order to refresh himself and gather strength. He understood the importance of exercise and was an avid swimmer well into his eighties. It is possible that his love of exercise contributed to his very long and productive life span of ninety-two years.

Third, and perhaps most important, Dewey's hometown was a major lumber depot employing many immigrants, including French-speaking Canadians.

GARRISON: Burlington is lovely, but the Burlington that Dewey grew up in was already an industrial city, quite diverse for its time. Ample records reveal its vice and horrible working conditions. The place where young Dewey delivered newspapers and tallied lumber was a far cry from today's small, idyllic Vermont town.

HICKMAN: Dewey's life in Burlington prepared him for the massive waves of immigration and the brutal industrialization he would encounter in Chicago between 1894 and 1904. It was during this period, of course, that he served on the board of Hull House, the famous settlement house founded by Jane Addams, who would later be awarded the Nobel Peace Prize.

IKEDA: Starting as a place to teach immigrant workers and help integrate them as active members of society, Hull House later became a center of support for the poor and efforts to improve labor conditions. In those days in the United States, the rapid development of capitalism bred poverty and discrimination, aggravating social tensions and contradictions, destroying established values, and leading to conflicts and schisms. The situation foreshadowed present social problems and inequities.

Dewey was eager to participate in Jane Addams's welfare work, and he sought new social and educational models. His actions in these directions must have greatly influenced his people-centered, practical, pragmatic philosophy.

Professor Garrison, do you perceive any similarities between Dewey's personality and thought and your own life?

GARRISON: No! My life and John Dewey's life are very different. I feel a deep affinity, however, with the way his insights help satisfy a need for unity—not a static but a dynamic, ever-evolving unity, a process of equilibrium followed by disequilibrium and finally restored equilibrium. This is the rhythm of growth.

I think many people find him and his works attractive because he seeks unity in difference and diversity, not reduction of difference to uniformity. That is why he appeals to people from all kinds of places, all walks of life. Dewey is read and appreciated in many cultures, because his notion of unity includes diversity and never strives to homogenize divergent viewpoints. It is an evolving and dynamic unity, and people have an affinity for it.

MORAL COURAGE

IKEDA: Dewey's philosophy offers a creative integrating force. He sought a way of living that vibrantly embodies the dynamism inherent in life itself. His concept was indeed a dynamic, evolving unity recognizing differences, harmonizing diversity, and restoring equilibrium. It is sure to be an important outlook for the creation of a peaceful society in the twenty-first century.

Professor Hickman, do you agree?

HICKMAN: You have made a very important point, without which we cannot fully appreciate Dewey's contribution to global ethics and world peace. Regarding the matter of diversity in the United States, for example, he wrote that he had always found the "melting pot" metaphor distasteful. The same feeling that leads us to recognize and respect one another's individuality should also lead us to recognize and respect different cultural traits.

I believe that it was this attitude that made him so popular during his visit to China. He is still regarded by many Chinese as the personification of a cultural bridge between their country and the United States.

IKEDA: I have discussed the same thing with many Chinese scholars. We can learn an essential quality for global citizenship from Dr. Dewey's greatness as a human being.

Earlier, we mentioned common points between John Dewey and Tsunesaburo Makiguchi, who, twelve years the younger of the two, lived in a world of upheaval similar to the one Dewey knew. Hypothetically, the two men might have met: In 1919, Dewey, fifty-nine at the time, was conducting a busy, three-month lecture tour in Japan. He arrived in February and, while in Japan, he and his wife stayed mainly at the home of Inazo Nitobe, educator and later under-secretary-general of the League of Nations. At the time, Makiguchi was on close terms with Nitobe and attended monthly meetings at the Nitobe home of the Kyodo-kai, a study and research group on Japanese regional and folk culture.

HICKMAN: It would be wonderful if evidence of a meeting between Dewey and Makiguchi could someday be found. Whether or not they met, however, we can be fairly certain what they would have talked about. At that time, Japanese schools were suffering from an excess of patriotic fervor associated with emperor worship. Dewey reported that elementary-school teachers were among the most fanatical nationalists. He even reported that some teachers had been burned or had allowed children to be burned trying to rescue portraits of the emperor during fires. Of course, since Makiguchi was opposed to militarism and fanatic nationalism, he and Dewey would have had some very important conversations about how to improve Japanese schools and, especially, the role that democratization of the schools would play in reforming the larger society.

GARRISON: I enjoy imagining what they would have talked about. It would be nice to know if they met, but in a way it doesn't matter, because their ideas have led to this present exchange. They would have had plenty to say, first of all, about Immanuel Kant, who influenced Makiguchi and was the topic of Dewey's dissertation.

Another very likely topic of conversation would have had to do with Dewey's deep dislike of militarism and a rigid, feudalistic class structure. Makiguchi got into trouble for refusing to treat upper-class children deferentially. In fact, he refused to acknowledge social class distinctions in a society obsessed with them. The same thing bothered Dewey deeply. In many of his written works, he uses the phrase *moral courage*, a trait he found lacking in Japanese intellectuals of his day. He does, however, argue that nowhere else did it require as much moral courage to speak out as it did in Japan.[12]

Makiguchi died in prison in opposition to the militarism in Japan. Makiguchi's own great moral courage is evident in his willingness to die for his convictions.

IKEDA: The starting point and fundamental spirit of the Soka Gakkai International movement derive from Mr. Makiguchi's courageous struggle—his committed action, even to the point of giving his life, for the sake of human happiness and peace. The Tokyo Makiguchi Memorial Hall in Hachioji, where Soka University is located, is a monument to this great teacher.

GARRISON: I was deeply moved by the Memorial Hall when I was in Tokyo, not only by the grandeur of the building itself but also by what it has to say of Makiguchi's personal victory. To me, the contrast between the physical dimensions of the tiny cell in which he was imprisoned before he died and the splendor of the building symbolizes the victory of a vast spirit over not only material obstacles but also dangerous ideology.

Makiguchi was victorious because he had, in Dewey's terms, moral courage. We may say the same for the SGI. Oftentimes, human beings are victorious just because they refuse to be defeated. Makiguchi didn't win against the militarists: He died. But he was not defeated. He perished in jail helpless to escape, but he was not really helpless at all.

IKEDA: I am delighted by the depth of your understanding of Makiguchi's life and ideals. Unconcerned with the praise or blame of the world, Dewey, too, pursued the path of his convictions and triumphed. I believe that the nucleus of his life and philosophy was courageous moral action, striving with the people for the sake of social justice. The two of you, as educators and intellectuals of action, are steadfastly embodying and transmitting this noble spirit to future generations.

I am heir to the philosophies of two great teachers—Tsunesaburo Makiguchi and Josei Toda, our second president, who shared Makiguchi's prison struggle—carrying on their philosophies and convictions, and putting them into practice with courageous people, especially our young people, to whom the future belongs.

HICKMAN: My dear friend and colleague Jim Garrison and I are constantly inspired by Dewey's example, which motivates our respective efforts to realize the goals he formulated for democracy and education. We have also been inspired by the vision—and the sacrifices of tireless efforts—that have characterized your work and that of your wife, Kaneko Ikeda.[13]

CONVERSATION TWO

Learning Together

IKEDA: Let's begin this conversation with an incident illustrating the high estimation in which the American people hold John Dewey. In 1949, when he was turning ninety, a little girl who met Dewey told him with a smile: "Oh, so you're Mr. Dewey. We have John Dewey education at our school." Dewey was delighted.

When and how did the two of you first become aware of John Dewey?

HICKMAN: I believe that my own spiritual odyssey retraces Dewey's: from a somewhat narrow religious perspective, through the liberation I found in Georg Wilhelm Friedrich Hegel's thought, to a broader humanistic outlook. I, too, was heavily influenced by a devout, evangelical Christian mother, who in some ways resembled Dewey's mother.

It was not until graduate school that I began to read Dewey in a systematic manner. I soon perceived something interesting: No one had noticed that he had a lot to say about technology. So I wrote a book called *John Dewey's Pragmatic Technology*,[1] which introduced his work to people who were interested in technology.

GARRISON: I vaguely remember somebody in graduate school mentioning John Dewey. I asked him, is that the guy who invented the Dewey Decimal System used to organize libraries? The answer was no.[2] People often ask me the same question and are shamefaced and embarrassed about it. They relax after I tell them how I once made the same mistake.

Despite his larger cultural influence, when I was in graduate school, almost no one in American philosophy departments studied Dewey at all. This was because philosophy was then dominated by technical, analytic thinking divorced from the daily concerns of life. Fortunately, since my student years, traditional American pragmatism, and especially that of Dewey, has experienced a renaissance.

I discovered Dewey two years after I earned my doctorate in philosophy. By then, I had degrees in physics and psychology as well as a master's in humanities and was working on a National Science Foundation grant in mathematical logic.

At the risk of suggesting some kind of conversion experience, I can say that the discovery of Dewey in 1983 stunned me. Our school had a good philosophy-department library. Significantly, the book I found was an original 1925 copy of *Experience and Nature*. As soon as I started reading the introduction, everything made sense to me. I had read a great deal of Charles Sanders Peirce, the father of pragmatism; I wrote a dissertation on the history and philosophy of science that drew considerably on Peirce. However, I had never read a single thing by Dewey, who belonged to the same philosophical school.

IKEDA: So, both of you encountered Dewey's philosophy in your eager, youthful pursuit of learning. Professor Garrison, fortuitously picking up a library book changed your life and launched you on the path to your lifework in the study of Dewey's thought.

A great book has the power to affect one's life enormously. Indeed, an encounter with a good book can ignite a flame in a youthful heart to provide power for a new journey in life.

We Are Creators

Garrison: Yes, *Experience and Nature,* which I casually pulled off a shelf, stunned me because it was what I had been looking for the preceding seven years. Dewey taught me how to say what I had been struggling to say even to myself: We are creators performing acts of creation without end, generation after generation, perhaps until the species passes. This concept explains my interest in an organization that titles itself "Value-Creating Society."[3]

Ikeda: The fact that the concept of creativity is both part of the name of our organization and a key element in Dewey's philosophy is indeed a fascinating connection and correspondence. The term *soka* ("value creation") emerged from the mentor-disciple dialogue between our first two presidents, Makiguchi and Toda. The disciple, Toda, used his own funds to publish *Soka kyoikugaku taikei* (The System of Value-Creating Pedagogy), the groundbreaking work that sets forth the pedagogic principles of his mentor, Makiguchi. When the decision to publish was made, Mr. Makiguchi described the purpose of education as "value creation." Mr. Toda thereupon suggested the term *soka kyoiku,* or "value-creating education." The Soka Kyoiku Gakkai, later renamed Soka Gakkai, came into being on the day the book was published, November 18, 1930.

As we have already seen, its founders, Makiguchi and Toda, entertained the deepest respect for John Dewey. I can't help but feel that in some way my encounter with both of you was arranged by Mr. Makiguchi, Mr. Toda, and Mr. Dewey.

GARRISON: Perhaps they did through the words that drew us to them. What I like about Dewey is his commitment to the classical Greek notion of *poiesis*; poetry in the deep sense of making, creating, or calling into existence, with or without rhyme or meter. For Dewey, philosophy and poetry are close, cut from the same fabric. You can distinguish between them, but you cannot separate them.

IKEDA: Dewey's own poetry is an important element in understanding Dewey in his totality. Among his ninety-eight poems that survive, "Truth's Torch" strongly expresses Dewey's thoughts and convictions:

No course is lit
By light that former burned
From darkness bit by bit
The present road is learned.

Tho space shines bright
And paths are trodden clear
Never to thy searching sight
Does the true road appear

Till dart th'arrows
Of thine own lifted flame
Through clinging fogs that close
And hide the journey's aim.[4]

I am fond of this poem. Dewey penetrated the darkness and illuminated the future with the light of his life force and passion. It is essential to impart the light of courage and hope to the young lives that will follow after us.

Education at Home

Ikeda: Many of our readers,[5] especially mothers with young children, have asked to learn more about your families and how you were encouraged to study and read at home.

Garrison: My dad had a sixth grade education, and my mother an eighth grade education. They were not well educated. But they both read. When I was growing up, we read books and talked to one another about what we read. There could be no better foundation for literacy than the one provided by my parents. There just wasn't anything better.

According to a great deal of research, parents often think that their job is only to start their children reading; the rest will take care of itself. But that is a limited way of looking at things.

My parents and I exchanged books. On his way out to the car, Dad might say to me, "Hey, do you want to read this?" I would read the book he offered, and a few days later we would discuss it.

Ikeda: Yours is a wonderful model of reading education. Reading the same books and sharing reactions not only promotes heartwarming communication between parents and children but is also an important form of home education, offering precious spiritual sustenance to children in a natural, unforced way. It also helps children learn about family sentiments and attitudes toward the world. At times it can also be a source of discoveries and surprises for parents. It's a way in which parents and children can learn and grow together.

Today, television and the Internet have made their way into the family, too, but it is impossible to stress too heavily the importance of reading. The decline of the culture of the printed word can be seen as leading ultimately to the destruction of humanity itself. A popular saying, sometimes attributed to Cicero, tells us that a "room without books is like a body without a soul."

Hickman: My brother and I were encouraged to read by my mother, just as Dewey's father encouraged his reading. My father was very occupied by his job, which required him to travel a great deal. His hobbies included geology and archaeology, however, and I suppose I inherited my interest in the sciences from him.

Since we lived near the Texas-Mexico border, my family visited Mexico many times during my youth. We always had books about Mexico as well. It was through books and travel that I came to love that country and its people.

Ikeda: Parents play an important role in encouraging children to become avid readers. I can tell that you grew up in a home blessed with parental love, Professor Hickman.

Garrison: The power of love in the home is immeasurable. I was adopted. I was wanted by my adoptive parents. I had correspondence with my natural mother until I was twenty-four.

My history is not so much about place as about people. Until my thirteenth birthday, every night after she turned off my bedroom light, my adoptive mother told me she loved me. The power of knowing I was loved was incredible.

My adoptive father was a career Marine. He was heavily decorated for action in both the Pacific and Korea, but he drank and was never at ease. Like most warriors who have seen the horrors of war and found them difficult to deal with, he did not like war and did not consider it an ennobling experience. I got that lesson from him.

After I was adopted, I didn't have any chance to meet my natural parents. But knowing for certain that I was wanted empowered me tremendously. It's a great gift. Many of the sons and daughters of privilege at the large state university where I teach lack the great gift of such certainty.

IKEDA: I am grateful to you for sharing these precious personal experiences, Dr. Garrison. They seem to me to be the source of your deep commitment to peace.

As you have said, nothing is as important as parental love in giving children strength, courage, and peace of mind. Your comment that many students lack the certainty that they are loved and wanted by their parents represents an important issue that modern education needs to address.

Opening the World

IKEDA: To move ahead, I want to mention the immense significance Tsunesaburo Makiguchi, as a geography scholar, attached to education in geography and local history and customs. Mr. Makiguchi's idea in this respect closely corresponds to Dewey's philosophy.

When you were students, did you like geography?

GARRISON: As a boy, I hated it—rightly so—as a lot of inert facts to memorize and regurgitate on a test.

HICKMAN: Geography was one of my favorite school subjects. I loved spending many hours examining maps. I still do.

I also collected stamps from all over the world and enjoyed learning about the countries they came from. That can lead to all sorts of discoveries. For example, collecting some of the stamps issued by the Weimar Republic (of Germany) in the 1930s taught me about the terrible effects of inflation. I recall a single stamp that cost several million marks! That is just one example of the many ways that the study of geography opens up the world to learners, young and old alike.

IKEDA: Remarkably, in 1899, when Dewey was forty and Makiguchi twenty-eight, both lectured on emphasizing geography in educational reforms. Four years later, in 1903, Makiguchi published his monumental *Geography of Human Life*.

HICKMAN: Dewey thought that the study of geography was one of the most important aspects of a school curriculum.

IKEDA: For Makiguchi, the study of geography was not just about place names or a tool supporting imperialism and colonialism. Mr. Makiguchi felt, as Professor Hickman suggested, that it helps the individual become aware of his or her place in the world and promotes independence. It is an essential subject for helping people lead fulfilled, value-creating lives and become stalwart global citizens.

As such, Makiguchi's stress on the importance of reforms in geographical education necessarily led to his sharp criticism of Japan's slide toward militarism. I believe that, in the context of the globalization of the twenty-first century, this emphasis on daily life and geography deserves reappraisal.

HICKMAN: Dewey thought of geography as a tool for understanding the many complex factors linking humans together in terms of the uses of materials, trade routes, foodstuffs, and many other factors. He defined geography broadly and considered it intimately connected with the study of history. In his 1916 masterwork *Democracy and Education*, he devoted an entire chapter to geography and history.

I personally am quite concerned about the ignorance of geography among some young people in the United States. In a 2006 survey sponsored by the National Geographic Society, 33 percent of young adults, eighteen to twenty-four years old, couldn't identify the state of Louisiana on a map. Fewer than 30 percent thought it was important to know the locations of countries in the news, and just 14 percent considered it important to speak another language.

We have to ask ourselves what sort of global citizens these young people will be if less than half of them can find India on a map. Of course, the study of geography involves much more than locating places on a map. But it is that, at the very least.

IKEDA: It is extremely important to have an interest in world affairs, and a deep understanding of the connections between one's homeland and the world is indispensable. The Buddhist doctrine of dependent origination teaches that nothing exists independently of other things, and all things mutually influence and are interrelated with one another.

In his *Geography of Human Life*, Makiguchi wrote that experience, observation, and analysis of even a tiny plot of land—"no bigger than a cat's forehead" in the Japanese turn of phrase—lead to the understanding of whole nations and the entire world. In other words, solidly anchoring oneself in one's own place and observing it carefully enables one to perceive, within each phenomenon, the connections to the larger world, leading eventually to a global perspective.

Likewise, understanding the relationship between the world and one's self leads to a better understanding of one's self. This is what makes studying geography and one's local region an important requirement for the cultivation of global citizens.

In both your opinions, what significance do Dewey's teachings on geography have for the future?

A Middle Way

HICKMAN: As we know, geography lessons were a central feature of Dewey's educational philosophy. His ideas about the importance of geography and history are increasingly relevant to us today as we seek to educate the future leaders of our rapidly globalizing environment. For one thing, knowledge of geography and history allows us to discover and build on strands of human commonality that trump the radical postmodernist emphasis on difference and discontinuity.

Second, since the study of geography and history employs scientific methods, it allows us to appreciate mild forms of cultural relativism without giving up objective judgments about competing claims, including competing moral claims. It is now undeniable, for example, that we live in a world in which the links between cultures and peoples are increasingly intimate. If we are to avoid the dogmas that lead to the type of authoritarianism that is often expressed as virulent nationalism, then it is important that we understand the historical and geographical factors that have contributed to what other cultures regard as their defining qualities.

But it is also important that we understand the times and places in which cultural practices have developed historically, and consequently that some cultural practices have come to be more evolved compared to others (when "more evolved" is understood as capable of creating greater value and opportunity for the growth of individuals and communities). Charting a course for this Middle Way cannot succeed without individuals who are well informed about historical developments and cultural choices as our geographic spaces shrink to form a global village.

GARRISON: In spite of my childhood dislike of the subject, I had an experience during graduate school that exemplifies what Dewey and Makiguchi had in mind about teaching geography. Running through the city of Tallahassee in northern Florida where I went to graduate school was a large ditch that had once been a river. When I discussed the geographic feature with him, a local explained that the old river once divided the black community from the rest of the town. Eventually, we realized that most of the town was built according to the geography of the river that cut through it. I came to understand how the local geography structured the town, including its commerce.

For both Makiguchi and Dewey, the subject was human connectedness and unity and wholeness across difference. That's the spirit that should come out of geography. That's how Dewey's spirit could work in the twenty-first century—overcoming differences while not reducing everything to the same. He helps us understand our connectedness and our disconnectedness as well.

Your question regarding Dewey's teachings on geography for the future leads to an astute understanding of Dewey's spirit. In the Deweyan tradition, it is about getting connected in the right ways, including getting disconnected from some of the wrong ways. Geography helps us do that.

IKEDA: Thorough investigation of one's local environment not only establishes external connections, it also helps cultivate recognition of the inner universality of life and the consequent universal dignity of all people. President Makiguchi examined the influence of geography and the natural environment on human life and character formation from many different angles. In succeeding conversations, I hope to examine this more fully.

CONVERSATION THREE

From Mentor to Disciple

IKEDA: What is the force that creates history? In a memorable observation, British historian Arnold J. Toynbee described it as the "deeper, slower movements."[1] He meant that history is ultimately not what newspapers think makes good headlines but these "deeper, slower movements."

Humanistic education based on the worth and dignity of life is what leads, with strength and rectitude, the will and power of the people—the force that creates history—toward world peace and happiness for all humanity.

I understand that the John Dewey Society, in which you both play leading roles, was formed by about sixty educators in 1935, five years after the formation of the Soka Gakkai. Both organizations came into being at the time of the Great Depression.

The Ikeda Center for Peace, Learning, and Dialogue and the Institute of Oriental Philosophy,[2] two organizations I founded, have collaborated with the John Dewey Society in publications, symposia, and scholarly and educational exchanges. In the summer of 2008, your organization conferred on me honorary life membership, for which I am grateful.

John Dewey was in his seventies and rounding out his life's work when your society became the heir to his thought and philosophy. It was a time of great troubles: President Franklin D. Roosevelt was implementing New Deal policies to stimulate the economic recovery of the United States, in the grips of deep depression, while the ominous footfall of militarism was starting to be heard again throughout the world.

Hickman: As you say, the John Dewey Society was founded in 1935, during the depths of the Great Depression, by a group of young, progressive educators who were eager to effect changes in American education. In the midst of that crisis, they saw great opportunity. The founders named the society for Dewey in honor of his lifelong efforts to address the real problems of education by engaging in an unflinching study of the interdependence of school and society.

Garrison: Dewey himself was not involved with the society, the full title of which is the John Dewey Society for the Study of Education and Culture. The name *John Dewey Society* was chosen because the founders thought his life and work exemplified the kinds of values they wanted to uphold. Many of John Dewey's friends and associates were either founding or very early members.

Ikeda: How did the two of you learn about the John Dewey Society?

Hickman: I became aware of it when I began to study Dewey's works in a systematic way and was deeply honored when I was invited to stand for election as an officer.

Ikeda: For America and the whole world, Dewey's philosophy is a treasure, and your organization is a spiritual guidepost for humanity.

GARRISON: I cheerfully chugged along for a long time before I knew it existed. Once, I went to a lecture by someone I especially wanted to hear. When I arrived, I discovered the lecture was sponsored by the John Dewey Society. So I joined, and I became involved with it.

The Dewey Society remains robust and active after all these years. Given the prevailing rate of change among organizations, for such a society to last this long is quite surprising. It stays active because it was founded on Dewey's commitment to reflective intelligence and the spirit of diversity and inquiry.

IKEDA: I respect the noble efforts your society has made. According to an ancient Chinese saying, "The farther the source, the longer the stream." A movement or organization that prizes its noble origins, like a great river flowing along and watering fertile fields on its way, will transcend the age and greatly develop. As long as the founding spirit remains vibrant, boundless future development is possible.

But without people capable of studying and transmitting its spiritual tradition, any philosophy or organization is sure to become a mere facade and eventually disappear. This is why I believe that universities and similar institutions play a vital role in devising ways to increase the flow of wisdom that enriches the human mind, ensuring that this wisdom continues to flow into the future. To perform this role, such institutions require wisdom adapted to the times.

What are the current activities of the Dewey Society?

HICKMAN: The Society meets each year at the annual meeting of the American Educational Research Association, where it sponsors lectures, panels, and various other activities. In addition, the Society's Commission on Social Issues has a presence on the Internet. The journal we publish, *Education and Culture*, is a widely read, biannual journal.

In addition, officers and members of the Society are active in promoting the work of John Dewey in a variety of venues. During the last fifteen years, for example, I have presented an average of one lecture per month and have helped to establish international Dewey centers in China, Italy, Hungary, Poland, and Germany, and of course at Soka University in Japan.[3] Professor Garrison also lectures widely and is very active in promoting the work of the Society.

GARRISON: In an important sense, in promoting the philosophy of John Dewey, the Society encourages education concerned with the social justice and amelioration he desired.

I always tried to put on the rostrum speakers who sometimes disputed Dewey. After all, the Society was founded on his commitment to reflective intelligence and the spirit of dialogue and respectful dissent, and I thought that those who could respectfully express dissenting opinions would help promote the spirit of John Dewey. Things have evolved well during the nearly sixty years since Dewey died, and, as someone committed to adapting to changing circumstances, he would want to honor intelligent growth and change.

THE MENTOR WITHIN

IKEDA: Dewey's philosophy is epitomized by the cultivation of a flexible, creative intellect and seeking mind, responsive to the changing times, and the striving for limitless advancement and continuous growth.

When I met the two of you in Nagano, Japan, in the summer of 2008, Professor Garrison said that education consists in succession, in its transmission from generation to generation, the role of young people being crucial. I was pleased to hear you say that; I always strive to treasure young people, share their joys and sufferings, and develop together with them. The essence of any philosophy or the founding spirit of any institution can only be transmitted to the next generation and its future development ensured through a creative, constructive effort enjoined with youth.

As a youthful disciple, I inherited and perpetuated the Soka spirit of dedication to the well-being of all humanity to which Makiguchi and Toda devoted their lives. Professor Garrison, you have spoken of the "everlasting unity of mentor and disciple"; the profound shared vow and actions of mentor and disciple are what ensure the immortality of their spiritual relay.

GARRISON: At the beginning of this three-person exchange, when we discussed your initial meeting with President Toda, I sensed profound consideration and extraordinary energy in your eyes and voice (see Conversation One). The first thing that came to my mind was immortality.

I have been interested in your thoughts on the mentor-disciple relationship, which I understand in terms of the teacher-student relationship of shared inquiry.

IKEDA: The observation that the mentor-disciple relationship is one of shared inquiry is perceptive. Looking back in history, the mentor-disciple relationship between Socrates and Plato shines above all others as the model pedagogical bond. It is due to Plato that the essence of the philosophy of his teacher, Socrates, has been passed on to us today, nearly two-and-a-half millennia later.

HICKMAN: In 1930, in a brief autobiographical essay, Dewey wrote that Plato "still provides my favorite philosophic reading."[4] What was it in Plato that he found so engaging? He tells us that he is captivated by the

> dramatic, restless, cooperatively inquiring Plato of the *Dialogues*, trying one mode of attack after another to see what it might yield; . . . the Plato whose highest flight of metaphysics always terminated with a social and practical turn.[5]

This is surely the Plato who was so greatly inspired by his teacher, Socrates, whose own restless inquiries are still of great interest and value to us today. It is not, Dewey added, the Plato "constructed by unimaginative commentators who treat him as the original university professor."[6]

IKEDA: Dewey deeply sympathized with Plato's unflagging, sincere inquiry and vigorous search for truth. In the *Second Epistle*, Plato wrote the following: "There is not and will not be any written work of Plato's own. What are now called his are the work of a Socrates grown young and beautiful."[7] Scholars have long puzzled over this controversial passage, but the famous Japanese pedagogue Takeji Hayashi thinks that "Socrates grown young and beautiful" refers to the Socrates living within Plato.

In other words, the mentor continues to live forever within the life of the disciple. Countless examples throughout history, as well as my own experience, lead me to believe this to be true.

I am who I am today because of my mentor, Josei Toda. My thoughts and achievements would not exist if I had not benefited from his instruction. Even after his death, I constantly converse with the Josei Toda existing in my heart and can honestly say that I have depended on his guidance in overcoming all kinds of difficulties.

I am sure that, even after the execution of Socrates, Plato continued to engage in intense mental dialogue with him. The fruit of this exchange produced an immortal light of wisdom for humanity.

So it is that we find a wondrous conversation between mentor and disciple and an immortal transmission of their shared spirit in the origins of Western philosophy. The mentor-and-disciple relationship is the inexhaustible wellspring of learning and the light illuminating humanity's future.

HICKMAN: The wonderful relationship between Plato and Socrates has been much celebrated. Other famous mentor-disciple relationships that come to mind in the field of philosophy include Albert Magnus and Thomas Aquinas; Jeremy Bentham and John Stuart Mill; and Ralph Waldo Emerson and Henry David Thoreau. Each of these relationships occurred at a time of significant change. For Magnus and Aquinas, the crucial issue was how to reconcile the texts of Aristotle, newly recovered from the Muslim world, with the doctrines of the Roman Catholic Church. For Bentham and Mill, the question was how to release women and workers from the grip of an old system that favored the aristocracy. For Emerson and Thoreau, the problem was how to open up the cloistered religious practices of conventional Christianity so that each person could get a sense of participation in a larger self.

Of course, there are many well-known mentor-disciple relationships in other fields besides philosophy. For example, although Wolfgang Amadeus Mozart was already a success by the time he met the much-older Franz Joseph Haydn, Mozart was clearly influenced and instructed by the latter. In turn, Haydn expressed great admiration for the younger man, once telling a friend that Mozart was "much my superior."[8]

THE DISCIPLE'S TRIUMPH

GARRISON: Perhaps the addition of a third party makes the relationship more important still. Unquestionably, the most important triplet is that of Socrates, Plato, and Aristotle. Very few people would deny that this is the most important teacher-student inquiry or mentor-disciple relationship in the history of Western thought.

Of course, the triplet of Makiguchi, Toda, and Ikeda, too, is interesting because it shows the continuity of the mentor-disciple relationship. You have followed the path they trod before you and, in doing so, have made a highway that others, too, can follow. In a certain sense—much as Socrates' greatest achievement was his student Plato, and Plato's his student Aristotle—Makiguchi's greatest achievement was Toda, and Toda's greatest achievement may have been Ikeda.

IKEDA: I am grateful for the depth of your understanding of the Soka Gakkai vision of the mentor-disciple relationship. In our movement, we find the mentor and disciple persisting through three generations to be extremely significant, because in the continuity attained by transmitting the intense, person-to-person bond between mentor and disciple to a third generation, the immortality of the mentor and disciple relationship is ensured.

During the winter vacation of 1919, as a nineteen-year-old primary-school teacher on the northern island of Hokkaido, Toda traveled to Tokyo. There he met Makiguchi, the principal of a primary school. In the spring of 1920, Toda moved permanently to Tokyo and found employment as a temporary teacher at that primary school.

Directly after that, Makiguchi, who refused to capitulate to unjust pressure from authority or power, was transferred to another school through the unscrupulous interference of an arrogant politician. Young Toda organized a movement among faculty members who revered Makiguchi to protest this unwarranted action. Parents and guardians, too, sincerely respected Makiguchi and supported him.

From this point on, our first two presidents formed an unbreakable mentor-disciple relationship. Ten years later, on November 18, 1930, Toda introduced his mentor's educational philosophy to the world, financing the publication of Makiguchi's great work *The System of Value-Creating Pedagogy*. For the next dozen years or so, the two men progressed from educational reform to religious reform, championing freedom of thought and faith by resisting Japan's militarist government founded on state Shinto.

As a result, amid the turmoil of World War II, they were unjustly arrested and imprisoned, accused of violating the pernicious Peace Preservation Law of the time. President Makiguchi died in prison on November 18, 1944.

When Toda learned of Makiguchi's death, he tearfully vowed to carry out his mentor's dying wishes. Released among the devastated ruins of defeat on July 3, 1945, shortly before the end of the war, Toda began rebuilding the Soka Gakkai. During ceremonies to commemorate the second anniversary of his mentor's death, Toda declared, "In your vast and boundless compassion, you let me accompany you even to prison."[9]

I still remember how moved I was upon hearing Mr. Toda's account of these events, and I firmly resolved to proudly follow the same noble, immortal, mentor-disciple path for the sake of peace and human happiness. It is my greatest honor and happiness to have broadened the network for peace, culture, and education throughout the world in keeping with this vow.

HICKMAN: There is nothing rarer or more precious than the type of relationship you have just described. It is remarkable that it has persevered across successive generations.

In our own time of relative stability and plenty, it is especially important to recall and celebrate the types of relationships that persist and even grow in the face of crisis—when doubt and despair stalk isolated individuals, when the odds against success seem overwhelming, and when it is especially important for us to share clarity of goals and unity of purpose.

Your account is a reminder that each of us has an obligation to extend an extra effort to be the best mentor, or the best disciple, that we can.

GARRISON: In Tokyo, looking at the massive memorial building named after Makiguchi, who because of militarist oppression had died in a little prison cell, I thought that the important thing is that Toda and Ikeda and, more important, the Soka Gakkai, turned his apparent defeat into victory and immortality. The building symbolizes the immortality of the mentor-disciple relationship.

I think of that relationship in terms of two components. The first is fundamental moral equality, the unity between mentor and disciple. In other words, they both have the potential for growth and development, such that the teacher, or mentor, is resolved to help the disciple move further along the path of inquiry. Sharing an inquiry—or, in your terms, being on the same path—is very important. The mentor may be further along the path, but both are still bound in a profound unity.

There are no causes without effects, so that in a sense the effect is the cause of the cause. There are no mentors without disciples: The disciple helps the mentor to emerge and advances him along the path as well.

IKEDA: Buddhism considers the disciple the cause and the mentor the result. Though we say "mentor and disciple," the disciple is the key, and everything depends on the disciple. The two are inseparably united and nondual. Thus, the disciple's triumph is the mentor's triumph and vice versa. This is a profound formula, and the oneness of the mentor and disciple is the quintessence of Buddhism.

Mentor and disciple, Makiguchi and Toda were united both personally and by the spiritual bond of comrades in a shared struggle. Through these bonds, Makiguchi transmitted to Toda the depth and development of the philosophy that is Nichiren Buddhism. In my encounter with Mr. Toda and our shared struggle as his disciple, I received detailed instruction in the contemporary articulation of the Wonderful Law to which he had awakened while in prison. In this manner, the personal relationships and philosophical transmission carried through three generations of mentors and disciples remain vitally alive in our people's movement based on Buddhism.

The Wonderful Law

GARRISON: The second of my two components concerns the teaching partner. Whereas in your terms the Wonderful Law governing the life force of the universe is always the ultimate teacher, for Dewey the experience of nature shared with the student is always the teacher. Dewey's idea and yours seem analogous. In the experience of nature, both mentor and disciple cooperate and inquire along the way.

IKEDA: For Nichiren, the Japanese Buddhist thinker and reformer whose teachings we of the SGI uphold, the enduring, unchanging Law was the direct and immediate teacher that instructed him in his faith and philosophy. He said:

> The word "Law" (*ho*) here stands for *shoho,* the various phenomena of existence. The word "teacher" (*shi*) indicates that all these various phenomena act directly as our teacher. That is, the varied and numberless phenomena of the three thousand realms[10] can act directly as our teacher and we can become their disciples.[11]

President Makiguchi, too, deepened his faith through inquiry into and practice of the Law.

At the same time, generally speaking, the mentor-disciple relationship is characterized by the transmission of a one-to-one, personal, existential experience between two individuals.

When teachings are transmitted to posterity solely as writings, the absence of that existential experience to inform their content can result in the teacher's thought degenerating into lifeless, empty words. On the other hand, if too much emphasis is placed on the existential experience, and there is no deep inquiry into and practice of the Law, a mentor's real teachings may never reach people prevented by space or time from coming into direct contact with him or her.

The tension between these two considerations can be seen as one of the difficulties of the mentor-and-disciple relationship throughout history. This is an issue that our Buddhism-based peace, culture, and educational movement, now active in 192 countries and territories around the world, will have to face in demonstrating its true value in the years to come.

GARRISON: Dewey disapproved of people who spoke not of mentors but of masters. Clear distinctions must be made between the relationship between a mentor and a disciple and that between master and servant.

Your concern is the same as Dewey's regarding what he called *masters*. They think they can get to something supernatural beyond the natural; they assume a privileged access to the realm of heaven or nirvana—only they know the will of God or the Buddha. And, once they achieve supernatural access, or at least get a lot closer than other, normal people do, then they believe they have the one true dogma. For them, the notion that the master learns from the disciple as the disciple learns from the master is unthinkable.

In much the same way, the priests of Nichiren Shoshu[12] resemble masters. They wanted a master-slave relationship and sought those disciples who would follow them in silent obedience.

On the other hand, when Makiguchi discovered Nichiren Buddhism, he, like Nichiren himself, wanted to share it with the people so they could explore it together. Makiguchi, Toda, and you created mentor-disciple relationships. In a sense, your organization, which tried to work with the priests of Nichiren Shoshu, may have been fated to encounter a break in the relationship from the beginning.

IKEDA: I am grateful for your keen insight and profound understanding.

Continuous Human Community

HICKMAN: Following William James, who influenced him greatly, John Dewey advanced the doctrine that a belief is true when it satisfies both personal needs and the requirements of objective conditions (such as what we are physically able, or unable, to do). This doctrine is no less true in the area of mentor-disciple relationships than in other, more abstract areas of human endeavor, such as mathematics and the natural sciences. As I understand matters, this idea resonates with your remarks about the relationship between personality and the Law as sources of insight.

The balance about which you spoke is especially important at the level of the university, where a professor must balance the needs of research and teaching. Too much emphasis on research can cut off the many important insights that come from interacting with, and learning from, students. And too much emphasis on day-to-day teaching can cut short systematic inquiry into the realities of the world outside the classroom.

Teachers must have time to recharge their energies and follow new paths of inquiry. A true balance between personality and the Law is, I believe, what Dewey had in mind when he wrote that experience, in its fullest sense, is

> free interaction of individual human beings with surrounding conditions, especially the human surroundings, which develops and satisfies need and desire by increasing knowledge of things as they are.[13]

It is this type of experience that we must strive to promote both for ourselves and for our students. And it is this type of experience that I find apparent at Soka schools and universities.

IKEDA: As founder, I am happier than I can say to receive such a profound assessment from an heir to the essence of Dewey's philosophy.

As a diamond can be polished only by another diamond, so human beings can be refined only by other human beings. The creation of new values and human progress itself depend on fostering our successors to surpass us, all of us sharing in the quest for universal truth and working together to improve and elevate ourselves. This is also the quintessence of education. As Dewey rightly wrote, "What one person and one group accomplish becomes the standing ground and starting point of those who succeed them."[14]

GARRISON: Professor Hickman and I have both visited Dewey's hometown of Burlington on several occasions. His remains are buried outside the old library there at the University of Vermont. On the grave marker are some lines from the closing paragraphs of *A Common Faith*, which I know you admire:

> The things in civilization we most prize are not of ourselves. They exist by grace of the doings and sufferings of the continuous human community in which we are a link. Ours is the responsibility of conserving, transmitting, rectifying and expanding the heritage of values we have received that those who come after us may receive it more solid and secure, more widely accessible and more generously shared than we have received it.[15]

We must preserve for future generations what we have inherited. A self-professed master would merely hand the heritage over to his successors. But, if we lead like good mentors, we will join those successors on the path of inquiry to improve that heritage and enhance its value.

This is the true immortality of the mentor-disciple relationship: Both pursue the same path of inquiry—preserving, rectifying, and creating value. This is the real meaning of the inscription on Dewey's grave marker. The Soka Gakkai accomplishes it completely.

CONVERSATION FOUR

Growth Is the Goal

IKEDA: "One may find happiness in the midst of annoyances; be contented and cheerful in spite of a succession of disagreeable experiences, if one has braveness and equanimity of soul."[1] This is one of my favorite examples of Dewey's life wisdom.

Many people imagine philosophy to be abstruse and difficult. But, far from abstract, Dewey's philosophy is directly relevant to our lives and has human happiness as its goal. It is an unpretentious philosophy for the ordinary person, a living philosophy of the people, aflame with the courageous American pioneer spirit. And it is a philosophy of action for a vibrant way of life, a treasure house of the wisdom and vitality the twenty-first century requires.

In this conversation, I want to explore the origins of Dewey's philosophy. Dewey's thought is usually described as pragmatism. Why?

GARRISON: The word *pragmatism* derives from the Greek *pragma*, which means deed or action. Charles Sanders Peirce, the originator of pragmatism, was inspired by Kant but reconstructed his work to develop pragmatism as placing more emphasis on practical worldly action.[2]

Likewise, Makiguchi reconstructed Kant's value spheres of truth, beauty, and the good to get beauty, gain or benefit, and the good. Both Makiguchi and Dewey consider right action critical. Truth obviously has a great deal to contribute to right action, but it is not the central thing because theirs are philosophies of action.

IKEDA: Our fundamental challenge as human beings is to lead a life of value creation through right deeds. How can philosophy make this possible? Pragmatism's appeal derives from directly addressing this question.

In *The System of Value-Creating Pedagogy*, President Makiguchi declared children's happiness to be the goal of education. He insisted that children's growth and development can only take place within a happy life. As corroboration, he introduced Dewey's philosophy of placing living at the heart of education.

Makiguchi's life-based philosophy was also evident in his Buddhist faith. He believed that religion must always make a concrete contribution to human growth and people's happiness, to peace and development. We of the Soka Gakkai are the heirs to this spirit, committed to developing the philosophy of happiness, peace, and value creation among the people through our religious practice.

As I mentioned (see Conversation One), I spent my youth in an ardent search for the correct way to live amid the collapse of the Japanese value system following World War II. During this search, I encountered Josei Toda. At our initial meeting, I asked him how we should live our lives. Remarking that mine was the most difficult of difficult questions, he honestly and succinctly answered:

> You can of course ponder on what is the correct way of life if you have that much leisure time. However, you would do better to practice [Nichiren's] teaching. You are still

> young, after all. Through your own practice, you will come to realize that you are paving the correct path of life. I can assure you this.[3]

Believing these words, I became his disciple and a practicing Buddhist.

HICKMAN: You describe a wonderful mentor-disciple relationship and raise an issue that goes to the heart of Dewey's philosophy. As a pragmatist, he thought that philosophy should be more than rarified speculation or preoccupation with mental puzzles. He was a sharp critic of what he termed "empty abstractions." His method accomplishes this by beginning with real, experienced difficulties and then attempting to apply the tools that are required to restore equilibrium.

IKEDA: By referring to himself as practical, Dewey clearly states his belief that philosophy is never a goal but always a means to human growth and improvement.

HICKMAN: Yes, but the goal is not just the solution of an isolated problem—it is promotion of the growth of each individual human within his or her social environment by the enrichment of the meaning of his or her life. When this is successful, we can say that value has been created. So it seems clear to me that Makiguchi's concept of value creation and Dewey's notion of growth are very similar.

IKEDA: President Makiguchi said that things that impart the power to expand our lives have value. In other words, the primary aim, from the perspectives of both the individual and society, is to promote the growth and personal enrichment of each human being. The aim of education is to develop character in both the self and others that can contribute to the mutual benefit and welfare of the individual and the whole. This was his personal conviction and philosophy.

GARRISON: Dewey didn't care much for philosophy as recondite study, although he certainly was a master of high abstraction. He admitted that was his natural tendency. In one of his most famous works, "The Need for a Recovery of Philosophy," he put it wonderfully:

> Philosophy recovers itself when it ceases to be a device for dealing with the problems of philosophers and becomes a method, cultivated by philosophers, for dealing with the problems of men.[4]

For Dewey, and I think for the Soka Gakkai as well, philosophy's purpose is the amelioration of suffering. Deweyan philosophy is a living philosophy. Deweyan pragmatism is a philosophy of life and social amelioration. The goal is growth, after all.

He clearly argues that growth is the aim of education and of life. For Dewey, the meaning of life is to make more meaning, which is close to saying that the meaning of life is constantly to create more value. In this way, Dewey's idea of endless growth resembles the aims of the Soka Gakkai.

DEWEY'S TEACHERS

IKEDA: This is the essential mission of both education and philosophy.

At the age of eighty, to an interviewer's inquiry about how he lived in a world of insecurity and manifold problems, Dewey replied, "My philosophy of life is based essentially on the single word *patience*."[5] Dewey both described and practiced his philosophy of pragmatism as a form of patience or forbearance. Perhaps it is not too much of a stretch to see in this quality a similarity to the Soka Gakkai philosophy of value creation, aimed at the happiness of both self and others.

Among the many people who influenced him in evolving this philosophy, we must not overlook the three teachers who did much to improve and elevate him as a scholar and individual: H. A. P. Torrey of the University of Vermont; William Torrey Harris, who gave him a place to publish his philosophical thesis; and George S. Morris of Johns Hopkins University, who helped him both officially and personally.

GARRISON: Dewey was literally a pupil—in your sense, a disciple—of Torrey and Morris. In his sense, he was their student in a shared inquiry, and they were his teachers. He was very grateful.

Torrey encouraged him to go on to graduate school at Johns Hopkins. Significantly, in his autobiographical essay "From Absolutism to Experimentalism," Dewey wrote that Torrey was constitutionally timid and would never give his mind free rein, and that, if he had, he might have done great things. Dewey also said that, often in their talks together, just the two of them, Torrey would let his mind go.[6]

I think this is an interesting case in which a devoted and capable disciple could actually have helped the mentor go further down the road. But as Dewey said, Torrey's constitutional timidity was an obstacle in his own path. Dewey was gentle with that criticism because he clearly admired Torrey and knew the debt he owed him. He was not an ungrateful student, but the truth is Dewey was correct.

When George Sylvester Morris died suddenly and at a relatively young age, Dewey wrote a memoriam in which he praised both the man's incredible power and the quality of his character. He also said that for Morris, the spirit of poetry and the spirit of philosophy were the same.[7]

HICKMAN: When Dewey returned to Burlington after two years of teaching high school in Oil City, Pennsylvania, he once again turned to Torrey for counsel. And without the advice and support of William T. Harris, who was the founder of the first journal of professional philosophy in America and who would become the U.S. commissioner of education, Dewey might never have pursued philosophy as a profession.

George Sylvester Morris was Dewey's main professor during his graduate studies at Johns Hopkins University. When Dewey completed his doctorate in 1884, Morris offered him a position at the University of Michigan.[8]

Shortly after Morris's untimely death on a camping trip in 1889 (at the young age of forty-eight), Dewey wrote about the ways in which his teacher's philosophy had fused with his personal character, about his love for all that was beautiful in life, and about his great capacity for sympathy. Dewey took pains to point out that Morris had taught that the conventional split between the natural and the supernatural revealed a deeper truth—that of the unity of the natural and the spiritual (in the sense of the best of human insights and aspirations).

The Deweys named their third child, born in 1892, Morris. Dewey's wife, Alice, had been a student of Morris at the University of Michigan, and both she and John were eager to acknowledge their affection for their wonderful mentor.

These three mentors served Dewey well as he began to establish himself as a professional philosopher. But there was something more. Dewey was by all accounts a very shy and retiring young man who suffered from a substantial deficit of self-confidence. The support these three mentors provided helped him establish a certain professional trajectory, to be sure, but must also have helped him develop the personal traits he would need to work with the wide range of people, especially those outside academic circles, that he would eventually encounter in his role as an educational reformer.

Fellow Seekers

Ikeda: You bring up an important point, vividly communicating Dewey's respect and gratitude for his teachers and their enlightenment and support. The influence they had on the development of his naturally self-effacing personality provides abundant, profound food for thought. With his ingrained humility, Dewey communicated candidly not only with students and other scholars but also with people from all walks of life—laborers, social activists, women, and children—with whom he formed strong friendships, in the process elevating his own thought and philosophy.

He also developed his philosophy through joint projects with trusted scholarly colleagues such as George Herbert Mead and James Hayden Tufts. Dewey's life testifies to the truth of Emerson's words, "Life would be twice or ten times life, if spent with wise and fruitful companions."[9]

Having good friends is a jewel that enriches life and enhances its value. Exchanges with close friends expand one's capabilities and bring them to flower. Buddhism calls the comrades who join with us in seeking the Buddhist way "good friends" and teaches that associating with such good friends deepens one's faith and increases one's wisdom. I believe the presence of a network of such good friends in Dewey's life is a noteworthy factor in considering his philosophy.

Hickman: As you indicate, Dewey enjoyed the support of close friends, among whom were George Herbert Mead and James Hayden Tufts. Dewey and Mead were especially close. They were together on the faculty of the University of Michigan, and when Dewey moved to the University of Chicago in 1894, he brought Mead with him. They collaborated on experiments in psychology during Dewey's years at Chicago, and their friendship and professional collaboration continued until Mead's death in 1931. I think it is fair to say that many of the ideas that Dewey expressed about the importance of communication in his 1925 masterwork *Experience and Nature* came from his discussions with Mead.

IKEDA: What you say will be helpful to all young scholars. As a result of each having a trusted friend with whom to engage in fruitful dialogue, Dewey and Mead refined, polished, and matured their philosophies. Their earnest conversations opened a new intellectual realm for humanity.

Buddhist practice is also a form of communication—that of mutual inquiry among comrades. The Soka Gakkai places great importance on its tradition of monthly discussion meetings, in which members gather to discuss their lives and experiences in faith, increase their understanding of Buddhism, and encourage one another.

President Makiguchi started them as "Discussion Meetings for the Empirical Verification of the Life of Great Good." Participants explain and offer empirical verification of the benefits that they, their families, and society experience through Buddhist practice. President Makiguchi studied and was deeply sympathetic with the principles expressed in Dewey's *The School and Society* and other works. Ideas similar to Makiguchi's concept of the discussion meeting as a venue for "empirical verification" and dialogue can be found in Dewey's philosophy. This deserves further study.

GARRISON: That is something to look forward to.

In the fuller sense of "fellow seekers of the Way," I would mention Ella Flagg Young, Jane Addams, and Dewey's wife, Alice. It is evident that he was influenced by women, including Alice, who had tremendous influence on him intellectually. This is important. Anyone's wife is going to have tremendous influence. We are married men; we can acknowledge that.

IKEDA: I have come to see that with the great men I have met, there have always been great women standing shoulder to shoulder with them. As an example, the father of modern chemistry and great peace activist Linus Pauling told me that it was because of his wife, Ava Helen Pauling, that he became involved in the peace movement: "I felt compelled to earn and keep her respect. She always understood the reasons for all my actions. And I did not want her to think I was a coward."[10]

The voice of courageous women striving in earnest for the happiness of others has the power to move history and reform society.

HICKMAN: I should be remiss not to mention an instance in which Dewey himself served as a mentor. He received a great deal of correspondence and tried to answer as much of it as he could. *The Correspondence of John Dewey* contains more than 22,000 items. In 1916, an admiring teenager from Alabama named Myrtle McGraw wrote him a short letter. His response began a correspondence with this high-school girl that would last for many years.

He encouraged her to pursue a career in psychology. After receiving a degree from Columbia University, she became a well-known researcher at Babies Hospital (today the New York-Presbyterian Morgan Stanley Children's Hospital, part of the Columbia University Medical Center) in New York City.

IKEDA: It's a beautiful story.

A word of encouragement can be incredibly important, a precious seed of inspiration that develops into something grand and wonderful in the future. People blessed with outstanding leaders and teachers are fortunate, because such encounters can enable them to develop and demonstrate their potential to the fullest.

What memorable mentors did the two of you have?

GARRISON: The first relationship of this kind I can remember is with Miss Goode, my twelfth-grade history teacher. I might add that I only got a C in her class. But she always accentuated the love of learning. Once, near the end of the year, in front of the whole class, she looked at me and said, "Jim, of all of my students, you are the only one I know who has the love of learning."

She understood that, although I was not a good student, I was a reader. My friends and I read and talked about books. In fact, on one occasion, when I got caught skipping school, I was actually reading in the library.

Modern schooling, not education, operates largely on a deficit model. It's pathological; it's like medicine. It wants to see what is wrong with you. The wrong with me was very plain for anyone to see. But Miss Goode was interested in what was right about me. She was always my favorite teacher.

IKEDA: Your story warms the heart. Miss Goode is a brilliant example of the way praise can become a force for development and growth. It is important for us to look for children's good qualities. Once we find their good points, we should immediately, sincerely praise them.

At the ceremony where Shakyamuni Buddha expounded the Lotus Sutra, he repeatedly shared praise: "Excellent, excellent!"[11] The Buddha praises living beings as a way of awakening and strengthening the Buddha nature inherent in their lives. I see a correspondence between this attitude of the Buddha and that of the educator who praises students judiciously to stimulate their growth and development.

I, too, have many recollections of this kind. Immediately after

World War II, I went to work at a small printing company to augment the family finances, as my father was incapacitated by rheumatism. To keep up my studies, I attended night classes at Toyo Commercial (now called Toyo High School), where I had some wonderful teachers.

I did well enough in most of my classes, but I had difficulty learning how to calculate on the Japanese abacus, or *soroban*. One day, when I got a bad mark in that subject, the teacher kindly invited me out for a cup of coffee. Instead of scolding me, he skillfully encouraged me, "I know how bad you must feel about your poor marks in abacus calculation, especially when you are doing so well in your other subjects." He knew I was studying while working and understood how hard that must be. I deeply appreciated his warmth and sincerity, and I cherish the memory to this day.

Teachers can have a tremendous effect on our lives, and I am sure that many other people could cite similar unforgettable experiences.

GARRISON: I imagine so. One of my teachers in graduate school was a renowned analytic philosopher named Jaakko Hintikka. He is a technical thinker and a mathematical philosopher, but what I learned from him was how to let your mind go. He taught me to go ahead and think any crazy thing that comes to mind, then later to review it, adjust it, or do whatever else was necessary. The idea was first to play with ideas and then clean them up later.

But my true mentor in life was Jim Macmillan (C. J. B. Macmillan), and no two people could have been more different than us. He was closely related to the British Macmillans, one of whom was prime minister during the 1950s. Jim was tall—six foot three—and aristocratic. As you know, I am not a tall man and have neither aristocratic bearing nor an aristocratic background. Jim Macmillan taught me how to handle myself in genteel company and made me a part of his family.

He, too, was a renowned philosopher of education, in the technical, analytic tradition. When I started leaving analytic philosophy and wandering into pragmatism and places like that, he never approved, but he never disapproved either. He never once said anything about it. That's a mentor, not a master.

A master, of course, would have abandoned me. Allowing the disciple to actualize his or her unique potential along a unique path is a tremendous—perhaps the ultimate—gift from a mentor to a disciple.

Bluer Than Indigo

Ikeda: In *The System of Value-Creating Pedagogy,* President Makiguchi wrote:

> Teachers must not arrogantly set themselves up as great models for students to emulate. They must humbly lead their disciples and encourage them to progress as their teachers do, taking as their role models, not their own teachers, but those who are far greater than themselves. This is the right path for teachers to follow.[12]

First-rate people in all fields, not just education, are modest and humble; without humility, you cannot continue growing. Stagnation sets in the instant people decide that the status quo is good enough. "Not advancing is retreating"—when you're in retreat, you can't inspire passion in the young and move forward with them toward ideals.

Hickman: In terms of my professional life, I have the good fortune to have had a series of mentors, each of whom seemed to appear at just the right stage of development. The director of my doctoral dissertation, for example, Professor Ignacio Angelelli, opened my eyes to the fascinating complexity of the history of philosophy and the wonders of international scholarship. At home in several languages, including Spanish, Italian, German, Latin, Greek, Polish, and Russian, he challenged me to a more disciplined study of languages. He insisted that by the time my doctoral thesis was complete, there should be no one in the world who knew more than I about the subject I had chosen.

IKEDA: That is powerful encouragement! And you have fully justified it.

As my mentor always told me:

> You must study more, much more.... Otherwise you cannot accomplish your future mission. I'm not talking about your faith alone. You must also become well-versed in all the affairs of society. Furthermore, you must place yourself within the destiny of the entire world and formulate all of your ideas from this perspective.[13]

My discussions with intellectuals from all over the world have made me even more intensely aware of the weight of Toda's words.

Leaders who, like your mentors Ignacio Angelelli and C. J. B. Macmillan, can encourage young people from the broadest possible perspective, pointing out lofty peaks of ideals to them, have the power to build the world of the future.

HICKMAN: They certainly do. In terms of my private life, I should also mention Lee Freeman, a progressive Baptist minister in Austin, Texas, during the 1960s. Many public facilities in Austin were still racially segregated at that time; he was a prominent voice for progress in racial relations, for equal rights for women, and against American military involvement in Southeast Asia. He and I spent many hours in his study discussing those issues, as well as some of the thorny theological issues that concerned me at the time. His patience and support were crucial to my own thinking and to my maturation as a person.

One of the most important lessons that these two mentors, Ignacio Angelelli and Lee Freeman, taught me was the importance of creating a platform that the disciple can use to go beyond the accomplishments of his or her mentor. Both were so secure in their sense of self that they were never threatened by the possibility that their students might achieve greater things, follow a different path, or take on disciples of their own. They considered such results testimony to their success as mentors. I think it is important that teachers adopt that attitude with their students, and I have attempted to follow their example.

IKEDA: Learning about your two mentors has moved me deeply, Professor Hickman. The noble spirit of affection you describe is essential to a true leader who wants his disciples to live a better life and accomplish more than he or she has.

An ancient Chinese saying employs the metaphor of dyeing fabric with indigo to express the idea of the disciple surpassing the mentor. Indigo leaves were used to dye textiles blue in ancient times, and repeated steepings of the fabric created a color deeper and more intense than the dye itself. The simile also appears in some Buddhist texts.

President Makiguchi often referred to "from the indigo, an even deeper blue" as describing the special character of Soka education. Disciples inherit ideas and spirit from their mentors, then go on to revitalize and further develop them for the sake of limitless growth, thus making enduring contributions to human happiness. It is in this sense that the bluer-than-indigo spirit is so important.

CONVERSATION FIVE

The Cost of War

IKEDA: My mentor perceptively observed the astonishing development of American society, the best of which is exemplified by John Dewey's philosophy. In contrast, Japan's reliance on state Shinto ultimately led to the launching of a reckless war that plunged people into misery. Who would win and who would lose the war, Mr. Toda said, was crystal clear before the fighting began. With this bold assertion, he was casting into sharp relief the vitality of American democratic society based on pragmatism while highlighting the fearsome results of a mistaken philosophy and education, and their power to wreck a whole nation and bring misery to the masses.

GARRISON: In the beginning of our discussion, I spoke of the subject matter that a conversation between Dewey and Makiguchi might have had if they had ever met and suggested that Japanese militarism and social class structure would form the most important part of their talk (see Conversation One). Dewey would certainly have shared the profound concern entertained by Makiguchi and Toda about undervaluing human life and existence.

HICKMAN: Opposition to official Japanese militarism during the 1930s and 1940s involved acts of courage that are very difficult for most of us today to appreciate fully. The lesson that Mr. Makiguchi found in the writings of those who influenced him, such as Nichiren and Dewey, and that he put into practice at the eventual cost of his own life was that the measure of our experience must come from within human practices themselves.

For example, Makiguchi rejected the dogmas that the Japanese educational establishment sought to impose on teachers and students. He instead experimented with novel forms of teacher-student interaction and learned from the concrete experiences of the classroom.

IKEDA: Before and during the war, under the infamous Peace Preservation Law, freedom of speech and belief were taken away from the Japanese people, and their fundamental human rights were thoroughly violated. The philosophical pillar of Japanese imperialism was a view of the nation based on state Shinto.

This was recorded in the *Kokutai no hongi* (The Cardinal Principles of the National Body), compiled by the Ministry of Education in 1937 as Japan moved toward greater militarism. This document speaks of an everlasting, immutable Japanese empire eternally governed according to decrees of the forever unbroken, imperial ancestral line. It sweepingly criticizes Western philosophy and learning, specifically rejecting the idea of the individual as the origin and arbiter of all values, which determines the basic personality of modern Western culture. The teachers' schools (normal schools) of the time were compelled to use this as a textbook in their compulsory curriculum, and the values it preached were incorporated into the moralistic textbooks for elementary-school children.

As Japan prepared to go to war, such thought control intensified. The militarist government employed education as a tool to incite the people to war and encourage their utter self-sacrifice. It was this militarist philosophy and education—denying the liberty and dignity of humanity—that President Makiguchi was fighting against.

HICKMAN: When Dewey was in Japan in 1919, he was appalled by the educational situation in much the same way that Makiguchi was appalled by it. Dewey was particularly upset that teachers were putting more emphasis on obedience to the emperor than they were on learning. He reported that Japanese society seemed to have little or no private or public institutional structure between the family and the supreme state authority.

IKEDA: In a truly democratic society, fundamental citizens' rights are protected, and various civil institutions stand between individual families and state authorities. These autonomous civil institutions not dependent upon the state stand guard against state abuse of power and serve as a deterrent force. In a totalitarian society, however, the state absorbs everything and oppresses the populace.

In Japan during the war, diverse organizations effectively acted in complicity with the militarist government. Even Nichiren Shoshu kowtowed to state authorities and attempted to compel Mr. Makiguchi to enshrine Shinto talismans.[1] His refusal to do so was one of the reasons advanced for arresting him on suspicion of lèse majesté and violating the Peace Preservation Law.

Sound, balanced education is important to ensure that society never again lapses into that kind of extremism.

HICKMAN: Dewey recognized that education is one of the most powerful tools at our disposal to overcome the forces of extreme nationalism, bigotry, and intolerance, which, as you indicate, are among the forces that often lead to war. Dewey was highly critical of the Japanese educational system that he found in 1919, because he thought it overly authoritarian. He saw that the schools had been captured by powers moving the country toward a militarist stance with respect to its neighbors. Dewey was so displeased with what he found that, when the government offered to award him the Order of the Rising Sun (Japan's third highest award), he declined as a form of protest.

Ikeda: Nothing is more frightening than misleading education. When I was a teenager, our heads were crammed with the idea of sacrificing our lives for the nation's sake.

Under the influence of this propaganda, behind my parents' backs, I volunteered for the air corps of the preparatory pilot training course. When he found out, my father strongly opposed the idea. Four of his sons had already been drafted by the military, and he could not bear to send any more children to war. Ordinarily a taciturn person, he lost his temper and scolded me so harshly that I abandoned the plan.

If I had joined up then, I might in due course have been assigned to the Special Attack Units. Toward the end of the war, members of the air corps who knew how to take off but had not yet been taught how to land an aircraft were sent on missions and sacrificed.

Dewey and Makiguchi

Hickman: You, too, clearly had experiences of the kind that Dewey reported.

If Dewey and Makiguchi had met, I am convinced that they would have talked about the need to organize institutions that could help individual families, like your own, deal with such problems. And they would probably have agreed that schools are ideal places for establishing and nurturing institutions, such as parent-teacher organizations and those that provide social services, as well as the student clubs that foster opportunities for democratic exercises.

GARRISON: Only a pluralistic and communicative democratic education releases the unique potential of all individuals that they may make their unique contributions to society. This idea is crucial to Dewey's educational philosophy.

President Ikeda, your idea of "human revolution"—meaning self-motivated, positive change within the life of an individual that can also bring about a change in his or her environment—is an important aim of structured and methodical formal school education as well as of the kind of spontaneous, everyday, informal education you received from Toda.

Japan's militarist government sought only mindless indoctrination, conformity, and sacrifice to predetermined ends, which is the worst form of mis-education. Your father was right to be angry.

Because they fail to release the unique potential of every individual to make a creative contribution to the greater good of society while also benefiting themselves, militarist nations are unable to employ their citizens' abilities fully and are, therefore, unable to evolve and adjust to changing conditions.

IKEDA: During his 1919 visit, Dewey delivered a famous series of lectures at Tokyo Imperial University (today Tokyo University). Although his coming to Japan caused a great stir and generated high expectations, reactions from the Japanese academic world were disappointing. Japanese modern history might have been quite different if our society had studied Dewey's thought with greater depth and humility, and embraced it more broadly.

During that period, when militaristic, chauvinistic thought prevailed in Japanese society, Makiguchi paid keen attention to Dewey's philosophy and emphasized the excellence of his ideas.

In his celebrated *The School and Society*, Dewey advocated "living primarily, and learning through and in relation to this living."[2] President Makiguchi incorporated this aspect of Dewey's philosophy in what he called "the Life of Great Good," the practice of life-reformation that was the Soka Kyoiku Gakkai's goal. In its journal *Kachi sozo* (Value Creation), Makiguchi wrote that the merit of the life of great good must be verified within and by means of daily living.

This statement appeared in the issue published on December 5, 1941, a couple days before the Japanese attack on Pearl Harbor that started the war in the Pacific. At a general meeting of the Soka Kyoiku Gakkai in November 1942, after Japan and the United States had been at war for nearly a year, Makiguchi made a similar statement:

> One's way of life cannot be understood until one actually lives a life. According to the American pragmatist philosopher John Dewey, the way of life is verified in and by daily living. There is no reason to doubt this truth.

In an age when praising an enemy's ideas and philosophy was inconceivable, President Makiguchi made this bold public declaration. This was an act of courage nearly beyond our capacity to imagine today.

HICKMAN: When they are subjected to an external authority—to an edict of the government, to those who claim to speak for a deity, or to any other type of alleged norms imposed upon experience from without—the meanings of our lives are diminished. It is only by free and open interaction with our environments—natural as well as social environments—that we can continue to grow and to create value.

Whenever and wherever there are people who think it is in their interest to obstruct the growth of intelligence, then extraordinary individuals are often called upon to make extraordinary sacrifices to set matters right. It is altogether proper that we honor Mr. Makiguchi and Mr. Toda, along with others who have resisted the iron heel of authoritarianism, for their sacrifices.

IKEDA: Reflecting on twentieth-century history, I am compelled to reaffirm the important mission and responsibility of education. Moreover, with the increasing globalization of contemporary society, the significance of education for world citizenship grows proportionately greater.

In Dewey's words,

> What are our schools doing to cultivate not merely passive toleration that will put up with people of different racial birth or different colored skin, but what are our schools doing positively and aggressively and constructively to cultivate understanding and goodwill which are essential to democratic society?[3]

This question conveys Dewey's energetic spirit. He made the effort to foster people of understanding and goodwill, build a network of like-minded individuals, and contribute to the creation of a peaceful society. Educators need to be brimming with this overflowing dynamism. This is the way to engender the energy to carry out the noble mission of schooling and education.

An overview of Western educators who have focused on children and the education of global citizens for peace starts with Johannes Amos Comenius and progresses through Jean-Jacques Rousseau, Immanuel Kant, Johan Heinrich Pestalozzi, and Johann Friedrich Herbart to John Dewey. President Makiguchi placed major emphasis on Kant, Pestalozzi, and Herbart. The educational philosophies of these individuals are pillars of our intellectual heritage.

We could discuss their philosophies from various perspectives, but I am especially interested in your opinions on the importance of educating global citizens as a force for preventing war.

GARRISON: If the question is determining the importance of global citizens as a force for peace, you can scarcely overestimate it.

For two decades beginning in 1919, Dewey was the chief intellectual of the Outlawry of War movement. Basically, people active in this movement wanted to make war an international crime. That meant fundamentally changing our thinking about war.

He came to realize that it was going to be an education function. We know and talk readily about war—the fact that many war colleges (such as the Army War College in Carlisle, Pennsylvania, the Naval War College in Newport, Rhode Island, and the Air War College at Maxwell-Gunter Air Force Base in Montgomery, Alabama) exist but peace colleges generally do not is revealing. It is much harder for people to think about peace. Since no strong rhetoric surrounds it, even enabling the citizenry to hold an intelligent and thoughtful discourse on peace requires a great deal of educational work.

IKEDA: It is no exaggeration to say that the fate of the twenty-first century depends on our success in meeting this difficult challenge. Grass-roots dialogue and consciousness-raising movements are indispensable to this end. The idea of peace colleges inspires immense hope.

We of the SGI are engaged in pacifist activities around the world. For example, we have compiled the testimonials of victims of the Hiroshima and Nagasaki atomic bombings, collected the signatures of more than 13 million people opposed to nuclear weapons, and sponsored exhibitions and lectures all over the world advocating the elimination of the atomic arsenal.

On their own initiative, many members of our women's division in Japan study and discuss peace in what they call *peace schools*. In connection with the 2010 Nuclear Nonproliferation Treaty Review Conference in May, our young people started collecting signatures calling for a Nuclear Weapons Convention that would ban the development, testing, production, use, and threat of nuclear weapons.

I believe that concrete action and dialogue to teach people about the horrors of war and inculcate in them the spirit of nonviolence are important elements in global-citizen education.

HICKMAN: The question is how to estimate the importance of educating global citizens. You have identified one of the most vital tasks of educators. In traveling to many countries and speaking to young people from many different cultures, I have encountered a remarkable idealism and generosity of spirit. I have found a natural curiosity about other cultures and their peoples.

Even though we know that it suffers from obvious defects and creates many problems, I am convinced that the Internet can be an enormous force for cross-cultural understanding. Because of it, people are now able to ignore political boundaries as they organize themselves around specific interests or form various support groups. At the level of universities and even high schools, I am convinced that the future of peace studies will depend on the success of study-abroad programs.

IKEDA: Yes, many institutions are attempting to educate people about diverse cultures and values.

At Soka University of America, we have a program requiring all students in their third year to spend a semester studying abroad. They choose a language—Chinese, Spanish, or Japanese—and then spend that semester living and communicating with people in countries where that language is spoken. (SUA expanded the study-abroad program to include French in 2013.)

Studying abroad in this fashion provides a surprising experience, especially for students born in the United States. They say that witnessing firsthand different cultures and traditions, and the gap between the rich and the poor, makes them painfully aware of the limitations of what they have come to consider accepted truths. They also attest that it expands their horizons and makes them want to do something for the world's people.

HICKMAN: The international programs at Soka University of America provide a wonderful example of what can be done to educate, as you say, global citizens as a pacifist force. SUA students come from many different countries. They live, study, and play together. They form friendships and alliances that will continue as they return to their respective countries to become leaders of government, business, industry, and education. International networks of communication built at SUA and other universities that value such programs will have effects for decades to come.

GARRISON: I have visited Soka University of America twice now and both times found the commitment to international dialogue impressive.

DEWEY TODAY

IKEDA: This discussion is providing our students with much food for thought.

Now, to change the subject slightly, I would like to know whether Dewey's philosophy remains alive in America and how it is studied there today, 150 years after his birth (in 1859).

GARRISON: Dewey is very much alive in American society today, and he is certainly studied in many ways. Often, however, his influence is so deep and all-pervasive that it goes unrecognized by those who otherwise owe him a great debt of gratitude.

Ironically, it is very well recognized by those who would oppose him. In some ways, the significant thing is whether your enemies know you are important. In 2005, the national conservative weekly *Human Events* ranked Dewey's *Democracy and Education* as fifth among the ten most dangerous books published in the last 200 years, ahead of Karl Marx's *Das Kapital*.[4] That this publication felt the need to make such a ranking is a subtle indicator of Dewey's tremendous cultural influence.

Of course, in the civic life of my nation, Dewey lives on in institutions that he helped found, like the American Civil Liberties Union and the American Association of University Professors. These and other institutions with which he was involved, such as the New School for Social Research, constitute legacies that continue to be important in the American social fabric.

HICKMAN: I think it is fair to say that interest in Dewey's philosophy is now enjoying a revival after several decades during which his ideas were eclipsed by strands of Cold-War positivism, existentialism, and other movements. His influence is now being felt in the areas of social and political philosophy, public planning and administration, medical ethics, environmental and agricultural ethics, and even in the policies of the Obama administration in Washington, D. C.

I have some friends and colleagues who work for the Center for American Progress, which is a think tank run by John Podesta, the fourth and final White House chief of staff under President Bill Clinton, serving from 1998 until 2001.[5] I understand that CAP was influential during President Barak Obama's transition to the White House and in helping the Obama administration plot a new course. CAP was stocked with people who knew Dewey's work very well. One of my colleagues told me that many of them now work for the Obama administration.

IKEDA: Dewey's philosophy is a treasure of American society.

During his visit to Tokyo in November 2009, President Obama delivered a speech setting forth his Asian policies. Although I was invited to attend, my schedule necessitated sending someone to represent me. Many Japanese follow with great interest and sympathy his bold efforts toward the elimination of nuclear weapons and his challenge to build harmonious bonds among diverse cultures and ethnic groups. I am encouraged to learn that many people in the U.S. government are conversant with Dewey's philosophy.

Hickman: During his lifetime, Dewey was the target of a great deal of criticism. He was attacked from the political left as well as from the political right.

Today, most of his critics are from the extreme right, especially religious fundamentalists. He is still regularly compared to both Hitler and Stalin. If you go to the Internet and type in his name, you can see how his ideas are misunderstood and even feared. There are fundamentalist Christian home-schoolers, for example, who think that Dewey held a form of "anything goes" relativism or the view that all ideas are of equal value.

That is, of course, nonsense. Instead, what he argued is that even our most cherished norms tend to be abstractions that require interpretive contexts in order to be applied.

Ikeda: This is proof of Dewey's greatness. Throughout history, all movements seeking reform have been, to a greater or lesser degree, targets of misunderstanding and criticism. Nichiren said, "Worthies and sages are tested by abuse"[6] and "To be praised by fools—that is the greatest shame."[7]

The Soka Gakkai and I have often been misunderstood and defamed—the natural result of our continued struggle against the evils threatening human happiness and dignity. We have considered this a badge of honor for our peace movement and have persisted in our efforts, certain of our convictions.

"If people wish to laugh at me, let them laugh away. If they wish to jeer at me, let them jeer away. Empty slurs and criticisms are beneath me." From my youth, this indomitable pledge has always filled my heart.

HICKMAN: Your persistence in the face of opposition and defamation is a matter of historical record, and it is admirable. Although Dewey could at times be very direct when responding to his critics, he understood that the best response was to lead an exemplary life that put his ideas into practice.

GARRISON: The thing Dewey most stressed was lived reality, the realistic necessities of everyday life. Both the Soka Gakkai and Dewey adopt action-oriented philosophies, not epistemology-oriented philosophies. They are bound to be misunderstood.

The advantage of Dewey's pragmatic, action-oriented life philosophy is that it understands that right action is even more important than knowledge. Although right action requires knowledge, knowledge alone will not lead to right action.

IKEDA: Truth is the supreme vindication. Dewey's life proves this, as do all great people's lives.

Finding Balance

GARRISON: One of the things that Dewey does magnificently well is to coordinate the individual self with society, to bring out the best in each. On the one hand, he rejects the egotistic, atomistic individual of a modernity—certainly at least Western modernity—where the individual is conceived as cut off from society. On the other hand, he says that genuine individuals develop by contributing to society.

While doing away with the egotistic, atomistic individual,

Dewey insisted that only individuals create. This effort to balance unique individuality with the social nature of the individual has led to criticisms of Dewey from both the political left, which often thinks he underemphasizes the social, and the right, which often thinks he denies human individuality.

IKEDA: Dewey held an unsympathetic view of nationalism and totalitarianism, which deny human dignity. As Professor Hickman mentioned, Dewey refused in 1919 an honor offered him by the Japanese government as a protest against its policies. Then, visiting China and witnessing Japanese aggression firsthand, he declared that Japan was in need of a complete revolution.

In *Democracy and Education,* Dewey stated that the reason the "few set in authority" needed to impose a condition of intellectual subjection on the people was to fit the

> masses into a society where the many are not expected to have aims or ideas of their own, but to take orders from the few set in authority. It [intellectual subjection] is not adapted to a society which intends to be democratic.[8]

Such was the very danger he sensed in Japanese society.

Later, Japan was to invade several Asian nations, leaving profound scars. We Japanese must remember this part of our history. In order not to repeat this tragedy, education of world citizens is vital.

HICKMAN: Yes, in terms of his work, Dewey was certainly not pro-war. He was pro-education, because he thought that education was the best way to prevent war. I think that he would have agreed very much with your statement. Dewey was clear about it: In terms of war, everybody loses; nobody really gains. But if you have a strong, vibrant education, then everybody gains.

GARRISON: When lecturing in Denmark, I was told that the song students were singing one morning was written by the Danish educator N. F. S. Grundtvig. My host said that his favorite line in it translated into English as "God protect us from the spirit that would have us march in lines like ants." People sometimes become mindless cogs in the war machine.

Dewey has a very functional, very organic notion of education, in which individual and social growth is the aim of education. The only ultimate value is life itself.

The basic contrast is simply that war kills. What war does is to sever ties, destroy things and people, and wreck relationships.

IKEDA: After World War I, the Outlawry of War movement spread among the American people, initiating a great wave of popular support that resulted in the Kellogg-Briand Pact in 1928. Evaluations of the significance of the agreement to outlaw war vary, but one of the biggest public demonstrations in American history was organized in connection with the pact's conclusion and ratification. A petition in its favor with more than two million signatures was presented to the Senate.

Because war robs humanity of dignity in every sense, it is the ugliest of acts, the destruction of life. This is why we of the SGI have expanded a worldwide network of people dedicated to peace, culture, and education, based on the Buddhist principle of respect for the dignity of life.

In August 1942, in the midst of World War II, Dewey wrote of the need for a new kind of peace for a new age. I also believe that a new kind of education based on a new foundation of humanistic philosophy is needed to build a new force for peace. The Indian champion of nonviolence, Mahatma Gandhi, said, "If we are to reach real peace in this world and if we are to carry on a real war against war, we shall have to begin with children."[9]

CONVERSATION SIX

All Children Unique

IKEDA: Education is a focal point of the twenty-first century. Progress in education equates to progress in society and hope for humanity. One of Dewey's unshakable articles of faith was that "we must take our stand with the child and our departure from him."[1] This is an immortal guideline for the future.

In a similar vein, President Makiguchi asserted that the fundamental purpose of education is the student's "realization of happiness."[2] Both of these pioneering educators made working for the sake of children their starting point. We must always embrace in our hearts the key question, "For what purpose?"

HICKMAN: As you suggest, Dewey thought that education was an end in itself. It is tragic when schools and universities abandon that ideal in order to serve the transient ends and interests of the state. For example, in 1918, during World War I, all universities in the United States were virtually nationalized, and all healthy male students over the age of eighteen effectively became soldiers of the United States.

At Dewey's own Columbia University, some of his closest colleagues were dismissed for engaging in such allegedly unpatriotic activities as questioning American involvement in the war. As we know, Dewey encountered a similar situation in Japan during his visit in 1919. As we have discussed, he was highly critical of the emperor worship he found in Japanese schools.

GARRISON: Many people misunderstand *happiness* as meaning pleasure or success. That is not what Makiguchi and Dewey meant.

Recently, two of my friends, Stephen M. Fishman and Lucille McCarthy, shared with me some of their work on Dewey and happiness. As they point out, Dewey thought of happiness as a stable condition of personal development involving moral courage and calm self-composure. A happy person is one who has actualized his unique potential to respond to physical, biological, and social situations in ways that create meaning and value. The aim of education is growth in the sense of actualizing one's unique potential to achieve a stable, courageous, and composed character capable of making unique contributions to the community.

IKEDA: Abundance and material satisfaction alone do not determine happiness.

At the end of the nineteenth century, Dewey made this keen observation about school education:

> The aim is . . . the development of social power and insight. It is this liberation from narrow utilities, this openness to the possibilities of the human spirit, that makes these practical activities in the school allies of art and centers of science and history.[3]

Dewey envisioned expansive educational horizons. President Makiguchi also regarded the goal of education as educating the whole person, fostering a wholesome, open mind transcending narrow self-interest.

GARRISON: Dewey's thoughts on the utility of education are close to Makiguchi's. That two people so far apart in distance could share such insights shows how profoundly timeless was the truth they realized.

Every human being has unique as well as generic social and biological needs, desires, and purposes. Students learn and grow by creatively exercising their capacities to overcome obstacles and transform their environments, thereby creating value. In this way, they acquire a wholesome discipline quite different from what is imposed by authoritarian teaching, which assumes that students are passive and require external motivation to act. Habits of independence emerge as students learn to exercise their capacities intelligently under careful supervision.

IKEDA: At a time when education in Japan was predominantly authoritarian, President Makiguchi established its goal as bringing into flower the limitless possibilities of the human spirit, cultivating them, and enabling the full, vibrant manifestation of these possibilities.

A century ago, both Dewey and Makiguchi envisioned a new age and advocated the need to create a humanistic education founded on children's happiness. Their philosophies were in diametric opposition to education as subservient to the state or the economy.

Good Nutrition

HICKMAN: Today, at a turning point in history, it is important for everyone involved in education to realize this. The future, to a large extent, depends on whether we have people to take the helm and guide us in this connection.

At the moment, the growing influence of economic ends in schools is a particularly difficult problem in the United States at all levels of education. A recent report on the website of the University of Virginia, for example, listed state appropriations at less than 10 percent. Nationwide, the trend in state support is downward, according to the State Higher Education Executive Officers Association. Per student appropriation in 1987 was about $8,500. In 2012, it was a bit less than $6,000. That's a decline of almost 30 percent. American universities are increasingly reliant on business, industry, and the military for funding.

But it is far from clear that the interests of business, industry, and the military coincide with the interests of sound pedagogy. This situation is related to some extent to increasing tuition costs, with attendant stresses on low-income families who wish to send their children to college.

At the level of primary and secondary schools, the interests of business often take precedence over those of good pedagogy. Some schools, for example, have supplemented their budgets by replacing traditional healthy lunches with fast-food franchises. American students are now noticeably more obese than they were even a decade ago. This is a situation that is just beginning to be apparent in other countries, too.

Effective pedagogy requires good nutrition, and good nutrition requires that schools not sell out to the interests of the fast-food industry for a share of their profits.

IKEDA: The issue of nutrition, with its direct link to children's health, is very important. There has been much concern about children's nutrition in Japan, and in 2005, a law was enacted to add dietary education to other core focuses such as intellectual, physical, and moral education. Greater efforts are also being made to improve the nutritional quality of school meals.[4]

It is important for society as a whole to recognize this problem and support efforts to promote better diets for our children. In recent years, Japanese schools have adopted the motto "Early to bed, early to rise, and a good breakfast" to stress the importance of healthy daily habits and meals. This is a result of studies that have shown the powerful effect enough sleep and a good breakfast have on such factors as children's concentration, vigor, and physical and intellectual powers.

Nichiren wrote: "Food has three virtues. First, it sustains life. Second, it enlivens the complexion. Third, it nourishes strength."[5] Children cannot grow strong if proper nutrition is neglected.

In the early 1920s, when he was principal of Mikasa Primary School, Makiguchi used his own money to buy healthy snacks for children too poor to bring their own lunches to school. Inspired by the penny-lunch project of some Chicago suburbs, he also used monetary donations to provide free bread and soup—a fact that was reported in the *Yomiuri Shimbun*, a leading Japanese newspaper, on December 8, 1921.

Mr. Makiguchi strove tirelessly to enable students to attend school and enjoy the learning process. I am reminded that a deep, abiding love for children must underlie every aspect of education, even a single school meal.

GARRISON: I am pleased that you have so many useful things to say about children's good health. Dewey, too, emphasized life and the living creature in not only his theory of education but also his aesthetics and his logic. In his presidential address to the American Philosophical Association, he even refuted abstract, philosophical idealists by asking what they will do when they realize that beings with bowels as well as brains influence reality.[6]

An important part of Dewey's educational philosophy involves rejecting the mind-versus-body distinction. Once we do that, we can realize that, properly understood, physical, intellectual, and moral education are all subfunctions of a single, organically unified system. We may also realize that a healthy lifestyle, including regular exercise and diet, are indispensable to proper growth and development. Therefore, they are important parts of good education.

HICKMAN: Another problem point in the United States involves television. Not long ago, some American primary schools received support from a so-called educational television channel for children called Channel One, which interrupted the children's day with advertisements. Our children are already bombarded by too much advertising outside the classroom. There is no place for advertising in the classroom.

Still another issue is testing. Evidence seems to support the view of many serious educators that much of the testing mania now replacing good pedagogy is driven by the financial interests of the companies that prepare tests. The interests of those companies are not necessarily those of the schools, the children, their parents, or the educational process.[7]

THE EARLY YEARS

IKEDA: These contemporary developments may seem isolated, but in fact they are manifestations of broader, underlying social problems. In my educational proposals,[8] I have consistently emphasized a society devoted to the interests of education, rejecting the paradigm of education that serves the interests of society. We need to work together as a society to foster our children, our treasures who will shoulder the future. In the process, we will also open the way to solving the problems afflicting contemporary society.

Skeptical about the merits of traditional educational methods at the end of the nineteenth century, John Dewey accepted the challenge of devising teaching methods that enhanced children's independence and individuality. As is well known, he conducted various experiments at the University of Chicago Laboratory Schools, of which he was in charge.

HICKMAN: Characteristic of his educational practice, the Laboratory Schools exemplified the idea that children are always most important and that abstract theorizing is meaningless.

IKEDA: All children are unique individuals. They cannot all be forced into some single, standard mold. Any serious effort at education must necessarily take their uniqueness and individuality fully into account.

The Soka Gakkai Education Department (for teachers from prekindergarten to high school) has compiled reports on field cases over the years, called the Educational Practice Record. The logs record teachers' creative, ingenious approaches in the classroom, as well as their tireless efforts to find solutions to problematic student behavior. Each account constitutes a kind of drama of the growth and sound development of students. More than 40,000 such accounts have been recorded (65,000 cases as of 2013). They have been well received and stirred tremendous interest among educators, both inside and outside our organization, as invaluable data.

One of the common themes of the case records is that faith in every child's potential is vital to education, and adults need to help children attain the independence to take an active part in solving their own problems. As Dewey put it, "The moment children act they individualize themselves."[9]

HICKMAN: I am particularly delighted to hear about the case studies in the Educational Practice Record. They indeed have the potential to provide invaluable examples of problem solving in the classroom. If they have not already been published, I hope that, when properly redacted, they will be made available to teachers everywhere.

IKEDA: Many of them have already been published in Japan and introduced in various educational journals. Thank you for your recommendation, which is sure to encourage the teachers who have been working on this project for many years.

HICKMAN: I am pleased by your emphasis on the uniqueness of each personal record. Dewey believed that educational testing should be treated like medical testing. Tests should be individualized with a goal of improving the educational experience of each student. They should never be used to compare one student to another.

GARRISON: The teacher's task is not inserting information into passive minds, which many mistakenly think resemble computers. Instead, teachers must rely on sympathetic compassion while studying students through personal observation, experimentation, and reflection.

Good teachers enjoy learning with and about their students. I am sure the Educational Practice Record is a storehouse of such observations.

IKEDA: Teachers and students put to use what they have gained through learning and growing together. It's also important to transmit these precious experiences and insights acquired through the actual educational process to the next generation. It is this continuous, unflagging effort that assures the steady progress of education.

In your opinions, what led Dewey to stress early childhood and primary education when he became a university teacher?

GARRISON: Rejecting the mind-body dualism, Dewey understood that physical, social, and moral development is as important as mental development. Indeed, he realized that in terms of human functioning, they are inseparable.

His deep commitment to developmental education, wherein endless growth is the ultimate aim, allowed him to understand that early childhood is critical. He also supported research on infant development, such as that by Myrtle McGraw and others for whom he helped secure research funding. Today we know that prenatal development, too, is important.

HICKMAN: President Ikeda, as you mentioned, Dewey turned his attention as a university professor to primary education. I think it was in part because he was such an observant and caring parent. He and his wife, Alice, had seven children, including Sabino, an Italian boy they adopted after their son Gordon died of typhoid fever when the family was traveling in Europe.

Even though they were always struggling financially, Alice would often take the older children to Europe on cultural tours. For John and Alice, travel to Europe was not a luxury but a pedagogic necessity. They thought it essential to acquaint their children with other cultures, other languages, and other ways of thinking about the world.

IKEDA: Dewey wanted to open his children's eyes at an early age to different cultures. The Soka Junior and Senior High Schools, which I founded, also place great importance on welcoming and carrying out exchanges with guests from overseas. I imagine that Dewey's wife contributed her own ideas on the family's educational approach, but what kind of parent was Dewey?

HICKMAN: To give an example of his approach to parenting, in 1894, when Alice and the other children were in Europe, John was left in full charge of their two-year-old son, Morris. It was very rare in those days for a husband to take such an extensive role in childcare, sharing those domestic responsibilities with his wife.

I should add here that John Dewey had a deep commitment to the social equality of men and women. He was a strong advocate of admitting women to universities and even graduate school when those practices were still quite controversial.

IKEDA: I want to discuss women's education at length later on, but let me just say here that President Makiguchi was also a pioneering advocate of women's education in Japan. He offered a correspondence course for women that, at its peak, had an enrollment of more than 20,000 students. In addition, to promote women's independence, he operated a women's business school.

HICKMAN: I am increasingly surprised to discover how much he had in common with Dewey.

But to continue with Dewey's concentration on primary education, he was an experimenter. He thought that if departments of physics and chemistry had laboratories, then his department of education should have one as well. His Laboratory Schools were never meant to be a model for others. They were meant to do the type of thing that has been done with your Educational Practice Record—to try out pedagogical ideas and to develop further insights into the processes of education.

Dewey thought that the school is a laboratory of social change. It is a place where the ideals of democracy can be inculcated, where social virtues can be fostered, and where old ideas can be transformed and reconstructed.

VALUE CREATION

IKEDA: Because both disciplines deal with human life, President Makiguchi considered medicine and education sister sciences. He argued that education and educational methods should continuously advance, just as medicine and medical technology do, and educators need to keep up with their field's progress, mastering the latest educational methods to provide enjoyable, easy-to-understand, efficient instruction. We can see that both men strove to improve and reform education with a scientific eye and a sense of social responsibility.

Makiguchi also directed his intense gaze at the realm of our inner being. Believing in our limitless possibilities and creativity, he focused on the creation of new values. Again, *Soka* means "value creation," the purpose of which is to enable people to become happy and to contribute to society's development and positive progress.

The more difficult the environment, the greater the joy resulting from discovering people's potential, bringing it into flower, and stimulating their growth and development as human beings. As an educator and scholar, Makiguchi perceived that happiness is to be found in the creative way of life, and it was his encounter with Buddhism that provided him the philosophical, practical foundation for and certainty of this belief.

HICKMAN: The problem, of course, is that in many educational environments, students are taught to be value *extractors*, not value *creators*. The idea of enriching the meanings of life, human as well as nonhuman, is the key to the pedagogies of both Makiguchi and Dewey.

In this connection, I recall a wonderful book by Viktor Frankl, an Austrian psychologist who survived the Nazi concentration camps. In *Man's Search for Meaning*, he argued that as individuals we can find meaning—create value, if you will—in all types of environments, even the most obscene and degrading ones.

GARRISON: I have learned a great deal by studying Makiguchi's ideas about value-creating education and believe he made unique contributions that equal and sometimes surpass Dewey's. A recent issue of *Educational Studies*,[10] for which you wrote an excellent introduction, helped me better understand the achievements of Makiguchi, who fashioned in a militarist context a magnificent theory of education, whereas Dewey had the immense advantage of working in a country that was already well on the road to democracy.

IKEDA: President Makiguchi would be pleased by your profound understanding.

Everyone has the power to create value. The question is how to tap this power. The proper environment must be created.

In the classroom, teachers are of prime importance. More than anything else, teachers' abilities determine whether education will succeed or fail. They need to share with and pass on to students the inner spiritual qualities they have acquired. Only through communication on this profound level can students discover their own enormous powers, awaken to them, and act with vitality and vigor. This process is the quintessence of humanistic education.

GARRISON: Dewey thought we only educate indirectly through the mediation of environment. We cannot directly insert learning into anyone's mind. We only learn through what we attend and respond to actively.

The role of the teacher is primarily one of forming an environment that allows students to respond creatively to obstacles within their capacity to overcome. The teacher must operate in a student-centered way that involves careful observation, study, and reflection on the student's physical and mental capacities, along with the needs, desires, interests, and purposes of the child. The teacher must then functionally coordinate the environment with the student's characteristics.

Makiguchi's writings provide exceptional practical guidance to teachers. Astute observations such as those most likely recorded in the Educational Practice Record can capture the details for achieving coordination.

HICKMAN: Dewey's call for a liberation of education from "narrow utilities" goes right to the heart of the role of the teacher in school education. I think that we must begin to teach social virtues in kindergarten, thus helping our children increase awareness of themselves as unique individuals within a community of similarly unique individuals. Moreover, we must abandon the highly structured regimen of teaching to the test that now dominates primary and secondary education in the United States and elsewhere.

IKEDA: In our discussion of education, Arnold J. Toynbee stressed the importance of the environment to very young children, especially since, in his view, the years up to age five are decisive to character formation.[11] As I have observed from founding Soka kindergartens in Japan, Hong Kong, Singapore, Malaysia, Brazil, and South Korea, the importance of providing a loving educational environment to small children cannot be emphasized too strongly.

Current studies reveal the powerful influence the environments in which young people develop have on them later in life. We now face a pressing need to reexamine earnestly the purpose and meaning of education.

CONVERSATION SEVEN

Educational Wisdom

GARRISON: I warmly remember how, when I visited the Soka schools in Tokyo, two first graders ran up to talk with me. That they were so comfortable approaching someone on an official visit, it seemed to me, spoke volumes about the democratic nature of Soka pre-college education.

HICKMAN: I have had the pleasure of visiting Soka schools on several occasions. I would first note that each had a unique personality. That is as it should be. Soka schools in Tokyo, for example, have a personality quite different from that of Soka schools in the Kansai region.

Pupils in both sets of schools, however, are not just passively absorbing information: They are active participants in the processes of their own education. As a result, even though curricular emphases may be similar in the two schools, each has a unique manner of appropriating and expressing the values of learning by experimentation and viewing the educational process in its larger context. Adjusting for local cultural values and institutions, of course, I would happily recommend Soka schools, based on the sound educational principles of Makiguchi and Dewey, as models for primary and secondary educators everywhere.

IKEDA: Your words give me the greatest pleasure. Greeting two such learned scholars of humanistic education as you has been a source of inspiration for the Soka schools faculty. Your visits have provided our students, too, with golden memories they will always cherish. As founder, I take this opportunity to thank you again. If you have any advice to offer the Soka schools, I am happy to receive it.

HICKMAN: I offer the Soka schools the same advice that I would offer other schools. First, honor the fact that children are natural experimenters, and that learning should be fun. Second, avoid overemphasis on testing, especially when tests are designed to compare one student to another or one school to another. And third, never stop experimenting with pedagogical processes. As Dewey pointed out, the norms of good pedagogy do not come from abstract discussions of pedagogical theories to be imposed on practice; they come from educational practice itself.

IKEDA: All three of your points are important. All human beings have an essential desire to learn. The pleasure and fun of learning are great sources of fulfillment in life. Igniting and stimulating the desire to learn are the starting points of education. Outstanding educators are constantly pressing ahead, acquiring through their tireless efforts in the classroom the wisdom and experience needed to develop and bring to full flower children's individuality and potential.

Education never reaches a stage of completion. The times change. Children's environments and their temperaments are always in flux. Naturally, education must also continue to grow and develop. Buddhism teaches that wisdom functions in accord with changing circumstances; educational wisdom must always respond to our ever-changing reality.

HICKMAN: Dewey was once introduced as a philosopher who *wanted to make intelligence practical;* to make abstractions applicable to the real world. He responded that he in fact *wanted to make practice intelligent*. By this, he meant that intelligence in everything, including education, must be grounded in the needs and interests of real people in real situations.[1]

I should add again that I was greatly impressed by the students I have met in the pre-college Soka schools, Soka University, and Soka University of America. I find them highly motivated, enthusiastic learners who are full of the focused energy that makes teaching and learning a pleasure.

I think the Soka students' attitude toward learning is—to put it one way—the spirit of the founder of the schools. The excellence of the curriculum and the way that the pedagogical process is carried out, too, are outstanding. The teachers understand the need to interact with students and even to learn from them.

What I've observed in the Soka schools I've visited suggests the students' strong sense that learning can be—and should be—fun. This attitude should remain with us not only in primary and secondary schools but throughout life.

Life and Knowledge

GARRISON: As I mentioned earlier, students at the Soka schools talked to me in a very friendly manner. On that occasion, I remembered my visits to Soka University of America, where I also encountered students engaged in rich dialogue with one another, staff, and faculty. As long as they continue to try new ideas and learn as much from failed experiments as from successful ones, each institution in the Soka system will prosper.

IKEDA: Thank you again for your warm encouragement, which I am sure will stimulate both our students and our faculty members. We are committed to further developing the existing culture of dialogue that you noted at our Soka schools.

In connection with student independence and volition, which Professor Hickman just mentioned, Dewey thought schools, instead of being places of passive learning following such traditional, authoritarian methods as rote memorization and testing, should become places where students actively and of their own volition engage in social activities and interaction. He stressed, "Anything which can be called a study, whether arithmetic, history, geography, or one of the natural sciences, must be derived from materials which at the outset fall within the scope of ordinary life-experience."[2]

In other words, he emphasized the importance of education rooted in the individual's life and experience, which he believed contributed to the sound development of the intellect and emotions. Unfortunately, however, a century after Dewey delivered this keen admonition, Japanese education remains tied to the traditional practice of cramming children's heads with information.

HICKMAN: I am afraid that the type of knowledge-cramming and excessive competition that you describe as infecting Japanese schools is increasingly a part of the educational situation in America, too. It is as if we in America were appropriating the worst of the Japanese educational system, ignoring the fact that it has not served Japan well.

IKEDA: Out of concern over this approach, efforts have been made in Japan to try out what was called a freer, less test-oriented educational method, but it did not go as well as hoped. We are still groping for solutions.

Another recent cause of concern is the Internet and video games. The concern is that children spend too much time shut indoors, engrossed in such occupations, enjoying little time playing outdoors, with deleterious influences on their physical health and personality development. Of course, since the Internet is becoming an indispensable tool in this information age, schools must devise ways to teach children how to use its technology skillfully—but without children losing themselves in a virtual fantasy world.

HICKMAN: Like you, I worry about some of the free-time activities of students, especially the Internet and video games. The Internet affords wonderful opportunities for learning but can lead to a terrible waste of time and talents. This is not meant as a criticism of video games per se, since many of them help to develop hand-eye coordination. But there is so much more to life.

IKEDA: Cultivating the intellect and personality to be capable of independent thought and value creation is vital to human growth. In this sense, schools should be learning environments where children can naturally acquire these strengths while enjoying life. As Dewey wrote,

> One may be ready to admit that it would be most desirable for the school to be a place in which the child should really live, and get a life-experience in which he should delight and find meaning for its own sake.[3]

President Makiguchi, reflecting on the educational failings of his day, observed that the great majority of Japanese minds, because of the failings of the educational system, were inflexible; the realms of learning and life had become completely divorced from one another, and this had "sundered our lives in a dualistic way."[4] When life and knowledge are divorced from each other, the knowledge we are supposed to have acquired in our education is useless in daily life.

This led Makiguchi to propose a system in which half of the

student's day was spent in the classroom and the other half in some kind of work, the aim being to deepen education's connection to society and put the knowledge attained through education to use in the real world.

A Porous Boundary

HICKMAN: Makiguchi proposed splitting the school day between the theoretical and the practical, between the abstractions of the more narrowly academic and the concrete realities of everyday existence. Dewey also promoted this type of extramural learning experience. He thought educators should ensure that the boundary between the school and the larger community remain highly porous.

IKEDA: Professor Garrison, what do you think are the salient points for preventing this divorce of learning from daily life?

GARRISON: Young children learn readily from those activities that satisfy curiosity in daily life. At first, they only playfully imitate adult action, but even before they start school, children engage in simplified versions of the sorts of structured activities that occupy members of their family and the larger community.

Dewey insists that the best kind of education is *through* the occupations but not *for* them. This is because work, including the use of tools (from wheels to computers), is inherently social. Organized action satisfies human purposes. In work, we learn to refer our actions to others in social situations. When working with others, we must coordinate with them directly. When we work alone, we must use materials and tools prepared by others to produce something others will use. For Dewey, good work never loses its playful aspect.

He thought we should break down the barriers between school

and community. In learning the various occupations of the community, the child becomes a socialized and productive member of the community.

Mere socialization, however, does not serve the needs of democracy and social justice. Therefore, in learning occupations, students should also learn how to critique them and be willing to reconstruct them.

IKEDA: As you say, this resonates with Makiguchi's idea of spending half the day in class and half at work. Children more thoroughly master their school studies by participating in various social activities and learning about society.

It is also important to learn a way of life that finds joy in getting involved in the welfare of others and society. In Japan in recent years, various efforts have been made to achieve this end, like taking primary- and middle-school pupils on tours of workplaces where they can gain experience and cultivate awareness of social connections. Sometimes local people with special skills, like carpenters and florists, volunteer to support school programs by giving special classes. There is renewed appreciation for the hands-on learning that cannot be acquired through testing and for interaction with the community. These are so important.

GARRISON: You are so right. In experiencing other people in local settings skillfully engaged in everyday activities of work and play, we learn many more things than just abstract ideas. The test of such experiential learning lies in our growth in feeling, action, and happiness, not just thought.

A major problem with scholastic examinations is that they test only a few cognitive domains of human functioning; they fail to consider many cognitive domains. Of course, among other things, they completely ignore emotional intelligence, physical ability, sociability, creative talent, a sense of adventure, and moral character.

It's clear to me that happiness and growth are in many ways the same things. Happiness is not just *in* growth but actually *is* growth. There are distinctions, but you will not have happiness if you do not actualize your unique potential. You cannot actualize your unique potential if you are not participating in, and contributing to, a larger community that allows you to teach and learn from others. In this sense, happiness is growth.

IKEDA: In terms of growth, it is important to teach the joy of striving together with one's classmates, learning from one another and engaging in positive competition as a motivator for realizing one's full potential. What are your thoughts on healthy, creative competition in education?

EVERYONE A WINNER

HICKMAN: I appreciate your concern about competition in education, an increasingly important topic. The real question is whether the competition is appropriate. We all know of situations in which inappropriate competition drains the energies of learners and creates the type of tension and anxiety that makes learning difficult.

At the same time, students will eventually compete for any number of things during the course of their lives. I believe that as educators we have an obligation to teach them how to deal with competition, how to understand their own strengths and weaknesses, and how to win and lose gracefully.

Properly managed, for example, competition in sports can be a marvelous learning experience. Competition in more academic settings, such as debate tournaments, can instill self-confidence.

However, it is important that our students understand that there are many types of intelligence. If someone is insufficiently talented to compete in one field, there will almost certainly be other fields in which he or she can succeed.

GARRISON: We often think of competition as what game theorists call a zero-sum game. As in poker, when one player wins, others must lose the same amount. In humanitarian competition, everyone may win. Said differently, we may all grow.

Dewey clearly argued that a person cannot grow without the opportunities the community provides. But he also said that a person has no potential until he encounters other people who are different from him, because your existence helps actualize my potential, just as mine helps actualize yours.

What is important is moral equality. For example, you may be physically superior or intellectually superior. On the other hand, I may have social skills that you don't have. I might lose in a math contest with you.

But if we engage in humanitarian competition, each of us may help the other find what we are good at doing. My growth depends on your growth, but we each must grow in a different way.

IKEDA: Buddhism has a saying, "cherry, plum, peach, and damson," meaning that each of these trees flower as they are, exhibiting their unique beauty, and this is what makes a garden beautiful. No matter how lovely a cherry tree may be, it cannot be a peach tree, nor should it. The same is true of people.

In other words, people should blossom in their own way, making the most of their individuality. One isn't the winner and another the loser. If we respect one another's individuality and do our best to rise to our unique challenges, we are all victorious in our own way.

This is competition for the sake of tapping our individual strengths to the fullest. And as you said, Professor Garrison, it teaches us that we are all moral equals—that all life is precious and worthy, and that it is important for us to trust, cooperate with, and support one another. This is the path to creating a garden of harmony accommodating many different people.

GARRISON: Dewey said that competition allows us to find out what we are best at doing. It allows each of us to actualize his or her own potential, and it need not be a zero-sum game. In the end, everyone wins if everyone finds his or her unique potential and can make his or her unique contribution to society. When you actualize your potential and I actualize mine, then we are going to be morally equal and equally happy, each in a different way.

We must remember, however, that some growth should be limited. If you want to grow a garden, you must weed it. Some things are lethal if not controlled and put in their proper context.

To Prevent Bullying

IKEDA: I see the problem of bullying as a prime example of what you're talking about. Allowing children's negative energy to remain unchecked can escalate into bullying and uncontrolled aggression.

School ought to be a place where children can study and enjoy themselves with peace of mind. Unfortunately, however, this is not always the case. Bullying is one of the causes. It inflicts deep wounds on children's personalities.

Tragically, in Japan, bullies' victims have sometimes taken their own lives. How is the issue of bullying perceived in the United States?

GARRISON: The report *Bullying Prevention Is Crime Prevention*[5] indicates that bullying is the number two problem reported by students in the United States. Only stress is reported more often. Of pupils who frequently bully others in middle school, 60 percent have at least one criminal conviction by the age of twenty-four.

Bullies pick on those they perceive as weak. Such behavior is a form of social violence, whether physical, emotional, or intellectual, and is perpetuated by groups as much as by individuals.

HICKMAN: I am pleased, President Ikeda, that you have broached the subject of bullying, as unpleasant as the topic may be. The formidable and growing literature on bullying addresses what parents, teachers, and support staff can do to deal with the problem. There are support groups on the web.

In the United States, the Centers for Disease Control and Prevention provide extensive information about the forms bullying takes and how to deal with them. These reports are extensive and should probably be in the hands of every teacher and administrator. There are also for-profit corporations that send professional counselors to schools to work with administrators, teachers, students, and community leaders to reduce bullying.

IKEDA: The problem is greatly aggravated in Japan because bullies tend to act in groups and often operate behind teachers' backs. Allowing it to continue amounts to tacit collusion, which is utterly unacceptable.

And it is even worse to assume, as is sometimes done, that victims bring bullying on themselves. It is crucial for teachers and other adults to make it completely clear to children that bullying is unacceptable, that it is an absolute evil, and that the blame falls 100 percent with the bullies.

Passive bystanders, too, are a problem because they actually aid the bullies, thus often unwittingly becoming assailants themselves.

HICKMAN: Of all the many dimensions to this problem, the one that I find most interesting involves the role of bystanders. Since they are the majority in any school, they have a great deal of influence. With the help of their teachers and parents, they can mount peer-based informational campaigns and report cases of bullying.

IKEDA: In many instances, bystanders aid the bullies by merely observing, feeling impotent to stop the violence. Afraid of getting involved and wanting to stay out of trouble themselves, they pretend not to see, thus effectively condoning the bullies. Other children, observing this, are in turn hurt by this passivity.

But it has been reported that when some observers—it need not be all—step in to arbitrate, the bullying stops. Even when that isn't feasible, the worst outcome can often be averted if someone in the child's life reaches out to and supports the child being bullied. How can we encourage onlookers not to remain passive?

HICKMAN: The question of peer mediation is an interesting but difficult one. In general, I believe that mediation techniques should be part of the curriculum.

Caution is required, however, since on-the-spot, peer-based intervention through attempted mediation sometimes leads to retaliation. Studies have shown that peer-based mediation must be used with care and on a case-by-case basis.

If I may speak personally, as a rather thin and bookish fourteen-year-old student, I was regularly bullied by the son of one of my teachers. His bullying of me and other students was so blatant that I could not understand how his mother could be unaware of what he was doing, and why she did not intervene. I am certain that, if bystanders had intervened, he would have made them his next target.

It is a tragedy when teachers turn a blind eye to bullying. It disrupts the learning process and creates distrust.

As I said, I think it's important that peer-based, on-the-spot mediation be used with extreme care to avoid possible retaliation.

IKEDA: Teachers and parents need to be aware of the sometimes almost imperceptible signals children give of being the targets of bullying and speak to them about what's going on. If children are confident that adults will take action when they bring such matters to their attention, they can find the courage to stop merely looking on and step forward to act. Children's willingness to condone bullying as passive bystanders is inextricably linked to their mistrust of adult society.

HICKMAN: Bystanders can actually incite violence. That's why we need a whole program that addresses teachers, students, support staff, and so on. Even the best-intentioned bystanders can sometimes act counterproductively. The important thing is for everyone involved to become closely acquainted with the available literature, like that provided by the CDC, which is very effective in terms of application.

Bystanders should learn to avoid actions such as incitement, inappropriate intervention, and indifference. Essentially, the issue can resolve itself when there is appropriate intervention in terms of mediation by peers and certainly by faculty, staff, and administrators.

GARRISON: Learning to prevent bullying is a form of peace education. Confronting bullies requires moral courage and intelligence on the part of individuals and nations. As Dewey and Makiguchi understood, educating for happiness is the best way to prevent bullying.

Remaining silent supports bullying. Victims should tell adults. Making friends or joining a club also is helpful. Students who witness bullying must tell adults and provide support. Adults must look for the signs of bullying, talk with students, and help them network socially. Ultimately, what makes for a good democracy creates a good school climate.

IKEDA: I established the following five principles for the Soka Junior and Senior High Schools: (1) Uphold the dignity of life; (2) Respect individuality; (3) Build bonds of lasting friendship; (4) Oppose violence; and (5) Lead a life based on both knowledge and wisdom.

The Soka schools strictly forbid despicable acts like violence and bullying. I have repeated this to our students on each of my visits to their schools.

Creating a healthy, caring learning environment in which we share one another's joys and sorrows is the first step in education. President Makiguchi said many times, "Unless you have the courage to be an enemy to evil, you cannot be a friend to good,"[6] and "One must not be satisfied with passive goodness; one must be a person of courage and mettle who can actively strive for good."[7] In Soka education, cultivation of such brave, good hearts is prized.

At the same time, we must always remember that children mirror adult society: Their problems are the problems of the grown-up community. No fundamental solutions are possible as long as we fail to solve those problems.

CONVERSATION EIGHT

Creative Families

IKEDA: I want to discuss education in the home, the starting point of all humanistic education. Professor Alice Dewey, John Dewey's granddaughter, with whom we of the SGI have maintained a friendly relationship for many years, discussed her grandfather's educational views with us. Her grandfather believed in respecting children as individuals, she said, and approaching them on equal footing. Precisely because of this, he saw to it that they acquired a correct understanding of their rights and responsibilities. He believed that this helped children speedily mature as human beings and develop their creative senses. She added that, of her own childhood experiences with him, she remembered most clearly how he always treated her as an individual.

We must never condescend to or spoil even small children. As Alice Dewey stressed, treating children affectionately and respectfully as individuals with a sense of responsibility gives them self-confidence and security, enabling them to advance toward independence with assurance. This spirit of respect from adults is an absolutely crucial requirement for an environment that promotes children's growth and learning.

HICKMAN: Making children feel very safe and providing a good learning environment are important parental roles. Parents must not only provide a safe environment to bring out their children's abilities but also take an active role in the educational process. They must both confer regularly with teachers and help with homework, talk with their children, and offer whatever support is needed.

IKEDA: Many parents worry about how to interact with their children. Dewey and his wife, Alice, had seven children. What were his thoughts on domestic education? How did he put them into practice? Our readers will be interested in your replies.

HICKMAN: John and Alice Dewey were keen observers of the behavior of their children. They avoided the two extremes that Dewey called "pouring in" and "drawing out." Of course, they avoided the "pouring in" or "cramming" model of domestic education that many parents now seem to accept without question. On the other side, they thought that what could be "drawn out" would not be of much value in the absence of their parental guidance.

The Deweys observed their children at home and at play—their intensity, zeal, and restlessness. They shared the task of attempting to find ways that those energies could be developed in each child according to his or her talents and interests.

The Deweys also thought that there should be a seamless connection between the activities of the child at school and at home. They took educational trips with their children. They attempted to establish close contact between their children and the realities of nature. They introduced their children to the practical skills that make domestic life richer. They thought that home-economics lessons were for their boys as well as their girls.

GARRISON: For Dewey, education always begins at home. It is by participating in the functions of the family that children's curiosity is first stimulated, and that they begin to investigate the world about them. The home and family are the setting in which the child first begins to learn cooperation and to refer her or his needs and actions to those of others. It is where habits of cooperation, industry, and responsibility are first developed.

Dewey wrote: "What the best and wisest parent wants for his own child, that must the community want for all of its children. Any other ideal for our schools is narrow and unlovely; acted upon, it destroys our democracy."[1] Much of what Dewey thought about what made a good school was actually based on what he thought made for a good home.

It is easy to infer much of Dewey's thoughts about domestic education from what he said about public education. There should never be a sharp separation between home and school. Schools and their staff, including teachers, custodial workers, cafeteria personnel, principals, and secretaries, should work closely with parents and, in many cases, grandparents, aunts, uncles, and other caregivers. It is difficult but important for the growth of the child. It is also rewarding when done well because everyone may learn from everyone else.

IKEDA: Dewey regarded the home as basic to children's education and also believed in the importance of continuity and consistency between the home and school environments—a fundamental point to bear in mind as we reconsider education today. In *The System of Value-Creating Pedagogy*, President Makiguchi expressed serious concern about many parents sending their children to school with no strong sense of the purpose of their children's education. Parents and schools need to hold shared, fundamental principles and aims for education, so they can work together to foster their children, the treasures of the future.

Another factor is that parents all too easily tend to adopt an authoritarian, negative attitude in interacting with their children, telling them what they must and must not do. When parents are annoyed or tired by work or under stress, they may, far from respecting their children's individualities, speak and act in a way that completely devalues the child.

In addition, marital discord is an aggravating factor in some families. As has always been the case, children's sensitive minds are deeply affected by conflict and dissonance in adult relationships in their world.

In recent years, many Japanese children have been reported as suffering from low self-esteem. Unfortunately, the number of young people who complain of self-loathing and lack of self-confidence seems to be on the increase.

GARRISON: Self-esteem and confidence arise from an appropriate sense of independence. Like good teachers, good parents must enjoy learning with and about their children. They must study their children and help them develop their unique capacities with care and compassion by creating appropriate tasks for them in the home, in the same way that teachers should work with students in school.

IKEDA: Parents and children should work together and share goals. This can be a very important experience. For example, parents and children can join together in sports or hobbies. Helping with domestic chores and work can teach children about the difficulties their parents face and the responsibilities of adult life.

When I was a child, my family produced *nori* (edible seaweed). I still remember getting up in the biting cold of early winter mornings—our busy season—to help in the harvesting. I also carried the carefully prepared seaweed on my back to the wholesale dealer, and I remember my friendly interactions with the people there.

In the family, sharing hardships and developing together promote understanding and create deeper bonds that provide a sure foundation on which children can grow and become independent.

A Japanese women's magazine once asked me to contribute an

essay about what kind of family life I thought we should strive for in our new age. This essay and several others I contributed to various women's magazines were later collected and published in English as *The Creative Family* (1977). I spoke of the importance of building what I call a creative family or creative household, in which parents and children grow and develop through mutual inspiration and shared value creation.

When I shared these sentiments during a meeting with Dr. Felix Unger, president of the European Academy of Sciences and Arts, and his wife, Monika, she expressed her complete agreement and commented with a smile that in the more than twenty years in which she had been a mother, she never felt that she had sacrificed her personal development for the sake of her children and family.[2]

Child-rearing is indeed demanding, but it is more than recompensed by the joy in witnessing children's growth. Approaching child-rearing with a positive attitude, employing one's full capacities, and drawing on the cooperation of others in one's life can be opportunities for tremendous personal growth.

A Circle of Action

Garrison: Sacrificing yourself disables you as a caregiver. Socially, caring never should be constructed as self-sacrifice.

On the other hand, to care for yourself, you have to care for your community, your environment, your significant others, your intimate relationships, your friendships, and all of the rest. Otherwise, you cannot maintain yourself.

Environmentalism, too, can easily fit into this way of thinking. Because we drink water, eat food, and breathe air, we must preserve our water resources, avoid poisoning the earth, and stop polluting the air. To care for yourself, you have to care for others, and to care for others, you have to care for yourself. It is a circle of action, where everything you do eventually comes back on you.

IKEDA: As Nichiren put it, "If one lights a fire for others, one will brighten one's own way."[3] In other words, doing one's best for others illuminates one's own path. In "On Establishing the Correct Teaching for the Peace of the Land," one of his major writings, Nichiren wrote, "If you care anything about your personal security, you should first of all pray for order and tranquillity throughout the four quarters of the land, should you not?"[4]

Human beings can only exist through mutual support. In addition, we must cultivate within ourselves the awareness of being a community member and should teach this fundamental truth to our children. Parents need to take the initiative and set an example in this regard, making a positive contribution to the community, teaching this truth to their children in a spontaneous, natural way.

Linus Pauling's son, Linus Pauling, Jr., a medical doctor in his own right, once told me something I shall always remember: Recalling the way his parents persevered in their peace work, unfazed by the harsh criticism and calumny heaped upon them during the Cold War, he said that children naturally inherit their parents' thoughts and ideas, sometimes in verbal form, sometimes nonverbally. This is why, he added, parents must always firmly believe in the need to advance the cause of peace and act accordingly.

GARRISON: Dewey had a profound understanding of the social nature of the self. He wrote:

> The *kind* of self which is formed through action which is faithful to relations with others will be a fuller and broader self than one which is cultivated in isolation from or in opposition to the purposes and needs of others. In contrast, the kind of self which results from generous breadth of interest may be said alone to constitute a development and fulfillment of self, while the other way of life stunts

> and starves selfhood by cutting it off from the connections necessary to its growth.[5]

In the modern family, economic necessity all too often leaves children alone and isolated from their parents. So parents must be faithful in their relations with their children. They must teach them to respond with a generous breadth of interest to the needs and purposes of others.

At the same time, children must acknowledge the sacrifices their parents are making to provide for their wellbeing. All people have a profound need for peace and security.

Because education begins at home, if children do not find peace in the domestic sphere, it will be much harder for them to find it in the public sphere. If they do not learn how to create and preserve domestic tranquillity, they will find it hard to pursue it in public. Peace education is important, and providing the primary experience of peace for our children in the home is the best way to initiate peace education. Such deeds speak much louder than words.

IKEDA: The famous humanistic educator Osamu Mizutani has devoted himself for many years to dealing with juvenile delinquency, school absenteeism, drug addiction, and suicide in Japan. He is affectionately and respectfully known as "Mr. Night Watchman," from his custom of walking the streets at night to talk with young people and convince them to mend their ways.

In a speech he delivered at a symposium held by the Soka Gakkai women's division in February 2010, he said:

> The home ought to be a place of complete safety and security, but it is often spoiled by marital strife and other tensions that seriously harm the minds of young children. I see conflict and unhappiness in the home as the reasons why children can find no strength to go on living.

He also said:

> Parents who want their children to study must be studious. If they want their children to be kind to old folks, they must demonstrate kindness to the elderly every day. If they want their children to live just lives, they, too, must live justly. You cannot merely describe the right way to live, you must demonstrate it.

As an educator who has been there for any number of despairing young people, has encouraged them, and has brought smiles back to their faces, Mr. Mizutani's words carry great weight. The only way to enable children to grow in a free, wholesome way is for adults to show them, by their own example, how to live with integrity and face life's challenges with optimism and courage.

HICKMAN: It is important to set a good example. Dewey followed Aristotle in holding that we become good by doing good, just as good grammar grows as a result of hearing speakers with good grammar and following their example. Dewey thought that moral behavior becomes easier as it becomes habitual, but that there are always novel situations requiring careful moral deliberation.

WORKING PARENTS

IKEDA: It is also essential for educators to serve as upstanding moral examples for their pupils in the school setting. In this connection, President Makiguchi wrote:

> Teachers should come down from the throne where they are ensconced as the object of veneration to become public servants who offer guidance to those who seek to ascend

> the throne of learning. They should not be masters who offer themselves as paragons, but partners in the discovery of new models.[6]

There is one more factor that we need to consider in terms of family education—the great changes that have taken place in families worldwide, as more mothers are working outside the home. This is a growing trend in Japan in recent years as well. The number of young women who list the ability to do housework as their top requirement for a future spouse is on the rise. As a result, the new family situation, with mothers away at work and fathers playing a new role in the home, is an important consideration when we discuss family education. What are your thoughts on this?

HICKMAN: The changing role of women in the home and the workforce is an important and fascinating topic. As you note, it has immense implications for education. The feminist movements that gained momentum in the 1960s and 1970s in Europe and the United States created new economic realities and responded in interesting ways to those changed economic circumstances. As a result, the structures of European and American societies have been greatly altered.

I recall returning to America in 1973 after a two-year postdoctoral fellowship in Germany. Driving home from the airport, I passed a road construction crew that included women workers. When I left the United States in 1971, such a thing would have been unthinkable. The changes that had occurred during my absence amazed me, and that was just the tip of the iceberg. I hardly recognized the society I had left just two years earlier.

IKEDA: In Japan, attitudes are changing, and young fathers are participating more in child-rearing—for example, taking paternity leave to care for their small children. More and more of them are reading picture books to their children. Indeed, publishers now produce parenting magazines targeted specifically at fathers.

Garrison: Did you have this kind of experience with your own children?

Ikeda: When my children were small, on the rare occasions when I was able to come home early, I used to read them stories, but I was so bad at it that the children never hesitated to say they liked the way their mother read better. I'm sure young fathers today are better at it than I was.

My very busy schedule meant that I left most of the actual child-rearing to my wife. Still, I tried hard to set my children's minds at rest with the assurance that their father was always looking out for them. When I traveled abroad, I sent each of them postcards. On their birthdays, my wife bought the gifts, and I presented them. With this kind of teamwork, I managed to be a presence in my children's lives. Even though our time together was limited, I created some memories for them.

My wife and I agreed on the importance of teaching our children to live for the sake of others and society, and to devote themselves sincerely to others. If you make an earnest effort to communicate, you can get your message across to your children, even when they are quite young.

Today, people are reassessing the balance between time spent on the job and time spent with the family. This line of thought has given rise to what is called a life-work-balance movement in Japan. How do fathers in the United States feel about this?

Fatherhood Today

Garrison: I am sure you were a profound presence in the lives of your children. That is what truly matters.

I know you deeply admire and respect your wife, Kaneko, whom I have met. It was evident by her presence that she shares, contributes greatly to, and fully understands your lifework. Thus, she rendered you present in thought and feeling to your children, even when your duties required you to be physically absent. Since Kaneko understood you were working for the welfare of others, she could convey that to your children. No doubt, this helped connect them not only to you, so that they experienced honor on your behalf, but also to the larger Soka community and the cause of global peace and happiness you serve. Thus, your entire family could find happiness together. As Makiguchi might have observed, any family that wished could find the same happiness and benefit for themselves by creating good for others.

In discussing fatherhood in America, we must remember that one out of every three children in the United States does not live with his or her biological father. According to several sources, the number of single-mother families in the United States has risen in the last fifty years from 8 percent to at least 24 percent. And according to the Population Reference Bureau, seven in ten children in single-mother homes are classified as poor or low income.[7] Remarkably, it seems to me that many Americans fail to acknowledge the seriousness of the problem, or else they place the blame on the unfortunate mother.

The National Fatherhood Institute of America surveyed men with at least one child and found that only slightly more than half felt they were initially prepared to be fathers, while 78 percent later felt properly prepared. Fathers identified their work as the greatest obstacle to good parenting. Finances were in second place.

Married mothers may help with financial issues by entering the workforce, but their entry means work will become an issue for them also. Of course, they work hard at home, too. Not publically acknowledging and rewarding this work is itself a social problem. It seems to me that, unlike yourself, most men and an increasing number of women do not see domestic labor as valuable. Men and women must come to feel equally rewarded in both the private and public spheres.

HICKMAN: The fact that women increasingly work outside the home places new stress on the educational process. It is difficult to take an active role in helping a child with homework, for example, after a full day at work. But such intervention is necessary. Although Americans have historically tended to think of themselves as "rugged individualists," it is arguable that the rising demand for more social services, such as daycare and improved preschool programs, is a direct result of the fact that in many households, both partners work outside the home, and that in many cases the householder is a single parent.

IKEDA: The numbers of single-parent households, nuclear families with no relatives living nearby, and families in which both parents have jobs outside the home have recently been on the increase in Japan. In the past, parents learned how to raise their children from living together with three generations in one household, in proximity to extended families, and through close relations with neighbors. Now, however, as housing conditions and lifestyle changes make the cohabitation of three generations difficult, many families consist only of young married couples and their offspring.

The result is that inexperienced parents must rely on books for help when they have questions about how best to raise their children. Although in local communities, certain official organizations sponsor classes for young prospective mothers and fathers, circumstances in our rapidly changing society make it impossible for them to cover everything.

HICKMAN: Some sociologists of religion have seen the rise of Protestant mega-churches—churches with thousands of members—as an effect of this new situation. In many (but by no means all) of these churches, intransigent theological dogmas have been replaced by a strong emphasis on social services, such as daycare, support groups, and social networking for children and adults alike. Although there is still a regrettable strain of narrow-minded, absolutist fundamentalism in many of these churches, there are also rays of hope, and I anticipate that we will see more and more of this move beyond rigid theology in the years to come. If this is true, then it is, in my view, a welcome phenomenon.

Rigid theological dogma tends to divide people, whereas social services tend to unite them. As Japanese society comes to include more single-parent families and households in which both husband and wife work outside the home, then demand for social services will probably increase from a wide variety of sources.

IKEDA: This trend is certainly growing stronger. There is an increasing need for a wide range of social services, from nursery schools and daycare centers to homes for the elderly. Various groups are offering activities to support child-rearing, and a rising number of nonprofit organizations are emerging and serving diverse functions.

The Soka Gakkai's Education Department provides educational consultation in thirty-four locations throughout Japan, where highly experienced teachers respond to the needs of countless parents and children in difficulties. Since operations started in 1968, some 350,000 people have turned to these services for help (380,000 people as of 2013). We engage in numerous other related activities in Japan, such as sponsoring community-based child-rearing seminars for young mothers and campaigns encouraging parents to read aloud to their children.

I have long advocated a systemic change from emphasizing education that serves the needs of society to the creation of a society serving the needs of education. Society as a whole must pool its wisdom and devote more effort to fostering our children.

HICKMAN: I applaud the commitment on the part of the SGI to equality of opportunity, including educational opportunity, for men and women. From what I have seen during my visits to Japan, the Soka Gakkai appears to be in the forefront of advocating for progressive change in Japanese society. The task will be difficult, but it is a necessary one.

What some regard as an educational crisis, others see as a great opportunity. In one case, Ira Harkavy, director of the Barbara and Edward Netter Center for Community Partnerships at the University of Pennsylvania, has found ways to locate various social services at neighborhood schools. For example, when parents come to register for food stamps or to pay a utility bill, they are encouraged to learn more about their child's school, to meet their child's teachers, and thus to become more involved in their child's education. Harkavy has targeted low-income neighborhoods in Philadelphia, and his program has achieved remarkable success.

IKEDA: This is a wonderful undertaking that provides much food for thought. It embodies a passion for improving educational efforts at the community level for the sake of children. By employing our creative powers and ingenuity, there are still possibilities for making great advances in building a society that exists for the sake of education.

We need to provide support at the community level for young mothers and fathers to help them create family environments in which children can grow and learn in wholesome ways. The home must be a safe, hope-giving haven for children.

Making it so depends on how society can manifest its wisdom to help create better domestic environments. This is the starting point to transition from education for the sake of society to a society for the sake of education.

CONVERSATION NINE

The University Experience

IKEDA: The university is the greatest open forum of the human mind and spirit on Earth. It is a place where truth and the future live.

I have visited and spoken at many institutions of higher learning, including Columbia University, with which John Dewey had close connections; the University of Bologna, the oldest in Europe; Moscow State University; Peking University; and Harvard University, the oldest in North America. Although Soka University is still very young compared to these venerable institutions, I have engaged in meaningful exchanges with their top leaders about such topics as the nature of the university. I have also had stimulating discussions with students on their campuses. Currently, Soka University is carrying out many academic and educational exchange programs with numerous universities.

There has been much discussion on the proper role of higher education in our changing times, and the concept of the ideal university has altered greatly. This is especially evident now as globalization and the development of a sophisticated, information-oriented society are dramatically transforming the college and university environment. In light of this, I want to ask you several questions on university education.

First, what role do Americans today expect institutions of higher learning to play? And are existing institutions meeting those expectations? As leaders in this realm, what are your thoughts?

GARRISON: In the past, students perceived the university as intrinsically valuable because it helped them cultivate their unique potential for personal and social growth. Increasingly over the last thirty years, however, higher education in America has become a private good purchased by students. Now, for too many, it has only exchange value; students purchase it and exchange the value added for a better job, higher income, and greater social status. They confuse *having* more with *being* more. At the same time, in the last few years, there have been signs that students again want a more value-creating education, although their desire has yet to have much effect.

At major research universities, the reward system is primarily keyed to grant-funded publication. This has become increasingly necessary as the government withdraws tax-based support.

TEACHERS DEFINE A UNIVERSITY

IKEDA: In the past in Japan, acceptance at a famous university had a great influence on getting a good job later in life. Students therefore studied as hard as they could to pass entrance examinations but, once in a university, frequently lost interest in study and just coasted along.

At the same time, it is hard to envision one's future at eighteen, when one typically enters university. It is a stage of life characterized by much trial and error. This is why it is crucial for university faculty members to provide students with intellectual stimulation and help them develop their interests and inquisitiveness.

In writing about what we can expect university courses to accomplish, Dewey lucidly commented, "The permanent and fruitful outcome of a college education should be the training of one's *human* nature."[1] This is a perennial challenge for the university. Teachers must employ ingenuity and strive to enable each student to rise to the challenge of learning and, through the university experience, refine and add luster to their character.

HICKMAN: My colleagues in the departments of philosophy and education at several Japanese universities have described the situation that you mention—that students tend to slack off once they have a secure place in a university. This is a tragedy of missed opportunities.

As you point out, ideally, universities are places of enhanced discussions, new ideas, and new possibilities for growth. It is imperative that we impress on our university students the precious nature of this period in their lives and the importance of availing themselves of the many opportunities university life affords.

Faculty should be well informed, committed to the intellectual and moral growth of their students, and, perhaps most important, willing to learn from their students as well as to teach them.

IKEDA: As I always tell Soka University teachers, the faculty defines the university. At our matriculation ceremonies in April 2010, I reiterated my conviction that teachers must take as much care of their students as they do of their own children, and that what students learn from teachers can be an asset and rare encouragement to grow as human beings and scholars.

Learning is the key to character formation and the way to victory and happiness in life. The noble mission and responsibility of faculty members are to help each student discover, develop, and bring to full fruition their talents, while faculty learns along with students.

HICKMAN: As for the purposes and motivations of American university students, I think it is difficult to generalize because there is such a wide range of institutions of higher learning. There are so-called research universities, liberal-arts colleges and universities, community colleges, and even universities that exist for the most part only on the Internet. Some colleges are specific to various disciplines, such as the famous Julliard School in New York City, where the primary emphasis is on dance, drama, and music.

TEACHING AND RESEARCH

IKEDA: Yes, a diverse society has diverse aims. Education must develop new possibilities to respond to them.

Another important point is that teachers need to deepen their own studies in order to become better instructors. In particular, they need to find the proper balance between their teaching duties and their academic research. What are your thoughts on this?

GARRISON: Personally, I see no separation between teaching and research. Each enhances the other.

My courses emphasize independent student inquiry. When students ask questions I cannot adequately answer, we research the issue together and share what we learn. In this way, they learn independent thought, while I learn more, not only about my subject matter but also about my students. Of course, a high level of knowledge accompanied by a sense of reverent humility is essential for good research and teaching.

HICKMAN: Jim Garrison and I agree about the symbiotic relation between research and teaching, as well as about the importance of joint research with students. The customary procedure, of course, is for thesis and dissertation directors to give their students lists of required or recommended reading. I provide such lists for my students, to be sure. But I also ask: "Do you have a list of readings for me? What have you been reading that I should know about, and that you and I can work through together?"

Given the current avalanche of books and articles even in highly circumscribed fields, it is no longer possible for a single individual to keep abreast of everything. A graduate thesis or dissertation should thus be a collaborative work. The same goes for undergraduates. I want to know about what they read, about their experiences with the Internet, and even how they spend their leisure time. All of that, I believe, supports effective teaching.

IKEDA: Your students are fortunate to have you as their teachers.

I am reminded of Linus Pauling's beliefs on education that he shared with me. Although it is often assumed that the most eminent professors should focus on teaching advanced graduate students, Dr. Pauling consistently advocated that they should instead be teaching the new students. He believed that having accomplished faculty members devote themselves to teaching new students not only provides the freshmen students with tremendous inspiration but also results in fresh discoveries for teachers, enabling them to learn a great deal as well. The world authority on genetic engineering Dr. Sarvagya Singh Katiyar praised Pauling's perspicacity and told me that he himself learned a great deal from questions posed by new students attending his lectures.

GARRISON: It seems to me that Pauling must have had a deep understanding of the mentor-disciple relationship. Just as the mentor and disciple in Buddhism must strive together to understand the Wonderful Law, so must the teacher and student strive to learn the laws of chemistry.

Further, as Dewey often noted, to teach effectively, we must know our students. Once we know our students, we must know the subject matter so well that we can completely rearrange our understanding to fit the students' needs as an expedient means for good teaching. Therefore, in teaching students, we must understand not only them but also ourselves in relation to them. In this way, mentor and disciple, teacher and student, create meaning and value together.

IKEDA: The essence of education lies in shared value creation. As I shall always remember, in our dialogue, Arnold J. Toynbee said that a researcher need not necessarily teach, but being totally engrossed in research and shut off from the currents of human life amounts to self-isolation. He also said that the most creative scholars relate their research to outside activities and draw powers of insight and wisdom from the experience.

Education and research are inseparably connected. This is an issue all universities confront.

Victor A. Sadovnichy, rector of Moscow State University, told me that at his institution, class loads are adjusted to enable researchers to teach and instructors to engage in research. Though this method presents administrative challenges, he acknowledged, he felt there is no other solution to the problem. Devising concrete ways to deal with the issue is indispensable to university reform.

HICKMAN: What I would add, with some confidence, is that student motivation depends in large measure on strong parental support and good teaching. Parents should encourage their children, not only financially, if possible, but in other ways as well.

Among sociologists in the United States, Asian-American families are often singled out for the high levels of performance of their children. It is clear that encouragement and support by family and friends play major roles in this success story.

IKEDA: I am aware of the great enthusiasm that Asian-American families have for education, and I know many outstanding young people brought up in such homes. As you point out, parental enthusiasm and support for learning greatly encourage children.

In Japan, during our period of rapid economic growth, young workers poured into the cities from rural areas in search of employment, and there was a rise in the number of nuclear families, replacing the multigenerational, extended families of former days. At the same time, community ties weakened, reducing the opportunities for adults to spontaneously interact with and encourage neighborhood children. These developments have made it increasingly important to exert our ingenuity to promote enriching communication, providing support and encouragement, both within families and the larger community.

GARRISON: In *The Public and Its Problems,* Dewey wrote: "Associated or joint activity is a condition of the creation of a community. But association itself is physical and organic, while communal life is moral, that is emotionally, intellectually, consciously sustained."[2]

This observation along with the following from Dewey provides profound philosophical guidance:

> In its deepest and richest sense a community must always remain a matter of face-to-face intercourse. This is why the family and neighborhood, with all their deficiencies, have always been the chief agencies of nurture, the means by which dispositions are stably formed and ideas acquired which laid hold on the roots of character.[3]

In the same work, however, Dewey acknowledged that it is "outside the scope of our discussion to look into the prospects of the reconstruction of face-to-face communities."[4]

Ultimately, the people in the local communities must empirically work out for themselves these concrete problems. Further, what works in one community may not work in another. Nonetheless, there are well-trained experts concerned community members may call upon.

The emerging field of community building will have much to contribute in the future. Experts in it have learned the importance of communicating with the families, the local community, and the entire region to learn its traditional beliefs and values. They have also learned how much ethics and spirituality matter.

SCHOOL SHOOTINGS

IKEDA: It is extremely important for families and community organizations to communicate smoothly and work together, not only for the development of education but for regional revitalization. Connected with this issue of community, I want to further consider issues confronting university education today from the perspective of social trends. In recent years, crimes, violence, scandal, and especially drug abuse have become increasingly common in Japanese universities. In addition, increasing numbers of college students are unable to communicate with the people around them and are becoming reclusive and depressed, prompting a call for universities to provide mental health care.

In the United States, on April 16, 2007, a horrifying shooting took place in Blacksburg, Virginia, at the Virginia Polytechnic Institute and State University, known as Virginia Tech, where you, Professor Garrison, teach. A twenty-three-year-old male student indiscriminately shot and killed thirty-two students and faculty members before committing suicide. This ghastly incident shocked the whole world.

I venture to ask you about the incident in the hope that we can learn a lesson from it. Where were you at the time? How did you first learn of the shooting? What are your thoughts on it now?

GARRISON: I was out of town the day of the slayings and first heard about it on the national news. Had I been there, I would have seen the events through my office window like so many of my colleagues. It was appalling enough having to watch events unfold across such a familiar landscape through the eyes of television cameras.

At the heart of the Virginia Tech tragedy is something lying at the core of the American experience. We are so infatuated with the isolated, atomistic individual that social services are unable to respond even when someone is clearly identified as deeply disturbed. Lucinda Roy, an English teacher at Virginia Tech, documents this in her book *No Right To Remain Silent* (2010). Silence is the great ally of violence, whether committed by bullies or mass murderers.

IKEDA: We need to build a society in which people make more effort to cooperate and relate to one another in a positive manner. When apathy and alienation prevail, society becomes both weaker and more dangerous.

GARRISON: Lucinda Roy worked one-on-one with the perpetrator, Seung-Hui Cho, after professor and world-famous poet Nikki Giovanni asked that he be removed from her class. It was easy to see from his writings and behavior that Cho was a threat to others and perhaps himself. He was eventually referred to counseling by the courts, but no one followed up, and he never went.

In Roy's opinion, the tragedy at Virginia Tech was institutional as well as cultural. Modern universities are simply too technocratically complex and university administration too focused on economic and technocratic efficiency to anticipate problems adequately or respond effectively to crises.

IKEDA: This extremely profound problem constitutes a serious warning for university education. What were some of the ways in which the university responded?

GARRISON: Since the tragedy, security and communications have been improved, as have mental health services. But national and state laws make it difficult to interfere with individual rights. The national gun lobby hindered passage of gun-law changes in the Virginia legislature.

Like most modern nations, the United States is constitutionally founded on rights, not responsibilities. The first ten amendments to the Constitution are often called the "Bill of Rights." Six of the first ten amendments explicitly use the word "rights" or the phrase "the right" of or to something. Of the remaining amendments, at least six also explicitly mention rights. The words "responsible" or "responsibility" appear nowhere among the amendments.

HICKMAN: After the tragic events at Virginia Tech, new emphasis was placed on counseling and safety measures at my own university. In general, it seems clear that schools and institutions of higher learning need strong psychological safety nets, and that students need to be taught how to monitor and report potential mental health crises among their peers.

Unfortunately, some legislators in the United States have used such tragedies to advance their own agendas. In my native state of Texas, for example, instead of emphasizing funding for counseling services, the state legislature has advanced a bill that will allow concealed weapons to be carried on campuses. It is probably a bit of an understatement to say that this seems to be a step in the wrong direction, especially given the abuse of alcohol on many campuses.

GARRISON: More positively, Virginia Tech now has a new Center for Peace Studies and Violence Prevention, headed by a professor who lost his wife on April 16, 2007. There is also a new Center for Student Engagement and Community Partnership, which coordinates the talents of diverse volunteers with the needs of the community in a constantly changing way while providing good mentoring.

IKEDA: It's important to take concrete steps of this kind. Building a sound, cooperative relationship between the university and the community is increasingly important to students' wholesome growth and the vigorous development of the local community.

Several years ago, Soka University of Japan students started a community safety and crime-prevention drive for the surrounding area. Their effort strengthened bonds among the students and also earned tremendous gratitude from the local population. The university also holds numerous public lectures and other events open to the community.

Soka University of America also stresses interaction with the local community, including sponsorship of an annual International Festival, reflecting the cultural diversity of the community. Opening the university to the community enables the university to incorporate a wider range of regional traditions and culture, which in turn broadens exchanges with the community, creating a synergy that local residents will welcome as a major source of stimulation.

I hope that Soka University will further deepen such community exchanges.

CONVERSATION TEN

The Twenty-First Century University

IKEDA: A life true to its vows to the end is noble and as radiant as a magnificent sunset. Such was the life of the physicist and president of the Pugwash Conferences, Joseph Rotblat, who devoted many years to the cause of eliminating nuclear armaments.

Speaking at Soka University of America, and on various other occasions, he insisted that university students in scientific fields should take something like the Hippocratic Oath before graduating. Dr. Rotblat called upon people with university educations to pledge, based on a strong moral conviction and sense of personal responsibility, to employ their knowledge for the good of humanity and society. In this idea, we can see his deep feeling of remorse and repugnance at the amoral science that engendered nuclear weapons.

Arnold J. Toynbee, too, said emphatically, "Before entering his profession, everyone who has received professional training ought to take the Hippocratic Oath that is prescribed for entrants into the medical profession."[1] What are your thoughts on this proposal?

Hickman: A requirement to take some version of the Hippocratic Oath would be a wonderful reminder to students in the sciences that their work is never completely value free. We can no longer afford the idea, still unfortunately current in the minds even of many educators, that the sciences are concerned only with facts.

Though we must never give up the idea that scientific laws are objective, in the sense that their experimental support is repeatable and verifiable, it is also true that scientists are often called upon to make value judgments of the utmost importance. It is essential that our students understand that training in ethics is not just tangential to their professional curriculum but integral to it.

Garrison: Rotblat and Toynbee are wise. I am also well aware that you, President Ikeda, are one of the world's leading advocates for nuclear disarmament.

We should honor the Hippocratic Oath in every domain of study. The first precept of the oath is a promise to "consider dear to me, as my parents, him who taught me this art." Disciples should always honor their mentors (just as the mentor must always honor his or her disciples).

The second precept urges the practitioner "never to do harm to anyone."[2] If every practitioner of every art and science would likewise swear to this principle, we would have peace in the world.

Liberal-Arts Education

Ikeda: A liberal-arts education that is truly liberal, in the original sense of the term, can foster the qualities required to carry out the oath described by Dr. Rotblat. Liberal education is the source of the fundamental strength to lead a more fully human life. It is a path of study that enables us to transform ourselves into more fully realized human beings.

Knowledge is not synonymous with wisdom. Only when we have the wisdom to use our knowledge correctly can we create abundant value. A liberal-arts education aims to produce wisdom in addition to knowledge. It is thus a force for creating new value in our lives as individuals and in society.

Soka University of America was founded as this kind of liberal-arts college. It aims to enable students to learn in a comprehensive, holistic manner, attaining a deep understanding of the interrelationships among fields of knowledge—not remaining limited to mastery of one specialized body of information. We seek to educate whole human beings, with open hearts and minds, an elevated moral sense, and outstanding cultivation and wisdom.

HICKMAN: You have described the virtues of a liberal-arts education so well that it is difficult to add anything to your remarks. I attended a liberal-arts university and have taught in departments of philosophy for thirty-five years. I continue to be grateful for the wonderful experiences and the opportunities for growth that the liberal arts have afforded me during those years.

Studies have demonstrated that liberal-arts graduates tend to advance more rapidly than do graduates who have been trained in narrow professional fields.[3] In addition, liberal-arts studies such as philosophy provide an excellent basis for future success in professional studies such as law. Dewey understood this quite well. A liberal-arts education involves more than training.

There was a joke when I taught at Texas A&M in the College of Liberal Arts: "Five years after graduation, what do you call a liberal-arts major?" The answer: "Boss."

Liberal-arts education is about learning to learn; it is about learning to develop the intellectual tools that provide the basis for lifelong learning.

IKEDA: President Makiguchi wrote:

> The aim of education is not to transfer knowledge; it is to guide the learning process, to put the responsibility for

> study into the students' own hands. It is not the piecemeal merchandizing of information; it is the provision of keys that will allow people to unlock the vault of knowledge on their own.[4]

Although many of us tend to associate university education with the mastery of specialized subject matter, I believe that the liberal-arts education described above is the true characteristic of university education. In an utterance that brilliantly encapsulates the importance of the cultivation supplied by a liberal-arts education, Goethe said, "Everything that is great promotes cultivation as soon as we are aware of it."[5] And Dewey wrote, "A student should expect from his college course a sense of the due proportion and right values of the various interests which may claim his attention."[6]

Cultivation provides the tools for discovering what are the most important values in life, as well as the criteria for making such judgments. The decline of a true liberal arts education and the degeneration of genuine cultivation into the mere trappings of being "cultured" are the equivalent of scrimping on the construction of that foundation. When it happens, both the individual and society lose sight of the values that should be their foundation.

A person lacking this cultivation, though he or she may possess knowledge, is not a learned individual. Universities must always begin with the development of cultivated intellectuals.

GARRISON: Dewey rejected any dualism between liberal education as pure knowledge that develops the mind and self as intrinsic goods and the idea of professional and practical studies that are only extrinsic goods. As Dewey often remarked, so-called pure knowledge is associated with a leisure class fit to rule, while practical knowing is associated with the lower working classes that must serve and follow. The natural sciences have helped break down this dualism, but we still strive to hold on to a separation of studies that seek to create intrinsic value for the student (commonly called liberal studies) from those that seek to help the student create extrinsic value for the world (commonly called vocational education).

Dewey believed in the unity of the self and its acts. We cannot separate thinking from doing in society any more than we can in the individual self. The only distinction worth making is between intelligent and unintelligent action.

IKEDA: The essential goal of education is then promoting the growth of integrated, whole human beings.

GARRISON: In overt worldly action, we express the present mind and self, and, simultaneously, we form the future mind and self, so there is no separation.

A truly liberal education is one that liberates. Thus, if properly taught, all education can be liberal education.

I see this notion of liberal education at work in value-creative education at the Soka schools, where students learn to develop and care for themselves by helping others. And, of course, the pursuit of peace is an external aim that simultaneously brings gain to the self and good to the world community. Genuine humanism does not separate being or knowing from doing.

An International Orientation

IKEDA: Let me express my heartfelt gratitude for your profound understanding of Soka education.

Dewey's emphasis on the connection between the self and the community and between the spirit and the deed expresses the essence of liberal education. In connection with this theme, let me ask your thoughts on the education we need for the age of globalization. I believe there is a pressing need for a program that we might call "global citizen education"—an education that enables us to understand the cultures and value systems of other peoples, humbly learn from them, and create value from the experience.

I believe that one element of such a program would have to be a new way of teaching history from a global viewpoint and with the aim of creating a better future. For example, during World War II, Japan invaded many Asian nations, inflicting great damage and loss of life. To build new relationships of trust and friendship with our Asian neighbors in the twenty-first century, it is more important than ever for Japan to make a sincere effort to demonstrate that it is confronting, rather than avoiding, this historical reality.

In *Democracy and Education*, Dewey wrote, "The segregation which kills the vitality of history is divorce from present modes and concerns of social life."[7] He goes on to say:

> Geography and history are the two great school resources for bringing about the enlargement of the significance of a direct personal experience. . . . While history makes human implications explicit and geography natural connections, these subjects are two phases of the same living whole.[8]

Josei Toda often told us that the study of history is actually the cultivation of a faculty of *historical insight*. Only by cultivating the ability to keenly perceive events as they are through the study of history can we employ the concrete happenings of the present as a mirror to help us envision the future. In this sense, the study of history is indispensable to a truly liberal education.

GARRISON: Makiguchi always starts with the personal, particular, and concrete. Dewey, too, reasoned from the concrete particular to the abstract universal while insisting we validate our abstractions in concrete practice.

This means we should teach history in much the same way as Makiguchi and Dewey teach geography. When the two are treated together, history does for time what geography does for space.

History is comprised of stories. When I teach it, I always begin with some item of personal history. We then move on to connect students' personal narratives to their family narratives. Having the students interview their parents and grandparents helps them learn about family history. Knowing a bit of family history, students then find it easy to connect to national events that influenced the lives of parents and grandparents. From there, the move to the global story is easy.

IKEDA: As you note, using young people's personal connections to history is an effective way of teaching the subject, because it makes it immediate and meaningful to them—it brings history to life.

Soka Gakkai youth, for instance, have interviewed family and acquaintances to collect the war experiences of ordinary citizens, which they have published for posterity in an eighty-volume series titled *Senso wo shiranai sedai e* (For Generations Who Have Never Known War). The volumes in this series include both accounts of the sufferings of war victims, including atomic-bomb survivors, and the horrors of enlisted men compelled to take part in the war. They echo the agonized cries of people enduring the misery and cruelty of war and reveal war's folly from many perspectives.

HICKMAN: I am very encouraged to learn about the eighty volumes of *For Generations Who Have Never Known War.* The Spanish-American philosopher George Santayana stated that "those who cannot remember the past are condemned to repeat it."[9] As educators, we must never cease to remind our students about the horrors of war—about the terrible waste that results from violence. That is one part of our task. Another is to help our students build bridges of empathy and understanding to other cultures, especially cultures that are the most different from their own.

Dewey wrote that geography and history are among the most important subjects in the curriculum, since so many other subjects radiate from them.[10] When our students understand their nations and their cultures in a broader context, then they will be prepared to deal with peoples and ideas in new and creative ways.

Dewey's experimentally based pragmatism provides tools for fostering global citizenship by indicating some of the ways in which global publics can be formed. Global publics will be based internally on shared interests and goals. Externally, they will be based on their ability to establish connections and alliances with other global publics. In all this, there is an important experimentalist component, since scientific methods are universally applicable, and when applied, they can bridge chasms of distrust.

Jane Addams's work at Hull House in Chicago during the early twentieth century, which I referred to earlier (see Conversation One), also offers examples of ways to build communities among the most diverse populations and under the most difficult circumstances.

Dewey's own commitment to evolutionary naturalism—his rejection of the divisive dogmas of supernaturalism—stressed the commonalities among the peoples of the world that can serve as platforms on which global publics can be built. By accepting a moderate version of cultural relativism (the idea that many cultural variations are significant, for better or worse), he was recognizing the obvious fact that what various cultures hold as good is much too rich and varied to be understood or judged in terms of one principle or set of principles. There are areas of experience where, as Dewey put it, knowing has no business; these areas are reserved for more immediate experiences, such as simple nonreflective delight in the music and cuisines of cultures other than our own.

IKEDA: Without doubt, encounters with other cultures lead to new discoveries, deepen mutual understanding, and act as a powerful force for value creation. In recent years, in particular, acquiring a global outlook and learning from diverse value systems has come to be seen as one of the important functions of a liberal education. In this context, I stress reading broadly and mastering languages, two pillars of liberal education.

Reading, in addition to practical information, can provide, through encounters with great literary works of all times and places, an introduction to the universality of the human experience that transcends the multiplicity of time and place.

And the importance of foreign language mastery is self-evident. I have frequently stressed language study at the Soka Junior and Senior High Schools and Soka University.

Language is the soul of culture. To study a language is to study both the values and thoughts that produce the culture of its speakers. Reading and language study cultivate a global view, enabling us to stand in another person's shoes.

I passed my youth during wartime, when studying English, the enemy's tongue, was forbidden. This is one of the great regrets of my life.

Although still a young institution, Soka University maintains contacts with 121 other universities in forty-four countries and regions (as of 2010) throughout the world. Every year, many of our students go abroad to study at schools with which we conduct exchanges, and students from other countries and regions come to the Soka University campus to study.

As I mentioned before, Soka University of America conducts a study-abroad program in which students spend one semester at a foreign university. Experiencing international exchanges of this kind is a significant inspiration in promoting students' development. As teachers at universities considerably senior to our own, what advice can you offer us?

GARRISON: Virginia Tech is a global university. The center of its strong international exchange program is the Cranwell International Center. It assists the more than 1,400 international students on our campus by acting as a hub of community activity and educational, cultural, and social exchange. It helps international students and their families adjust to life in the United States.

It also aids American students traveling abroad through the International Friendship Program. We have centers for research and study in the Dominican Republic, Switzerland, Egypt, and India.

The university also offers more than seventy student exchanges and more than thirty faculty-led programs for study abroad. Additionally, we offer a degree in International Studies emphasizing language learning and liberal education in a global perspective, which you, President Ikeda, spoke of earlier.

Meanwhile, Virginia Tech is an international leader in agriculture and engineering that sends consultants around the world and often hosts exchanges with visitors from other nations. While Virginia Tech strives to fulfill a global mission, it is a technical university focusing on economic activity. It lacks the compelling emphasis on humanism and peace education so essential to Soka education.

HICKMAN: Soka University has achieved well-deserved fame for its strong international program.

Southern Illinois University Carbondale also has a strong office of International Programs Services. It currently has exchange agreements with more than 150 universities. There are semester-long programs in Austria, Costa Rica, and the United Kingdom.

There are numerous short-term programs of two or three weeks in Ghana, Egypt, Italy, Greece, Germany, and other countries as well. These programs are continually evaluated by an advisory board.

During the 2008–2009 academic year, SIUC hosted some sixty-five Fulbright scholars. The university has a Center for English as a Second Language; a Global Media Research Center; programs of instruction in Chinese, French, German, Japanese, Spanish, and American Sign Language; and an interdisciplinary major in foreign language and international trade.

During the last fifteen years, the Center for Dewey Studies at SIUC has hosted more than 130 visiting researchers from thirty foreign countries, five of whom have been Fulbright scholars from, respectively, Denmark, Russia, China, Poland, and the Republic of Macedonia.

IKEDA: These are brilliant, far-reaching achievements. Projects like Erasmus Mundus[11] and the Socrates Program[12] sponsor millions of international exchange students, thus deepening mutual understanding and trust and greatly facilitating the building of a foundation for peace.

The Deweys, again, gave their children a chance to travel to Europe to experience different cultures. Having one's eyes opened to the world at a young age expands a person's horizons and naturally promotes learning from different cultures and value systems.

In this global age of the twenty-first century, cultivating understanding of different cultures among young people is going to be an increasingly important part of the university's mission.

GARRISON: Dewey rejected the notion that potential unfolds by itself. Instead, it requires something like dependent origination. Only by interacting with things different from itself can anything actualize its potential. Of course, the same thing holds for human individuals and individual nations.

This means that we should not only tolerate different cultures but must positively appreciate their differences as necessary to global prosperity and growth. Truly liberal, humanistic university education must embrace and cultivate differences in ways that create new global values of peace and understanding for the twenty-first century. Soka education is precisely the kind of value-creating education we need in this century of globalization.

I know that Cheng Yonghua, the Chinese ambassador to Japan (as of February 2010), is a Soka University graduate. I am aware that his appointment can be traced back to your efforts in the 1970s to break down the barriers of distrust between Japan and China. You first announced this initiative in 1968 at a meeting attended by 20,000 university students. It is a wonderful example of what a university with a truly global mission can accomplish for better relations between nations.

HICKMAN: You are surely correct, President Ikeda, that if they are to remain relevant, twenty-first-century universities must increase international initiatives such as study-abroad programs and student exchanges. Despite some logistical problems, the Erasmus program that you mentioned is already reaping great benefits in terms of cross-cultural understanding.

I believe that many of the disasters of the twentieth century might have been avoided if the world's universities had undertaken major, sustained efforts to support student exchanges. To learn another language is to learn about another culture, and to learn about another culture is to sow the seeds of peace. This is important even among nations with similar cultural values. I was greatly encouraged recently to learn of an Erasmus-type program that is being planned for exchanges among the students of Spain and the countries of Latin America.

The Founding Spirit

IKEDA: It is impossible to overemphasize the importance of contact with and learning from the unique qualities of different cultural values in one's youth. In the twenty-first century, we must, as you have just said, work with determination to create an unshakable network of peace based on exchanges among universities.

Now, I want to touch on the founding spirit of a university. I have visited and engaged in exchanges with many famous universities around the world—including Harvard, Moscow State, and Oxford—and in each case, I have been struck with the importance accorded to the university's founding spirit. When a university's founding spirit is deeply rooted and vibrantly alive in the minds of students, it is a priceless legacy and an inexhaustible source of strength. It promotes an appreciation of the university's history and traditions, and acts as a source of pride and inspiration, as well as provides a guiding philosophy and ethos for future development. Indeed, not just a university but any group or society that remembers its origins and frequently returns to its founding spirit is certain to develop and progress.

I have imparted three founding principles to Soka University of Japan:

- Be the highest seat of learning for humanistic education.
- Be the cradle of a new culture.
- Be a fortress of peace of humankind.

To attain these three goals, we put students first and make them the center of university life. Many of our graduates are wholly engaged in striving to make a positive contribution to society, based on the Soka University spirit. They have formed the Soka University Alumni Association as a network to promote the further development of their alma mater.

In addition, many of them make time to return to the campus

to give guidance and advice to current students. Every day, I receive letters from our alumni in Japan and abroad reporting on their activities, remaining true to the ideals and resolutions of their university days. As founder, I take supreme joy in learning of their activities.

GARRISON: The question of transferring a legacy is complex and difficult. Of course, rituals and remembrances are important. So is establishing continuity from founder to current students through a strong alumni association, such as the Soka University Alumni Association.

Still, much depends on the founding and what is best to pass on to the future and what not. Much depends on the wisdom of the founder. Both Soka Universities in Tokyo and the United States are very fortunate in that regard.

They are also lucky to have a founder who is still alive to communicate with them and serve as a mentor in their individual lives as well as the affairs of the institution. Within the larger unity of mentor and disciple, I know that you, too, must feel that you learn and grow from these young people, just as you did from your own mentor, Josei Toda. Indeed, as he is still alive in your spiritual life, so is he alive in theirs. Small wonder that you take such joy in learning of their activities.

Virginia Tech's motto is *Ut Prosium*, Latin for "That I may serve." As a land-grant university, Virginia Tech places special emphasis on service to the state, nation, and in recent decades, the world. This tradition is well maintained today.

From the beginning, the university has had a strong technical orientation intended to benefit agriculture, business, and industry by furthering practical education. This orientation is constantly referred to in the mission statements of the university and guides policy. However, the university has not always succeeded in making its practical education a liberating education.

Virginia Tech has a military history. At its founding in 1872, all students were members of the Corps of Cadets commanded by a former Confederate general. In 1973, Tech became the first cadet corps in the nation to enroll women. There is still a large cadre of uniformed cadets on campus, and their tradition pervades all aspects of the institution. Alumni of the Corps continue to provide strong support to the university.

Tech has an active alumni association, and its graduates contribute financially, intellectually, and socially to the benefit of the university. For instance, the Cranwell International Center was a gift to Virginia Tech from the William Cranwell family in 1986.

Universities that do not understand and honor their past will have no future, but which founding traditions to preserve and which to transform are questions every generation must ask.

HICKMAN: The founding principles of Soka University are both interesting and inspiring. They are interrelated, but they are also very different from one another. These founding principles are also reflected in SUA.

Being the highest seat of learning for humanistic education, for example, means being the very best university possible. Evidence indicates that SUA is already accomplishing that goal: A recent *U.S. News* report ranked SUA among the top ten liberal-arts colleges and universities in the state of California.[13]

Given the fact that SUA enrolled its first class in 2001, that is quite a remarkable achievement. It is clear that the stunning successes of SUA are due in large measure to your vision and unwavering support as founder and to the commitment of SUA President Daniel Y. Habuki to create extraordinary learning opportunities. The faculty-student ratio at SUA, for example (at this time about 1:9), is the envy of many institutions of higher learning.

To be the cradle of a new culture—this principle reminds us of the networks of support among SUA alumni that students may call upon after they leave the university to take their places in business, industry, and government. They will join networks of common values and common endeavor that transcend national and regional boundaries. It is a wonderful ambition to create a new culture that is not nationalistic but international and global, and reflects the values of peace and dialogue on which SUA is founded.

Finally, the third goal—being a fortress for the peace of humankind—recalls the wider values on which SUA and its sister institutions are founded and is an inspiration to work toward the continued flourishing of humankind.

Together, these principles constitute a marvelous reminder of what a university should, and can, be.

CONVERSATION ELEVEN

Education for World Citizens

IKEDA: New York is an international capital that stands as a microcosm of global society. It is also a city of education, at the cutting edge in fostering global citizens, a city where Dewey lived and worked.

The SGI-USA New York Culture Center is a historic building that once housed the Rand School of Social Science, a training center for citizens early in the twentieth century. Dewey delivered lectures there on at least seven occasions, when he was in his seventies.

Professor Hickman, in 2002, you delivered a lecture as part of an event held at the center to commemorate the fiftieth anniversary of Dewey's death. I thank you once again for your deeply meaningful contribution.

HICKMAN: Dewey was a great supporter of the work of the Rand School, which was founded to provide a broad education to workers, so I imagine that he would have been pleased to learn that the building now houses SGI activities that promote education for global citizenship. As you indicate, he lectured there on several occasions during the 1930s on topics such as "Education and Social Progress," "Politics and Culture," and "The Problem of Purpose."

It was a great honor to have been invited to make a presentation there in 2002, in the very hall where he had lectured some seventy years earlier. Attendees came from as far away as Italy and Japan to join us in celebrating his contributions to the advancement of democracy and education.

IKEDA: Coverage of your lecture in the Japanese newspaper *Seikyo Shimbun*[1] stimulated enthusiastic interest.

In May 2010, again at our New York Culture Center, Soka Gakkai youth representatives from Japan submitted to United Nations representatives 2,276,167 signatures calling for the adoption of a Nuclear Weapons Convention that would ban the development, testing, production, use, and threat of nuclear weapons. The presentation, with Sergio Duarte, UN High Representative for Disarmament Affairs, in attendance, took place during a nuclear abolition event at the culture center that coincided with the UN Review Conference of the Parties to the Treaty on the Non-Proliferation of Nuclear Weapons at the UN Headquarters. Ambassador Leslie B. Gatan, advisor to the president of the NPT review conference, also attended the SGI ceremony and read a message on behalf of UN Ambassador Libran N. Cabactulan of the Philippines, the president-elect of the 2010 NPT Review Conference. The petition was then submitted to the Review Conference and the United Nations.

Many have praised our young peace-builders for their positive actions and for the powerful message of hope they bring to international society in their efforts to build a world without nuclear weapons.

HICKMAN: I've had many opportunities to meet with students at Soka University in Japan and Soka University of America, as well as with young people at various SGI community centers, so I am well aware of the peace and human-rights activities of SGI young people.

There is an idealism among young people that can and should be nourished and directed toward realization of the values of peace and human rights. When that alignment occurs, many wonderful educational opportunities open up. And it is important to remind young people that the future is theirs, and that it will be what they make of it.

GARRISON: I also am aware of the impressive work on peace and human rights by the SGI. I know from my many interactions with students at both Soka University in Japan and Soka University of America, as well as the Soka students I met at all levels of K–12 education in Tokyo, that peace and human rights are constant themes not only in their education but in their lives as well. It should be for everyone everywhere.

Redefining Global Citizenship

IKEDA: I feel sure that your warm words will greatly encourage Soka youth. As I said, in his many years of work as an educator and social activist, Dewey left an indelible mark on New York City. For instance, he taught at Columbia University from the age of forty-four as a professor of philosophy, continuing until late in his life.

One of my unforgettable memories is the privilege of delivering an address at the Columbia University Teachers College in June 1996. In my talk, discussing the similarity between the philosophies of Dewey and Makiguchi, both of whom strove to create a new, humanistic education, I referred to the requisites for global citizens.

For many, the first image conjured up by the term *global citizen* is someone fluent in many languages or whose work takes him or her constantly racing around the world. In fact, the term is also a perfectly apt description for people who have no connections to international business, who are not globetrotters, but who, while firmly rooted in their local communities, think about things from a global perspective and take actions for world peace.

In my Columbia speech, I defined the following traits as the essential elements of world citizens: (1) The wisdom to perceive the interconnectedness of all life and living things; (2) The courage not to fear or deny difference but to respect and strive to understand people of different cultures and to grow from encounters with them; and (3) The compassion to maintain an imaginative empathy that reaches beyond one's immediate surroundings and extends to those suffering in distant places.[2]

These superior traits embody universal wisdom and spirit. I proposed their cultivation as one of education's major roles in the years to come.

GARRISON: I agree, but before going into the prerequisites of a global citizen, I would mention your comments on an axial line in the revival of humanity in your 1993 Harvard University lecture (in which you also referenced Dewey's insistence on the restoration of "the religious" in his book *A Common Faith*):

> It may be true that dependence on some external authority led people to underestimate both our potential and our responsibility, but excessive faith in our own powers is not the answer; it has, in fact, produced a dangerous overconfidence in ourselves.[3]

You also boldly asked the question, "Does religion make people stronger, or weaker?"[4] Unquestioning surrender to external authority as in dogmatic religion conceals interconnectedness, harms imaginative empathy, and causes fear of otherness and difference. The same holds for excessive confidence in our human powers, as in the case of people who believe in the omnipotence of reason.

IKEDA: Religion must always make people stronger, wiser, and happier. It must help people overcome their differences and promote working together for peace. This, in my belief, is the mission of twenty-first-century religion.

Reason is a two-edged sword. It is a fact that over-reliance on it can cause us to lose the human spirit—the openness of heart and mind manifest in compassion, trust, and friendship—and put our humanity at risk. This is why, as you suggest, we must strive for the Middle Way, inclining to neither extreme.

GARRISON: Those who have wisdom, courage, and compassion seek happiness in the Middle Way.

I might add a word about courage and compassion. I mean moral courage, not mere ferocity or bravado. With the ability to discern unique situations and with moral imagination—the ability to imagine the best possibilities—in a sense, you are already a citizen of the world.

Because all human beings are interconnected, wisdom, courage, and compassion travel very well. They are immediately understood by others everywhere.

In *A Geography of Human Life*, Makiguchi teaches geography in a way that discloses interconnectedness. It is not necessary to travel because, in a sense, the whole world converges on a person's little hometown through economic trade and global interconnectedness.

Community As Microcosm

IKEDA: Teaching that the things we wear and use all come to us thanks to the efforts of people in distant lands leads to Makiguchi's conclusion:

> The community, in short, is a microcosm of the world. If we encourage children to observe directly the complex relations between people and the land, between nature and society, we will be able to help them to grasp the realities of their homes, their school, the town, village or city, and to understand the wider world.[5]

Such an education is an important opportunity and foundation for fostering the wisdom to recognize the mutually interrelated nature of all living beings, the courage to engage fearlessly with different peoples and cultures, and the compassion to empathize with the sufferings of peoples of other countries.

GARRISON: I grew up in a small town, and my experience agrees with what you say; it was a microcosm of the larger world. If one has the ability to perceive connections and recognize the universal in the particular, then it does not matter where we are born—our experience will be large. Further, if one acquires moral courage and compassion while genuinely seeking wisdom, one can meet and learn from anyone anywhere on a footing of moral equality.

In the poem "Auguries of Innocence," William Blake wrote:

> *To see a World in a Grain of Sand,*
> *And a Heaven in a Wild Flower,*
> *Hold Infinity in the palm of your hand,*
> *And Eternity in an hour.*[6]

The macrocosm contracts into the microcosm. So, if you can read the ordinary world well and arrive at moral courage, compassion, and wisdom, no matter where you go in the whole wide world, you can entertain the desire for expanding experience, meaning, and value without being startled or thrown off balance.

IKEDA: With the poet's keen perception, Blake—a favorite of mine since my youth—splendidly reveals the true nature of things. All individuals are equally born to tread the precious path of life. Sadly, in all too many cases, people become obsessed with superficial differences, lapse into arrogance or servility or hate, and harm others.

Nichiren expressed it this way:

> Ultimately, all phenomena are contained within one's life, down to the last particle of dust. The nine mountains and the eight seas are encompassed in one's body, and the sun, moon, and myriad stars are found in one's life.[7]

The microcosm of the individual life contains everything in the macrocosm of the universe, all its measureless expanse and potential. We need to open young people's minds to this view of life and the universe.

It is essential for us, from the deepest level of our beings, to fully awaken to our inherent worth and dignity. We must humbly learn from our differences and, mutually enriching and elevating one another, grow together. The sure and steady way to achieve this is the continuous process of openhearted dialogue.

GARRISON: All of us are different, and differences are constantly about us. If you acquire and respond with wisdom, moral courage, and compassion, you will be well prepared to deal with the grander differences that might sail into your harbor one day.

HICKMAN: Makiguchi's description of community being a world in miniature is reminiscent of Dewey's idea that democratic institutions should function like the New England town meetings prevalent during his boyhood in Burlington and still an important feature of life in that part of the United States. The Internet offers many important educational possibilities, but it can never replace face-to-face communication. Participation in town council meetings, in civic organizations, and in clubs of various sorts, especially in a country as ethnically and culturally diverse as the United States, provides alternative ways of thinking about ourselves and reconsidering our assumptions about others.

IKEDA: I am in complete agreement with these concrete proposals from you both. Coming into contact with different languages and cultures is supremely important to the cultivation in our youth of the spirit of global citizenship.

RIGHTS AND RESPONSIBILITIES

HICKMAN: From the standpoint of Dewey's pragmatism, it seems important to emphasize the experimental component of global citizenship. Dewey claimed an experiential basis for his emphasis on continuity and commonality, thus rejecting the claims of skeptics, racists, and others that the primary features of human life are difference, discontinuity, and incommensurability.

He thought and taught that we must teach our students to understand that they exist as individuals only in relation to the connections and communities that enable them to be so. They are agents within a network of thick social morality and therefore within a network of thick social and political engagement that functions at its best when it is based on experimental methods and outcomes.

Moreover, since the aesthetic dimension of human experience plays such an important role within Dewey's account of experimental inquiry, he would doubtless have argued that aesthetic education would emerge as an essential component of global citizenship, as our students prepare themselves for broader participation in the new global publics.

IKEDA: Dewey emphasized the need for education promoting the commonweal and our awareness as members of the community. In connection with this, he noted the effectiveness of aesthetic education in forging connections among people. For this reason, he strenuously objected to the economically motivated elimination of music, drawing, and performing-arts classes in schools during the Great Depression. This is also an important point.

In line with this way of thinking, we can today consider human-rights and environmental education as keys to the cultivation of world citizens. Here, too, the starting point should be the local community. The spirit of mutual assistance and caring for others on the local level is the same fundamental spirit we need for world peace, and protecting the local natural environment is the starting point for global environmental awareness. Community action is indeed the starting point and foundation for global awareness. The interrelationship between the local and the global is extremely important.

GARRISON: Environmental education must emphasize the interconnectedness of humanity and human culture with biophysical systems. It should teach the Buddhist concept of dependent origination. It must also emphasize hands-on outdoor activities. Environmental education that expands the pattern for teaching geography and history as pioneered by Makiguchi and Dewey would be very promising.

Learning our rights is the first step. The United Nations Universal Declaration of Human Rights[8] provides a solid foundation for constructing a system of human-rights education. Often, we do not know our rights until someone names them for us.

For instance, I often point out in my classes that, unlike the Constitution of the United States, the Universal Declaration includes education as a human right. It is possible for states within the United States to withhold education from its citizens. Indeed, such a thing has happened. The Universal Declaration contains many rights not found in the U.S. Constitution. Exploring them over several class sessions has a dramatic effect on my students.

I have also found that visual images of rights violations help students create a sympathetic connection. Further, we should always ask not only who has rights but also who should defend them and how. It is important to talk about responsibilities, too.

Hickman: As an American who is deeply troubled by some of the actions of my government during the last decade and as a philosopher whose professional interests include the roles of science and technology in society, I am pleased to hear that you, President Ikeda, have linked these two concepts: human rights and environmental education. A part of the failure of my own government, and other governments as well, in these areas has been lack of transparency, narrowness of vision, and acceptance of environmental injustices as necessary evils or matters of little concern. Justice with respect to human rights is, in my view, a part of a larger issue: acceptance of the results of experimentation without, as we say, "putting one's thumb on the scale."

The past decade in my country has seen a remarkable corruption of science and technology policy. Data supplied by human rights organizations have been swept under the rug, good science has been either ignored or undercut, and environmental problems reported by career climatologists have been dismissed as "junk science" or as "needing further study." The nonprofit Union of Concerned Scientists collected thousands of signatures, including those of Nobel laureates and members of national academies, protesting these abuses.

On the positive side, this unfortunate period in our history offers important case studies that we as educators can utilize to help our students understand the importance of transparency, breadth of vision, and the benefits of environmental justice.

IKEDA: You raise important issues. It seems clear that with regard to human rights and the environment, darkness is crowding out the light. No matter how high-sounding the justification, we cannot accept any actions that lead to the sacrifice of the weak or the destruction of the environment.

It is thus increasingly important that, as global citizens, we acquire—through our schools and our daily lives—a system of ethics and a philosophy, both based on respect for life and the desire for humanity's welfare, that promote our dedication to others' happiness.

Further, in keeping with our rapidly changing times, we need to continue studying as long as we live to keep abreast of newly arising problems and to ensure our personal growth and ability to take appropriate action. Dewey wrote, "The aim of education is to enable individuals to continue their education."[9] This kind of education for global citizens is certain to become increasingly important.

CONVERSATION TWELVE

Ongoing Education

IKEDA: What is it that enables our humanity to shine in its full radiance? The desire to learn and the process of growth—both originating from education.

Dewey wrote, "I believe that education is the fundamental method of social progress and reform."[1] Based on this strong conviction, he involved himself in social action, living and working among the masses and devoting himself to developing education for them.

One of the arenas of his activity was the Rand School of Social Science in New York, which we mentioned before (see Conversation Eleven). Built with contributions from generous local citizens in 1887, it was a center of lifelong learning for all members of society, male and female, as its nickname, the People's House, indicates.

Today, too, lifelong learning and education—the process of study, self-improvement, and development throughout life—are indispensable. What are your thoughts on this?

GARRISON: The most important educational objective is learning the joy of learning and ways of pursuing it for a lifetime. Formal education often has the unintended consequence of teaching people to dislike learning. When we cease learning, we cease actualizing our unique potential.

As do people in the rest of the world, Americans largely see lifelong learning as a response to the new global knowledge economy and the necessity of continuously refining skills or retraining for new jobs. While it is useful, job training rarely develops the critical, creative, and reflective capacities that contribute most to personal growth and community welfare.

HICKMAN: The challenge to educators regarding lifelong learning is at least twofold. First, it is important that curricula reflect the needs and interests of a community. And second, it is important that people in lower socioeconomic sectors of society be afforded opportunities for which they may not be able to budget.

Of course, here I must return to the need for a strong infrastructure of social services, such as childcare. A vibrant, creative, stable, and peaceful society is a learning society.

DISTANCE LEARNING

IKEDA: Both of you make important points.

In 1930, Dewey retired from his teaching post at Columbia University and became an honorary professor of philosophy. The records of his lectures at the Rand School date from about that time. It was the year after the stock market crash that brought on the global misery of the Great Depression.

Dewey no doubt promoted lifelong education to encourage the people suffering in the Great Depression by introducing them to the joy of learning. He motivation must have been to do his share to help rebuild American society.

Lifelong learning can be a powerful, positive force for overcoming trying times. Our SGI movement, founded on Buddhist teachings, challenges us to pursue lifelong learning and is, in a sense, a school for life—one in which we continue to study, improve, and elevate ourselves as long as we live.

Professor Garrison points out the importance of "learning the joy of learning." Buddhism teaches that real joy is the existence of wisdom and compassion in both self and others. Truly inexhaustible happiness is to be found, in other words, in learning together, mutual encouragement, and striving in tandem with one another to develop our full potential. This is the way to build the active, creative, peaceful society of which you speak, Professor Hickman.

Of the many possible ways in which people can pursue lifelong study, correspondence education has been attracting great attention in Japan in recent years. You spoke of educational costs, and correspondence learning certainly meets the needs of people who, for one reason or another, cannot afford to attend school. What correspondence courses do your two universities offer?

HICKMAN: In the United States today, long-distance learning often employs the Internet. Some very large educational institutions are entirely web-based.

I myself participated in an early experiment during the 1980s called Connected Ed, which offered courses over the Internet. The difficulty then involved the need for more personal contact than typed messages can afford. I wound up spending a great deal of time on the telephone (long-distance calls were much more expensive in those days).

Today, with the aid of free long-distance phone service and video conferences, available through Skype and other programs, it is much easier to have person-to-person contact. This adds a rich dimension to the educational experience and allows learners who are geographically isolated or unable to travel because of disabilities to continue their education.

As a part of Southern Illinois University's commitment to

lifelong learning, its Division of Distance Education offers hundreds of courses in interactive, print-based, and web-based formats.

GARRISON: Traditional correspondence courses have evolved into online computer learning. The problem is that such systems limit distance learning to those who have the economic resources to afford the technology.

Virginia Tech is an international leader in online learning. Since 1998, it has delivered more than 6,000 courses for more than 130,000 total enrollments. It offers thirty-five graduate degrees, licensure programs, and certificates entirely online. Today, Virginia Tech Online delivers courses to students on campus, throughout the state, and beyond.

Modern technologies facilitate social interaction in many ways, but there is strong evidence that online learning is best when students form a sense of community with other students and with the professor. For instance, we know that distance education of all kinds works better if there are opportunities for the participants to meet with other students face to face.

IKEDA: Obviously, based on deeply held convictions and a commitment to responding to contemporary needs, both of your universities are enthusiastic about distance education.

Recently in Japan, growing interest in lifelong learning has stimulated an increase in correspondence education not only with universities but also in training for specific qualifications. The Soka University Correspondence-course Division opened on May 16, 1976. Since that time, it has conferred bachelor degrees on more than 13,000 students (more than 16,000 students as of 2013). Many of its participants have received doctorates or nationally certified qualifications as tax counselors, judicial scriveners, and notary publics.

In particular, large numbers of people are being qualified as teachers in our education courses. About 2,000 people (more than

2,700 people as of 2013) have qualified by passing the Faculty Appointment Examinations. Many correspondence-course students have rich life experience that, as a supplement to their studies, is enabling them to bring unique qualities to the challenges of the classroom environment and to shine as trustworthy instructors.

Today, Soka University is the prime correspondence-course university in Japan. In addition, for some years we have been strengthening correspondence-education ties with such overseas institutions as Open University Malaysia, among others.

Both Makiguchi and Toda emphasized the importance of correspondence education, and from the initial planning stages, I was eager for Soka University to include a correspondence-education department. I inherited from my two predecessors the belief that opportunities for higher learning should be equally available to everyone.

At present, our correspondence courses give people of all age groups—whether busy on the job, devoted to child-rearing, or adding enriching final touches to their lives—the chance to continue studying zealously.

Both of you believe in the importance of the human interaction provided by person-to-person meetings, and I agree entirely. Soka University correspondence education provides chances for such interaction in special summer and autumn school sessions, in which correspondence-course students from throughout Japan, as well as abroad, gather on campus to study together in a mutually stimulating way. Many of our correspondence-course students participate in these special sessions, which allow them to deepen their friendships with their fellow students, study together, and interact. This direct human interaction provides great encouragement, support, and reinforcement.

HICKMAN: Soka University is to be congratulated for its foresight. Correspondence courses are a growing part of the educational landscape.

WHEN FRIENDS GATHER

IKEDA: Lifelong learning is an important way to grow and progress as a person. Intellectual discovery is one of life's great joys.

The community has a very important role to play, in various ways, in the promotion of lifelong learning and education. Dewey thought of education "not just in the sense of schooling but with respect to all the ways in which communities attempt to shape the disposition and beliefs of their members."[2]

Establishing a positive environment for lifelong learning and education at the community level leads to an overall elevation of educational opportunities and promotes improved standards of school education in multiple ways. Such steps contribute greatly to fostering a society that exists for the sake of education. Consequently, providing a rich variety of opportunities for lifelong education at the community level is not only an important issue as far as education is concerned but an important challenge and source of hope for communities.

HICKMAN: Dewey believed that the reconstruction of social institutions is an ongoing project that is never complete, and that one of its chief engines is the school. That is why he rejected two ideas that are still all too common: first, that childhood is only a preparation for adulthood, and second, that education is designed to make us independent of others. He thought that growth, or the continuous reconstruction of experience, is the only legitimate end.

GARRISON: At the very end of *The Public and Its Problems*, Dewey refers to Emerson's conviction that we live in the lap of an immense intelligence but adds that "intelligence is dormant and its communications are broken, inarticulate and faint until it possesses the local community as its medium."[3] Dewey was convinced that the local, face-to-face community is necessary to form and sustain any public, including distance-learning communities, or organizations such as the SGI.

In "Creative Democracy—The Task Before Us," he wrote:

> I am inclined to believe that the heart and final guarantee of democracy is in free gatherings of neighbors on the street corner to discuss back and forth what is read in uncensored news of the day, and in gatherings of friends in the living rooms of houses and apartments to converse freely with one another.[4]

The Soka Gakkai grew out of precisely such gatherings. Indeed, it was in just such a setting that you met Josei Toda. I suspect that what guarantees democracy will also guarantee the future growth and prosperity of the SGI.

HICKMAN: It is my good fortune to have visited several SGI community centers. I've delivered lectures at centers in New York, Chicago, and Los Angeles. They are to be applauded as the kinds of institutions that strengthen the bonds of society. I believe that they provide models of what Dewey had in mind as institutions devoted to the growth of individuals and communities.

This is what Dewey was all about: forming institutions, developing institutions and what he called "publics," to which Professor Garrison referred earlier.

A public can be virtually anything. But there are two aspects of a public that he thought were important. First, a public must have a clear idea about what it wants to do, its own goals and purposes. Second, it should relate well to other publics.

In the case of SGI community centers, I see these two principles very much in evidence. If I may return to a topic that we discussed earlier, I would say that they are places where we can better learn to be value creators and not simply value *extractors*.

IKEDA: Thank you both for your warm understanding of the significance of our movement at the community level and the mission of our community centers. As you say, Professor Garrison, monthly discussion meetings, as opportunities for free, candid dialogue, are the pillar of our movement for peace, culture, and education.

I first met Josei Toda at such a meeting in the second summer after the end of World War II. As I have already said, I frankly asked him about things that were worrying me (see Conversation One).

On that occasion, Mr. Toda lectured on one of Nichiren's major works, "On Establishing the Correct Teaching for the Peace of the Land." I did not completely understand the content of his lecture or the discussion, but he answered my youthful questions clearly, precisely, directly, and in a way that embodied true justice and brilliant hope. Then and there, I made up my mind to learn under him.

President Makiguchi initiated discussion meetings before the war. He stressed the significance of such gatherings not only from the aspect of faith but in terms of education as well.

Once, when a young man asked him whether a large-scale lecture approach would not be better than the small discussion meetings, Makiguchi replied: "No, it wouldn't. Dialogue is the only way to communicate with another about life's problems. At a lecture, listeners inevitably feel uninvolved."[5] And he pointed out that even "On Establishing the Correct Teaching for the Peace of the Land" was written in dialogue form. Both Makiguchi and Toda hoped to make the masses wise and strong through meaningful, person-to-person dialogue and interaction.

One significant point about the discussion meeting movement is, without a doubt, the effectiveness of its vibrant, heart-to-heart communication in deeply connecting and reviving the lives of ordinary people, thus building a healthy society.

HICKMAN: It's important that the discussion meeting has an educational aspect. To function properly, however, such meetings need to be attended by people who are committed to active engagement with the issues, and it is also important to have some sort of institutional support that can provide structure. Otherwise, the meetings risk being disorganized and ad hoc.

Problem-Solving Power

Ikeda: Community-level support and interpersonal cooperation are essential if everyone is to progress happily and develop together. This is the purpose of the Soka Gakkai organization, an organization for the sake of the people, for the happiness of each individual.

In the years to come, the role of community organizations, community educational opportunities, and community networks for dialogue will grow increasingly important.

At the same time that Dewey was lecturing at the Rand School, Japan was, like the United States, affected by the Great Depression and confronting a tumultuous period. It was in these troubled times that, in 1930, President Makiguchi published the first volume of his great work *The System of Value-Creating Pedagogy*. In the introduction, he wrote:

> I am driven by the frantic desire to prevent the present deplorable situation where ten million of our children and students are forced to endure the agonies of cutthroat competition—perpetrated by the difficulty of getting into good schools, the "examination hell" and the competitive struggle for jobs after graduation—from continuing into the next generation. So I have no time to be concerned with the shifting vagaries of public opinion.[6]

His anguish at the thought of children suffering in the world's rough waves reveals the true nature of the father of Soka education.

Like Dewey, President Makiguchi believed that the only way to rebuild a troubled society was from the ground up, through the power of education. Establishing the Soka Kyoiku Gakkai (Value-Creating Education Society)—later renamed Soka Gakkai—he strove to reform society and acted to ameliorate the people's plight.

In an article titled "Introduction to Value-Creating Education," which he contributed to the November 1930 issue of the educational journal *Environment*, he wrote:

> The world is awaiting fundamental reform and advancement in the fields of politics, economics and the arts through the power of education. The solution to society's contradictions and problems is to be found in a basic transformation in humanity itself, and bringing about this fundamental change in human nature is ultimately the role of education.[7]

This conviction pervades *The System of Value-Creating Pedagogy.* Ultimately, the source of the illness afflicting modern society is to be found in us, its members. There can be no solution to the problem without the betterment and growth of human beings—and education is the basic force making this possible.

It is why I feel we must strive all the harder to realize Dewey's and Makiguchi's aspiration to employ education to rebuild society. This discussion with the two of you is a compass pointing the way to that future, I believe.

HICKMAN: Mr. Makiguchi's remarks were certainly prescient. Given the many problems that now confront us as a human race on our increasingly fragile and polluted planet, and given the dangerous and often inexcusable choices that humans continue to make—about their lives as individuals, their place in their communities, the roles that their social institutions play, and the long-term viability of their ecosystems—it now seems obvious that there will have to be a basic transformation of humanity itself, as he said so clearly.

Along with Dewey, he realized that there is no other way to effect the many changes that will be required than an increased emphasis on education, in the broadest sense of the term. It is my hope that the type of dialogue we have been privileged to hold will be multiplied many thousands of times over, among many thousands of individuals, and that the result will be new ways of thinking that will lead us to a human future that is bright with new possibilities for growth.

GARRISON: I want to comment on the subject of our current dialogue. In thinking about it, I came to realize that in some places I have some knowledge but no expertise. There are parts of this dialogue where I can say something relevant and valuable, but it became very clear to me that I was dialoguing with somebody important, who has created an entire Soka school system and two universities and literally knows the nuts and bolts of their daily operations.

It actually took me a while to realize that, in many ways, we are dealing with philosophical questions. I was shocked to see that ours is a dialogue between the East and the West. In fact, it is fascinating to see how Eastern Dewey's thinking actually is.

In our tripartite discussion, reasoning constantly begins with the concrete. As I started addressing these concrete questions, I was surprised at the level of universal insight to which they led. This is just an aside, but I find it fascinating.

IKEDA: You are both not only erudite scholars but also filled with a vigorous passion to learn and a youthful spirit of growth. This is why I am so grateful, knowing that our discussion is creating new value.

Dewey regarded an openhearted spirit of dialogue and a philosophy of democracy as requirements for a peaceful, happy society. Based on this conviction, he engaged vigorously in dialogue, encouraged others, and took action to build a better, more democratic society.

In the next conversation, I want to discuss Dewey's spirit of dialogue and philosophy of democracy at greater length.

CONVERSATION THIRTEEN

Dialogue and Transformation

IKEDA: A great dialogist is a great listener. Dewey was a splendid model of this. The American novelist James T. Farrell recalled him in this way:

> An interesting trait of Dewey's was that he would always listen to young people; he was extremely attentive to any young person. He was a good listener. You generally won't find philosophers—like Dewey, who listen as much as John would. Really, he'd listen, and listen, and listen.[1]

Dewey engaged in frank, open dialogue with ordinary citizens and young people, inspiring them with his shining character.

Both of you are vibrantly carrying on this spirit. In Japan, you engaged in stimulating dialogue with young people and students, and they were deeply impressed by how you embodied Dewey's philosophy of dialogue. In this conversation, I want to examine this philosophy and the convictions behind it.

GARRISON: In *Art as Experience,* Dewey wrote: "Language exists only when it is listened to as well as spoken. The hearer is an indispensable partner."[2]

Dewey himself practiced what he proclaimed in his theory of democratic dialogue. He was not easily upset or excited. Most of all, in dealings with other people, he emphasized broadmindedness and intellectual candor. He was cordial in personal dialogue and generally avoided a confrontational tone in public debates. Many who disagreed with him still respected his openness to dialogue with all kinds of people.

Ultimately, I believe his appeal lay in the common sense of his everyday, practical wisdom. He exemplified the virtues of his theory in his personality.

IKEDA: That Dewey put his philosophy into practice and manifested it through his character and behavior are proof that he was a true philosopher—the polar opposite of the image of the philosopher as an antisocial scholar, his head in the clouds.

HICKMAN: Yes, as you point out, Dewey did not fit the stereotype of the distant and disconnected philosopher, at home only in a realm of theories and able to talk only to other philosophers.

As you know, he was fully engaged on a number of levels: with schoolchildren, as he developed his humanist pedagogy; with professional colleagues, as he sought to reform academic philosophy; with like-minded political reformers, as he sought to steer a constructive course between the twin evils of Fascism and Stalinism; and perhaps most important, with the ordinary boys and girls, men and women, who wrote to him asking advice or seeking clarification of some complex idea.

Even though he was very busy and highly sought after as a lecturer and writer, the record of his correspondence reveals a man who exchanged letters with high-school students, the general public, and, in one notable case—which some researchers now think offers a remarkable insight into Dewey's views about religion—a U.S. Army private.[3]

IKEDA: He wholeheartedly encouraged each individual he met. Your description aptly communicates his great personal sincerity and warmth.

Many humorous incidents testify to his unpretentious, open-hearted character. For example, in his late years, he spent time at a country home, where he kept chickens and shared their eggs with neighbors. One day, the farmhand who usually did the chore was off, and Dewey himself undertook to deliver the eggs. On seeing a man in baggy trousers approaching her house, a wealthy neighbor asked him: "Is the usual deliveryman off work today? I suppose the Deweys sent you in his place." The man in the baggy pants did not identify himself. Some days later, Dewey was invited to dinner at the same woman's house. She greeted him at the door with: "Well, well! It's the egg man again." And the two of them shared a hearty laugh. I can almost see the pleasure on his face.

Never pretentious or conceited, he mixed comfortably with people and was a good conversationalist. This, I believe, deepened, strengthened, and broadened his philosophy.

My mentor, Toda, was a jovial, outgoing person, completely unlike the usual image of a religious philosopher. He, too, was a master dialogist, always listening to the troubles of others and, with ample wit and humor, offering encouragement and guiding young people. Even when discussing profound, complex Buddhist principles, he connected with people and daily life, and was completely accessible to his listeners. He was extremely convincing, and his words imparted deep certainty and determination, rousing courage in all with whom he spoke.

Nichiren said, "Teaching another something is the same as oiling the wheels of a cart so that they turn even though it is heavy, or as floating a boat on water so that it moves ahead easily."[4] This is the kind of masterful guide Josei Toda was.

An openhearted character of this kind, shining with love for humanity, is an important requirement for value-creating dialogue. How did Dewey cultivate and refine his character?

GARRISON: This is a good opportunity to reflect again on this aspect of his life. Dewey rarely revealed much of anything about his interior life. Therefore, he told us little about himself or how he became who he was.

There are only two published autobiographical statements. Allow me to call attention to a revealing passage from each. In the first, "From Absolutism to Experimentalism," Dewey wrote that

> the sense of divisions and separations that were, I suppose, borne in upon me as a consequence of a heritage of New England culture, divisions by way of isolation of self from the world, of soul from body, of nature from God, brought a painful oppression—or, rather, they were an inward laceration.[5]

What impressed him about reading Thomas Huxley's *The Elements of Physiology and Hygiene*[6] was a "sense of interdependence and interrelated unity" that served as a model not only for his later thinking but the healing of his hidden injuries.[7] This organic approach to the world recurs in many other major intellectual influences he mentions, such as the poet Samuel Taylor Coleridge and the philosophers G. W. F. Hegel and William James.

Second, in the biography edited by his daughter Jane, Dewey shared that his boyhood surroundings played a large part in forming his personality. As a boy and young man, he assumed a share in household activities and responsibilities and was thereby brought into contact with many occupations. These seem unimportant at first, but in *Democracy and Education*, Dewey declares that education *through* (not *for*) occupations is the best kind of education. All of this goes very deep when we remember that he said, "Philosophy may even be defined as the general theory of education."[8]

You are right: Dewey is a practical philosopher who found the greatest wisdom in ordinary, everyday occupations by which human beings learn to overcome the obstacles of life.

IKEDA: The important thing is to have hope and to courageously face life's challenges. To achieve this, people need a philosophy that provides a wellspring of wisdom. Casting his fate with the people and sharing their joys and sorrows, Dewey developed a philosophy that met their needs. I fully understand the respect that presidents Makiguchi and Toda had for Dewey.

Furthermore, Dewey's idea that the best education is one received through an occupation is important. Finding a purpose in life through one's work, learning and growing through work, and serving others and society—education focusing on this kind of social service leads to value creation and a fulfilling life. It is also deeply consonant with the spirit of Makiguchi's system—which I have already mentioned (see Conversation Seven)—of devoting half of each school day to classroom learning, the other half to work outside class.

GARRISON: Another aspect of his personal development, one that I have commented on before (see Conversation One), was parental influence. Dewey acquired a strong sense of social responsibility from his mother. His father was a gregarious merchant who was well liked in the community.

Also, the Burlington of Dewey's boyhood was an industrialized city characterized by class differences and ethnic and religious diversity, including an Irish and French-Canadian working class located along the lakefront where Dewey worked as a young man.

He was an energetic boy but shy. He was a very good listener from a young age. It was in Burlington that Dewey claimed he learned the value of democracy.

HICKMAN: At the risk of overlapping what has just been said, several factors come to mind when I think about the development of Dewey's open-minded nature. First, as I have already mentioned (see Conversation Eleven), he was heir to the wonderful tradition of the New England town meeting—a tradition of face-to-face communication that exemplifies democracy at its best.

Second, when he attended the University of Vermont, the student-to-faculty ratio there was such that students had the opportunity for extended dialogues with their teachers. Unfortunately, this is no longer the case in many research universities, where class size often runs to 200 students or more. I'm pleased that Soka University of America preserves this great tradition of faculty accessibility, with an admirable student-to-faculty ratio of about nine to one.

IKEDA: Everything begins with person-to-person dialogue. This is the way to produce limitless value. I also believe that we need to further stress the importance of education in small groups, where in-depth communication is possible.

You mentioned the democratic tradition of the New England town meeting. Recently in Japan, with the growing emphasis on regional autonomy, citizen participation is receiving renewed attention. As a young man, Dewey imbibed the grass-roots democracy of lively town-meeting discussions, thus acquiring the spirit of open dialogue.

HICKMAN: A third influence on Dewey's character development was his wife, Alice Chipman Dewey, who grew up in an environment in which Indians—Native Americans—were treated with respect and their cultural contributions honored.

A fourth influence was the profound insights he received as he observed the work of his friend Jane Addams, who seemed capable of overcoming even the most difficult impediments to dialogue. Addams founded Hull House, a settlement house for the waves of immigrants who poured into Chicago during the decades that straddled the turn of the twentieth century. She impressed Dewey with the importance of listening to others and respecting cultural difference.

Dewey's willingness to enter into dialogue would become enormously important during his twenty-six months in China, 1919–1921. It would play a major role in making his visit a success.

IKEDA: He was one of the American intellectuals who exerted great influence on the development of modern China. I have engaged in a dialogue with Chinese historian Zhang Kaiyuan, who told me about an earlier educator, Tao Xingzhi, who studied under Dewey in America. Zhang said that Tao helped modernize China's public education by expanding on Dewey's core ideas that education is life, that the school is society.

On the eve of revolution, Dewey lectured more than 200 times in various parts of China. Through positive efforts at dialogue, or creative communication, he enlightened, encouraged, and emboldened many young people, imparting the spirit of a new educational philosophy to China.

What did Dewey think about the significance of dialogue?

EXPERIENCE AND NATURE

GARRISON: Dewey is famous for saying, in *Experience and Nature*, that of all affairs, "communication is the most wonderful," for when it occurs, "all natural events are subject to reconsideration and revision."[9] He believed that to have a mind is to possess meaning, and that meaning arises through linguistic communication. Such communication implies two or more social beings reaching agreement in action regarding some third object or person.

We literally owe our minds and selves to our ability to incorporate others' attitudes toward the world. This is why good communication is critical to well-being.

Of course, dialogue is the supreme example of linguistic communication. For him, the main criterion of democracy was free and open communication. Any mode of life that limits communication limits democracy. Dewey thought much the same about dialogue and inquiry, including scientific inquiry.

HICKMAN: *Experience and Nature*, published in 1925, is one of his most important books. He begins the fifth chapter of that book with the following words, part of which Dr. Garrison quoted before:

> Of all affairs, communication is the most wonderful. That things should be able to pass from the plane of external pushing and pulling to that of revealing themselves to man, and thereby to themselves; and that the fruit of communication should be participation, sharing, is a wonder by the side of which transubstantiation pales.[10]

This statement is both simple and complex. In its simplicity, it says that participation and sharing are so richly productive that even alleged miracles pale by comparison. At a more complex level, it establishes a genealogical connection between human beings and the rest of nature—not only living things but inanimate objects as well.

It was in this latter sense that he suggested that it is only with the advent of human intelligence that nature comes to have a mind of its own.[11] Although there is communication in the rest of nature, dialogue—the ability to both put oneself in the place of the other and to view oneself as viewed by the other—appears to be a uniquely human capacity. There is an enormous responsibility implicated in that idea.

Dependent Origination

IKEDA: Thank you for your extended, thought-provoking remarks on the significance of dialogue and communication.

Further, as we have already mentioned (see Conversations Two and Ten), according to the Buddhist concept of dependent origination, all life forms influence one another and are inseparably connected.

Buddhism also teaches the oneness of life and its environment. A living being and its environment are nondual; they exist in a relationship of "two (in phenomena) but not two (in essence)." That is, they are distinct as phenomena but united at a more fundamental level. All living beings, moment by moment, are constantly changing and mutually influencing all other beings in accord with this principle of the nonduality of life and its environment.

In terms of our own lives, we are engaged in relationships of mutual interaction and influence—relationships with other people, with society, and with nature. In a sense, all our lives are communicating with one another as we undergo constant change.

The oneness of life and its environment suggests that, within this process of constant change and while engaging in value-creating communication, everything grows and moves in the direction of happiness.

As Dewey observed, "Planets exist and act in solar systems, and these systems in galaxies." Similarly, within the immense relatedness of all things, the "mind is nourished by contact with others and by intercommunication."[12]

Walt Whitman, the poet of democracy, also praised the wondrous interconnectedness of all things: "The whole referring, yet each distinct and in its place."[13]

Better communication is important precisely because all things, including human society, exist in inseparable relationships of mutual influence and interaction.

GARRISON: I am personally fond of Walt Whitman, as was Dewey. Dewey shared Whitman's reverent awe for what emerged in everyday communication. Whitman especially valued face-to-face dialogue as the stronghold of democracy.

IKEDA: His—and your—unshakeable conviction that face-to-face dialogue is the bastion of democracy resonates strongly with me. I shall always remember something that Richard von Weizsäcker, the first president of a reunified Germany, told me in 1991: "We should be concerned not just about material prosperity, but about the human being himself and the harmony and coexistence of humankind."[14] Having been a philosophical leader who experienced an age of great hostility, when the East-West Cold War divided a people and set them against one another, gives added weight to his words.

He was convinced that neither the capitalistic nor the democratic system alone could generate the virtue and sense of responsibility of which human beings, at their best, are capable. In this regard, he believed that the people have a crucial role to play. No matter what social system prevails, without the warmth of the human heart, the world is a savage place. To build the foundation for a harmonious society—a democratic society in which human beings respect one another equally and live up to the best of their potential—we need creative dialogue that brings people together in spirit and promotes their mutual elevation and growth.

Even during the harsh times of the Cold War, I engaged in exchanges with numerous people from the Soviet Union and East Germany. For example, at a time when many were antagonistic toward the Eastern Bloc, I shared dialogues with Mikhail S. Gorbachev, former president of the Soviet Union, and Anatoli A. Logunov, former rector of Moscow State University, which were later published as books. I believed that our shared humanity would make communication possible if we met and spoke candidly with one another.

Today, the once apparently impregnable Iron Curtain and Berlin Wall no longer exist. Their collapse demonstrates both the need to avoid allowing ourselves to be hampered by preconceived notions and the importance of a humanistic philosophy and the act of dialogue.

GARRISON: Philosophy must have a deep and abiding commitment to the infinite potential of a pluralistic, ever-changing universe. It must understand that existence is composed of fluid events and not lumpy substances or fixed identities, including personal identity.

This requires the realization of what Buddhism calls dependent origination. So the appropriate philosophy will seek to create value by creating good relationships. Devoid of fixed and final absolutes, it will see evil not as a thing or substance but merely as bad relationships that can be artfully translated into good ones.

Socially, it must have a commitment to each individual as a unique and irreplaceable nexus of relations. It must further recognize that each individual can only actualize his or her unique potential in transactional relations with other individuals.

Therefore, we must insist on moral equality regardless of all other differences. Such a philosophy must appreciate and cultivate differences, not merely tolerate them. It will constantly seek dynamic social relationships and strive to relieve suffering by transforming bad relationships into good through creative social action.

Ikeda: This is the kind of philosophy underpinning the creative democracy Dewey advocated. He saw democracy as a broader, deeper way of life transcending political and social systems. It meant transcending ethnic, religious, and ideological differences and perpetually striving to create a more human world, in which we are vibrantly engaged with others and with society.

Relationships can be either positive or negative. Through the exercise of our wills, we can reorient negative situations in a more positive direction. This is why, as we have already discussed, I stressed in my 1993 speech at Harvard University[15] that the great mission of religion in the twenty-first century is to enable human beings to lead wiser, stronger, better lives.

Ordered Richness

Hickman: Thank you for your profound statement of democratic ideals. Dewey continually characterized democracy as a kind of faith—faith in the ability of human experience to generate, as he put it, the aims and methods by which "further experience will grow in ordered richness."[16]

That means that we can join together in creating a better world on the basis of faith in the possibilities of our individual and communal experiences instead of having to rely on sources that allege supernatural or non-natural authority. Clarification and transformation of our experiences as individuals and communities is the lifeblood of democratic life.

Humanistic religious institutions such as the Soka Gakkai have an essential role to play in articulating and advancing this faith, in demonstrating and encouraging efforts to redirect "negative situations in a more positive direction," as you say. At bottom, the goal of philosophy, religious belief, democracy, and education alike should be the creation of value and the enhancement of the quality of human life.

GARRISON: A philosophy seeking to relieve suffering by transforming bad relations into good must advocate a constantly evolving, pluralistic democracy tailored to fit the needs of specific times and places for peoples with different histories and aspirations. Communication across difference will be greatly valued. Philosophy must always seek wisdom, which is always beyond knowledge alone and only expresses itself in right action.

Dewey's philosophy has all of the characteristics just described. Given my limited knowledge, it seems to me that the Soka Gakkai's philosophy does as well.

However, pragmatism and the Soka Gakkai philosophy developed in completely different cultures. This suggests that wisdom knows no special time or place. While they have many significant divergences of detail and expression, it is still rather easy for us to participate in dialogue. It seems to me that the Soka Gakkai extracted Nichiren Buddhism from feudal elitism and restored its fundamentally democratic quality to the people, thereby bringing it much closer to Deweyan pragmatism.

CONVERSATION FOURTEEN

Breaking the Cycle of Violence

IKEDA: Austregesilo de Athayde, the former president of the Brazilian Academy of Letters, played an important part in drafting the Universal Declaration of Human Rights. On one occasion, as if making a final testament, he told me, "Mutual understanding and solidarity created through dialogue is the force that will vanquish all threats of evils."[1] This force is in even greater demand today than it was when he made this statement.

Dialogue can range from grassroots discussions to dialogue between civilizations, but in all cases, the first condition is to come together. This can, however, be difficult to arrange, especially among different ethnicities and cultures in conflict.

Up to this point, the three of us have discussed Dewey's spirit of dialogue. What in your views is the force that propels dialogue?

HICKMAN: I agree that intercultural dialogues can be difficult. Your own extensive experience has shown you that these are very hard matters.

As I have already suggested, I think that we can benefit from looking at the work of one of Dewey's most influential mentors, Jane Addams (see Conversations One and Ten). During the 1890s, she and Dewey worked together in Chicago. She was an enormous help to him as he sought to form his ideas about the nature of conflict and its resolution.

Almost all of the more than 44,000 inhabitants of the neighborhood of about 200 hectares that Addams chose for her settlement house were immigrants. They represented some eighteen nationalities and thus a broad range of languages and customs. Addams had to find ways of dealing with racial and ideological conflicts, as well as those that were linguistic and cultural. Her successes, and her failures, provide important lessons for us as we face the prospect of an increasingly globalized world, in which hundreds of nationalities, languages, and customs are in ever-closer contact.

IKEDA: Women's compassionate acts to relieve the people's sufferings have a growing impact and shine with a brighter radiance over time.

Participating in the educational programs of Hull House together with associates from the University of Chicago was a valuable experience for Dewey. During her more than twenty years at Hull House, Addams fought against poverty and social injustice, and strove to bring together many different kinds of people.

I am especially fond of her following determination:

> The conviction remained with me, that however long a time might be required to establish justice in the new relationships of our raw industrialism, it would never be stable until it had received the sanction of those upon whom the present situation presses so harshly.[2]

HICKMAN: In a remarkably candid letter written to his wife, Alice, dated October 10, 1894, Dewey wrote:

> I asked her [Addams] if she didn't think that besides the personal antagonisms, there was that of ideas and institutions, as Christianity and Judaism, and Labor and Capital, the Church and Democracy now and that realization of that antagonism was necessary to an appreciation of the truth, and to a consciousness of growth, and she said no. The antagonisms of institutions were always unreal; it was simply due to the injection of the personal attitude and reaction; and then instead of adding to the recognition of meaning, it delayed and distorted it. If I could tell you the absolutely commonplace and unemotional way in which she said all these things, it would give some better idea of the most magnificent exhibition of intellectual and moral faith I ever saw.[3]

According to eminent Addams scholar Marilyn Fischer, Addams taught Dewey that without knowledge, attempts to enter imaginatively into the lives of others can be disastrous.[4] Addams herself wrote that "sympathetic knowledge is the only way of approach to any human problem."[5] And of course, sympathetic knowledge is a cornerstone of Dewey's philosophy of education.

GARRISON: Yes, in his *Ethics*, Dewey insists:

> It is sympathy which carries thought out beyond the self and which extends its scope till it approaches the universal as its limit. . . . Sympathy is the animating mold of moral judgment . . . because it furnishes the most efficacious *intellectual* standpoint. It is the tool, *par excellence*, for resolving complex situations.[6]

It is quite possible Dewey arrived at this observation through his many conversations with Addams, who, as Hickman points out, not only thought antagonism useless and harmful but unnecessary as long as we approached conflict from the "most efficacious intellectual standpoint."

Jane Addams seems to have provided Dewey with wonderful examples of practical intelligence in action on the streets of Chicago instead of the ivory tower of academia, along with helping him recognize the importance of intelligent sympathy, but never pity, in working with those less fortunate. It left an enduring impression.

BELFAST AGREEMENT

IKEDA: Both sympathetic knowledge and intelligent sympathy are important.

After the turmoil of World War I, Addams worked for women's solidarity all over the globe, including Asia and the Pacific region, as representative of the Women's Peacemakers Program, the first women's pacifist organization in the United States, and as president of the Women's International League for Peace and Freedom. In June 1923, in connection with her pacifist work, she visited Japan, where she was welcomed as a peace advocate.

She lectured in Japan, but after a brief stay, she became exhausted. Unfortunately, illness compelled her to return to the United States. Still, her ideas and deeds provided great inspiration and courage for the nascent Japanese women's peace movement.

She once said, "We...believed that justice between men or between nations can be achieved only through understanding and fellowship."[7] No doubt her many years of dialogue had made her keenly aware of the importance of mutual understanding and sympathy, both among peoples and nations.

My numerous discussions with thoughtful people from all over the world have led me to conclude that, no matter how problematic the situation or intractable the other party, dialogue is the vital first step to a problem's solution.

GARRISON: Undeniably, whoever the other party is, we must summon people to the discussion table. It is best to think in terms of friendly hospitality, where the guest and host show mutual respect.

We must avoid violently forcing anyone into a dialogue. Violence only perpetuates violence. Sometimes, circumstances may only briefly sanction forceful intervention (for example, military action) to stop even worse violence. Even then, we must use the greatest restraint possible and reconcile quickly.

The case of Ireland has become a beacon of hope for the entire world. There, the conflict involved religious disagreements (Catholics versus Protestants) but was even deeper and more complicated than that and had carried on for hundreds of years. Yet, on December 15, 1993, a treaty was signed that has held up well ever since. With the historic Belfast Agreement concluded in April 1998, an autonomous government and parliament were established.

IKEDA: Yes, these were epoch-making first steps. In the twentieth century—especially from the end of the 1960s—the protracted conflict in Northern Ireland became grave as hate-inspired acts of terrorism stimulated the desire for retaliation.

Through a campaign for dialogue based on respecting the ideas of local citizens, persistently listening to what they had to say, this historic agreement was reached and peaceful results steadily achieved. This is a great victory for nonviolence and courageous dialogue. SGI members in Ireland and England who prayed and spoke out for the earliest possible resolution of the conflict are rejoicing at this result.

In May 2009, Peter Gregson, president and vice chancellor of Queen's College Belfast, visited Soka University. His institution made considerable contributions to the conclusion of the conflict and the advancement of peace. As an example of the ways in which this was done, Professor Gregson mentioned the annual Belfast

Festival to employ art to connect the hearts and minds of local people. He expressed his belief that art and culture are important elements in building peace.[8]

In addition, I have carried on an extensive correspondence with George Mitchell, former chancellor of Queen's College. He is deeply committed to dialogue, based on his conviction that, since human beings start conflicts, human beings can conclude them.

Garrison: Let me say that while things vary in different times and places, we may generalize regarding the wonderful Belfast Agreement. Earlier, I mentioned summoning people to the peace table. In Ireland, this involved several things that seem to me to easily apply to other conflicts worldwide.

First, the large majority of the people themselves must wish to put an end to the conflict and show courage and determination.

Second, there must be wide recognition that violence will not resolve the conflict.

Third, leadership must comprehend the will of the people for peace or strive to educate them.

Fourth, the presence of a mediator like George Mitchell is often critical. Trusted intermediaries between parties unwilling to meet face to face are frequently necessary.

Fifth, outside parties that aid in peace efforts are helpful, while those that perpetuate conflict are harmful.

Sixth, negotiating parties must remain in constant contact. Modern communicative technologies can help.

Seventh, trust and patience are important.

Eighth, local, community-based organizations should be mobilized.

Ninth, there must be perceived mutual economic benefit. The changing roles brought on by participating in the European Union were important in Ireland.

Tenth, hope.

Eleventh, all parties must come to believe they are represented fairly and equitably, with power appropriately shared.

Twelfth, being able to tell one's story while listening carefully to the stories of others is always critical. George Mitchell, whom you just mentioned, was of Arab and Irish descent and a former United States Senate Majority leader and special envoy for Northern Ireland during the Clinton administration. All parties report that Mitchell was a magnificent mediator and unbiased listener whose patience gained the trust of everyone.

I am sure the foregoing is not exhaustive, nor must all of the things mentioned be present. The best place to start varies with context. Overall dynamic harmony matters most.

Loving One's Opponents

IKEDA: Each of your essential elements, Professor Garrison, is significant for the realization of peace. Whenever I have the chance, as in my SGI Day peace proposals,[9] I insist that the whole world should learn from the experience and wisdom shown in Northern Ireland. As you point out in your first generalization, the positive results achieved there manifest the power of dialogue based on courage and determination for peace.

HICKMAN: Mr. Ikeda, your point that there is no such thing as a conflict that cannot be ended is something we need to keep uppermost in our thoughts, especially when the prospects for peace appear to be at their worst. And Jim Garrison, you have done such a wonderful job of detailing and analyzing the many factors that went into the Belfast Agreement. Together, they can surely serve as a blueprint for the resolution of other conflicts, present and future.

Although each of the factors you mention is important, I want to emphasize the central role of the social services that provide the infrastructure for the education of children. The social and economic vulnerability of children, especially, tends to cut short educational opportunities. And where education is weak or fails, there is a corresponding lack of ability to envision life's possibilities, especially the possibilities of cooperative action toward shared spiritual goals.

GARRISON: We must engage in dialogue if we are to transform disharmony (conflict, evil, etc.) into harmony (peace, good, etc.), but that means recognizing creative possibilities. It is important that participants in dialogues across differences strive to understand one another's beliefs, values, and ways of life sympathetically.

However, substantial understanding is often not possible. Nonetheless, the novel meaning we create together sometimes forms mutual understanding, or at least constitutes a willingness to continue. It is important to retain a certain amount of respectful playfulness, by which I mean everything from cheerful banter and simply enjoying one another's company to exploring possibilities, all the while constantly respecting one another's difference.

IKEDA: Professor Gregson has adopted the convictions of Gandhi as his own. Gandhi is famous for being a person who laughed a great deal. Techniques such as the ability to negotiate skillfully are important for resolving difficult situations or breaking deadlocks; at the same time, it takes indomitable cheerfulness, mental positivity, and unfailing optimism to unite people emotionally.

To resolve the conflict in Northern Ireland, Betty Williams rose up with other mothers to conduct a historic peace march. She is a great mother of peace with just this kind of unflagging optimism.

I once asked her: "You have said that the example of Northern Ireland shows that the cycle of violence increases in viciousness with each passing generation. What do you think is the key to breaking this vicious cycle?"[10]

She replied, "For me, the only way I can work is to remain true to my beliefs and love my opponents into submission."[11]

Then, she related the following:

> I remember one situation in which a man was attacking me verbally. He was quite fierce, actually, and was standing so close to me that I thought he might bump me with his head or bite my nose off, but I just stood very still, without saying a word. Eventually, his mouth must have gotten tired. He started speaking more and more slowly, and then he backed away. And I looked at him and I said: "I love you." About two months later, that man became a peace worker.[12]

She also stressed: "As women, it is our responsibility to make sure that leaders who resort to brute force and oppression do not get elected. And that can only happen through education, education, and more education."[13]

What she said agrees with your opinion, Professor Hickman. Surely, education, cultural enlightenment, and exchange are essential to overcoming differences in cultural and religious background; they are the best way to cultivate an open mind and candid dialogue.

The Inner Voice

Hickman: The magnificent testimony of Betty Williams is reminiscent of the testimony of Jane Addams. She told of early resistance to her efforts to promote harmony among the culturally diverse immigrants of 1890s Chicago. When she was spat upon in the street, her active, loving response helped pave the way for her acceptance as a mediator among the various immigrant groups. For both Williams and Addams, *pacifism* was anything but *passivism*.

GARRISON: Back in the early 1990s, I began writing with Stephanie L. Kimball on the topic of listening in dialogues across differences. The single most powerful idea we developed was that even when two parties are almost completely incommensurate, it is still sometimes possible for them to co-create understanding in the space between them.

Stephanie has left academia but remains very active in her local community and committed to grass-roots democracy. Ultimately, dialogues across differences must succeed in local settings, as the case of Ireland illustrates.

Listening is the forgotten half of dialogue. We worry too much about the right of people to speak. Many times, what appears to be a dialogue is actually a soliloquy, because neither party is listening; they are only awaiting their turn to speak.

As Dewey said, "Soliloquy is but broken and imperfect thought."[14] Unfortunately, much of what passes for intercultural dialogue is really broken and imperfect thought. However, when participants are all listening attentively, we may achieve harmonious and unified thought or at least avoid violence. I do believe there are times when parties are not ready for dialogue, so it may be best to keep them apart.

Stephanie helped me understand that while sympathy is often valuable, it can be dangerous. Unless we strive to listen to others instead of just to ourselves, we might confuse our wants, needs, and desires with those of others. This can be disastrous if we seek to relieve the suffering of others in our terms instead of theirs.

IKEDA: As we have said repeatedly up to now, establishing a dialogue starts with listening and understanding the other party. Dialogue consists of sincerely listening to the person's inner voice. As we have two ears and one mouth, we should stress the importance of listening twice as much as talking. We must have our antenna tuned to other people's real meaning, considering how they came to think as they do, what they are trying to convey, and whether their real intentions have been verbalized.

In the Buddhist practice of the bodhisattva, listening to what others have to say is a manifestation of wholeheartedly empathizing with their sufferings.

GARRISON: When I first read chapter 25 of the Lotus Sutra and met the Bodhisattva Perceiver of the World's Sounds, I immediately recognized an ideal of deep, receptive, sympathetic listening that always seeks to comprehend and reduce the suffering of others in terms of *their* needs, desires, interests, and aspirations. When engaged in intercultural dialogue, we should all strive to imitate this bodhisattva.

IKEDA: Abandoning dialogue is tantamount to abandoning our trust in humanity. All that remains then is the logic of force. Violence and force breed hatred and retaliation, from which arises more violence, permanently preventing peacebuilding.

Dewey's philosophy is founded on trust in human nature. For this reason, it has sometimes been criticized as too optimistic. But history has shown that the logic of force cannot bring true peace and coexistence.

In this context, Jane Addams's and Northern Ireland's peace stand as radiant models of hope. This is why I go on loudly proclaiming courageous dialogue as true human victory.

CONVERSATION FIFTEEN

Creative Democracy

IKEDA: Democracy is one of the great treasures of the human race, won through the courageous deeds of countless forebears—among which Dewey's contributions are inspiring. I want now to turn to a discussion of his democratic philosophy.

Dewey visited Japan and China in 1919. His trip strengthened his faith in democracy.

Reflection on the terrible loss of life in World War I, in which more than ten million died, led to the convening of a Paris peace conference between January and June 1919, at which international society groped for ways to build a peaceful world order. Unfortunately, counter to this global current, Japan's shift toward militarism gradually intensified. As we have already said (see Conversation Five), Dewey was alarmed by the totalitarian indoctrination of the populace he observed in Japan. Meanwhile, in China, where Japan was steadily preparing to further its expansionist ambitions, Dewey witnessed a surging anti-Japanese, student-led movement. Finally, with the Marco Polo Bridge incident of July 1937,[1] the Sino-Japanese war broke out.

It was apparently Dewey's own idea to make this trip to Japan and China. Was this because of his great interest in Eastern philosophy?

GARRISON: You may be surprised to know that the answer is no. John and Alice simply wanted to experience Asia much as Western tourists do today. When two Japanese businessmen arranged for some lectures at Tokyo Imperial University, vacation plans began to change. While Dewey's ideas about democracy had little impact given the terrible militarist environment in Japan at the time, conditions were very different in China.

DEWEY IN CHINA

IKEDA: Yes, the two countries' situations couldn't have been more different. Dewey and his wife arrived in Shanghai, their first stop in China, on April 30, 1919, immediately before the May Fourth Movement of popular Chinese resistance against Japan's high-handed colonial domination. He was greeted by Hu Shi and Tao Xingzhi, who had been his students at Columbia University. On the third and fourth of May, he lectured to the Jiangsu Province educational committee on the topic "Democratic Education." In other words, he went straight to the people to deliver the educational thought China needed at that moment.

GARRISON: At the time, China was indeed in the midst of tremendous social unrest, and he was welcomed as the prophet of democracy, science, and modernization. He certainly found the situation in China much more promising than in Japan, whose militarism, state Shinto, and rigid feudalistic class structure perplexed and disturbed him. When Dewey accepted an invitation to teach at the National University in Peking for a year, it was the beginning of a two-year stay.

He wrote a colleague at Columbia that everything about the West looks different from an Asian perspective, and that his experiences made him feel youthful again. His experience in Asia transformed him. From his visit, Dewey acquired a critical distance from his own Western view of the world and an appreciation of Eastern thought.

In her book *John Dewey in China*, Jessica Ching-Sze Wang explained that, because he was a reflective thinker, Dewey soon realized that many of the political and economic concepts of the Western world did not apply to China. Dewey always preferred cultural, social, concrete, moral, and aesthetic notions of democratic community—that emphasized personal responsibility as much as personal rights—over political, abstract, formal, legalistic, and governmental structures.

She showed Dewey's appreciation for how the East internalized social control, in terms of personal responsibility in organic social relations, allowing one to actualize his or her unique potential through social interaction rather than the externalized mechanisms of formal jurisprudence that assumed the fiction of autonomous, atomistic individualism. Dewey appreciated that one could be profoundly ethical without belief in a supernatural deity. He also appreciated the way Eastern thought emphasized the artistic and aesthetic dimensions of culture and thought it could contribute to creative democracy.

Finally, his appreciation for the importance of a sense of closeness to nature in the East led him to an appreciation of Taoism and the Taoist notion of nondoing, which he considered a form of moral doing, conquering by yielding, and persisting "while nature has time to do her work." Dewey realized "active patience" is simply an especially thoughtful instance of pragmatic action. He thought that, given enough time, the "haughty and ambitious" often hang themselves in the "artificial entanglements they have themselves evolved."[2]

IKEDA: I was engaged in a dialogue with Professor Gu Mingyuan, president of the Chinese Society of Education, which was published as *Heiwa no kakehashi, ningen kyoiku o kataru* (Humanistic Education, a Bridge to Peace). In our discussions of Dewey's visit, he told me that the introduction of Dewey's philosophy and ideas on education into China, suffering under the oppression of feudalism and imperialism, inspired the drive for universal education for the Chinese people. Since the revolution, he added, there has been an evolving recognition of the value of Dewey's progressive educational thought, which promotes the autonomy of children in the educational process.

GARRISON: I am pleased to learn of a renaissance of Deweyan educational ideas in today's China after their suppression during the years of Mao Zedong's control.[3]

Unfortunately, it appears that during his visit, his Chinese hosts portrayed Buddhism as a passive, fatalistic religion seeking the extinction of desire, an otherworldly nirvana incompatible with his own active, world-transforming, ameliorative vision. It is productive to imagine what would have happened if the SGI had existed at the time, if Dewey could have had a creative dialogue with a version of Buddhism so agreeable to his own beliefs and values. In some ways, we three are having that dialogue now, decades later.

I believe Dewey's visit to the East started a value-creating conversation to which our dialogue today is a contribution. The surprising similarity between Dewey's philosophy and that of Nichiren and the Soka Gakkai suggests that, whatever may be the cultural limits of knowledge, wisdom is without borders. Although the task is never easy, if we search hard, we may find it arising in the East as well as the West or Middle East or anywhere else on earth.

IKEDA: The light of wisdom that illuminates truth knows no boundaries. It is the precious, universal spiritual heritage of humanity.

In all places, at all times, the ideas and philosophies that have served as the foundations for advanced cultures and civilizations have each, in their own ways, sharply observed reality and illuminated the boundless possibilities of human life. This is another respect in which Dewey's philosophy and that of Nichiren resonate deeply.

Professor Hickman, do you want to add anything on Dewey's visit to Japan and China?

HICKMAN: John and Alice loved to travel and had long wanted to visit Japan and China, so they planned a brief "working" vacation. Dewey was, of course, never strictly on vacation, since he was continually writing and lecturing.

In Japan, he lectured at Tokyo University, then known as Tokyo Imperial University. He and Alice had planned a brief trip to China following their visit to Japan, but while in Japan, he accepted an invitation from former students in China to spend a year lecturing at the National University and elsewhere in China. As it turned out, he and Alice indeed remained in China for two years, from 1919 to 1921.

It is not clear how much Dewey knew about Asian philosophy in advance of his trip. I was, however, able to locate a copy of a 1910 edition of the *Analects* of Confucius in his professional library, which is housed here at Southern Illinois University Carbondale. Although I have mentioned this before, it is worth repeating that Dewey was appalled by the militarism he encountered in Japan, and it is probably for that reason that he politely refused the emperor's offer of the Order of the Rising Sun.

IKEDA: Dewey had come to Asia for a vacation, but what he found were the live embers from which the fires of the next war would flare up. Back in the United States, from the end of 1921, he became involved in a movement to outlaw war.

The Soka Gakkai came into being in 1930, in the midst of the twenty years of crisis between the end of World War I and start of World War II, initiating its dialogue movement based on the Buddhist philosophy of the worth and dignity of life, with the aim of ensuring the happiness of children and all people. In 1943, Makiguchi and Toda were imprisoned by Japan's ruling militarist government.

Not long before, in the mid-1930s, the Nazi dictatorship emerged in Germany, which troubled Dewey deeply. But the Nazis were democratically elected under one of the world's most progressive democratic constitutions, that of the Weimar Republic. In his lecture "Creative Democracy—The Task Before Us," Dewey said:

> Put into effect it [democracy] signifies that powerful present enemies of democracy can be successfully met only by the creation of personal attitudes in individual human beings; that we must get over our tendency to think that its defense can be found in any external means whatever, whether military or civil, if they are separated from individual attitudes so deep-seated as to constitute personal character.[4]

Dewey emphasized the character, commitment, and moral sense of each individual as democracy's support.

A ceaseless spiritual struggle is necessary to enshrine the dignity and worth of the human being as the supreme value and enable each individual to realize the full potential of his or her creativity. This, Dewey firmly believed, is the only way to prevent democracy's corruption.

He also said: "Since it is one that can have no end till experience itself comes to an end, the task of democracy is forever that of creation of a freer and more humane experience in which all share and to which all contribute."[5] In other words, having neither an end nor any completion, democracy is an eternal process of advancement toward a better society. This is precisely why Dewey upheld democratic values and criticized the communism and fascism of the day. He was in turn criticized by misguided individuals, but his convictions remained unshaken.

HICKMAN: One of Dewey's most eloquent statements about democracy is in the address to which you refer, presented in 1939—a year during which fascism and Stalinism were on the march and a year that was not, therefore, friendly to democratic institutions. He characterized democracy as a way of life "controlled by a working faith in the possibilities of human nature." He added that this involved "faith in the potentialities of human nature as that nature is exhibited in every human being irrespective of race, color, sex, birth and family, of material or cultural wealth."

Democracy is thus much more than a matter of voting or legislation. It is a way of relating to our fellow human beings without interference by some authority alleged to exist outside of experience. In the same address, he characterized democracy as an evolving project that cannot be defined in terms of the life of one particular nation or culture, and he equated faith in democracy with faith in education.

Dewey and Whitman

IKEDA: Walt Whitman was one of those who influenced Dewey's philosophy of democracy. "Democracy is a name for a life of free and enriching communion," Dewey said. "It had its seer in Walt Whitman."[6] A poet of the people, Whitman loudly sang the praises of freedom and independence, a spirit that was vibrant in Dewey's character, too.

Whitman was one of my favorite poets in my youth. I remember reading *Leaves of Grass*, which I acquired after World War II, so often that I could recite it by heart. I often mention his poetry and way of life in speeches I make to students and young people. In front of the main auditorium at Soka University of Japan stands a bronze statue of Whitman.

GARRISON: I share your enthusiasm for the inspirational poetry of Walt Whitman. While visiting Soka University, I had my picture taken in front of that statue.

IKEDA: I am glad to have discovered another Whitman fan. Professor Garrison, you have already commented on the sympathy Dewey felt with Whitman.

"The genius of the United States," Whitman wrote in his preface to *Leaves of Grass*, "is not best or most in its executives or legislatures, nor even in its ambassadors or authors or colleges or churches or parlors, nor even in its newspapers or inventors . . . but always most in the common people."[7] The poet declares, in a hymn to a new age of democracy, that the people are the protagonists, the masters. Dewey and Whitman share many ideas in common. Did the two ever meet?

GARRISON: There is no evidence Dewey and Whitman ever met. I do know that in *Specimen Days* (which was in Dewey's library along with *Leaves of Grass*), Whitman mentions meeting William Torrey Harris, whom Dewey knew well.

Dewey has relatively little to say about Whitman in his published work. However, his calling Whitman the "seer," or prophet, of democracy says much about how highly Dewey thought of him. In Dewey's opinion, Whitman was one of the very few to realize that "democracy is neither a form of government nor a social expediency, but a metaphysic of the relation of man and his experience to nature."[8]

Dewey thought we lived in a diverse, pluralistic universe, wherein novel properties emerge with every unique interaction among its parts. Thus, Dewey's vision of democracy was part of his view of the very nature of existence.

He thought that when individual human beings or entire cultures interact, novel meanings and values will emerge. Hence, interactions based on good communication among individuals and nations will create novel meanings and values that contribute to sustaining human welfare and enhance our delight in being alive.

HICKMAN: One can only be continually impressed with the breadth of Whitman's democratic vision, which extends so much further than it does for most of us. He thinks in terms of the broader eye, the eye that comprises many people and many types of people. It's always a wonderful thing to read Whitman.

IKEDA: Whitman believed that "democracy too is law, and of the strictest, amplest kind" and that "law is the unshakable order of the universe forever."[9]

Some thirty years ago (in June 1981), I visited the house on Long Island where Whitman was born. Whitman's diary from the Civil War, copies of his manuscripts, and portraits and memorabilia were on display in the modest home. I said to the curator at the time that it seemed to me that Whitman's humble abode had much more of value to communicate to people than the towering skyscrapers of Manhattan.

The admirable spirit of that creative epoch continues to flow steadily as the undercurrent of American culture and society, inspiring people around the world.

In October 2010, friends from the SGI-USA met with representatives of the Walt Whitman Birthplace Association and engaged in a meaningful exchange.[10]

GARRISON: In a letter to his wife, dated April 16, 1887, Dewey wrote:

> I have been reading Walt Whitman more and find that he has a pretty definite philosophy. His philosophy of democracy and its relation to religion strikes me as about the thing. He is a good deal more of a thinker and less of an eccentric genius than I supposed before.[11]

Dewey recognized that poetry in its deepest sense unites with religion and democracy in the work of Walt Whitman. As Dewey said in *A Common Faith*, when poetry (in the sense of making, creating, or calling into existence) intervenes in affairs, it becomes religion.

Dewey must have admired Whitman's invention of what we now call *free verse*, with its unrhymed stanzas and lack of conventional meter. Like any good poet, Whitman used the usual poetical tropes (metaphor, metonymy, synecdoche, analogy, and such), but unlike other poets, the tropes were secondary to the intent. As he wrote, "All truths wait in all things." Whitman used tropes to show us something: "(I and mine do not convince by arguments, similes, rhymes, We convince by our presence.)" Tropes represent, mediate, and connect. Whitman said, "I send no agent or medium, offer no representatives of value, but offer the value itself."[12]

Whitman wished us to realize that everyday life itself is the greatest poem—and he wished individuals to realize this for themselves and then express it their own unique way.

Ikeda: When he wrote, "My heart is always with the people, in the thick of the struggle,"[13] Whitman was expressing his true emotions and convictions. The poet's boundless love for humanity and his pursuit of the answer to what makes a person great, a life meaningful, shine profoundly in his paean to the people.

Garrison: In "Creative Democracy," to which both of you have referred, Dewey repeatedly spoke of his "faith" in democracy as a guiding ideal. He shared this democratic faith in spiritual democracy with Walt Whitman.

It is a mistake to think we have secured democracy, when all we have secured are the conditions of its possibility. Democracy was an ideal for Whitman and Dewey that we should pursue in relentless good faith, grounded in the intelligent use of those relations that sustain our well-being. They both believed we live in a creative, pluralistic universe.

In *Democratic Vistas*, Whitman acknowledged that democracy first requires good constitutional government and, second, material prosperity. He thought that the United States had both of these from the beginning.

However, the true flower was "religious democracy," by which he meant intimate, caring (even loving) relations with the universe (especially other people) in which our creative (poetic) acts matter in the course of cosmic events. When Dewey commends Whitman's philosophy of democracy and its relation to religion, this is what he is endorsing.

Democracy and Religion

Ikeda: Whitman wrote, "For I say at the core of Democracy, finally, is the Religious element."[14] As Whitman said, democracy is founded on a humble respect for the worth and dignity of life, empathy for others' pain, and a spirit of self-transformation aiming for continual growth and self-perfection. Dewey's ideal of democracy, too, aims for a similar profound leap of the human spirit.

Garrison: I believe Whitman inspired Dewey's idea of creative democracy. Whitman mapped the proper relation between democracy and religion, where the creative powers of poetry become religion, when they creatively intervene in the world to ameliorate suffering and discord. Such poetry recognizes the possibilities of experienced situations and overcomes obstacles by creatively transforming them to realize our ethical ideals.

Dewey asserted, "Art is thus prefigured in the very processes of living."[15] Here, democracy and religion indeed become a "metaphysic of the relation of man and his experience to nature."[16] As Dewey said in "Creative Democracy—The Task Before Us," democracy is based on a working faith in the possibilities of human nature. Dewey shared this faith with Whitman. Like alleviating suffering, it is an ideal we must pursue endlessly and not a fixed and final destination.

IKEDA: What you say is important to any consideration of real democracy. Only through continuously striving for the individual's inner transformation and the building of a better society is true democracy attainable.

President Makiguchi was quick to recognize the potential of the United States as one of the world's great democracies. He saw the United States as promoting, from the individual to the international levels, the mutual interests of self and other as a builder of a new civilization of harmonious coexistence. He foresaw immense development for America, regarding it as a future meeting point of civilizations.

Praised by Whitman and idealized by Dewey, the image of the American as an animated, free, kindly, and industrious person with a sense of humor matches, I believe, the ideal image of the world citizen. It resonates deeply with the humanism for which we strive.

GARRISON: Earlier in our dialogue (see Conversation Eleven), we discussed the cultivation of global citizens. Your 1993 Harvard lecture asks the critical question: "Does religion make people stronger, or weaker?"[17] There, you map a "third path" suggested by the Nichiren perspective within the Mahayana tradition, which neither relies entirely on our own efforts (reason, egotistic self-confidence, etc.) or the power of others (tyrannical leaders, God, etc.).[18]

Here, you invoke Dewey as another who seeks to walk the humanistic Middle Way. That is true. Dewey thought we must each strive to recognize and actualize our inner potential. While perhaps not identical, this resembles Nichiren's notion that each of us has the Buddha nature whose beauty and wonder we express in our unique way.

We must have natural piety for the relations that sustain us, such as with nature, the family, democratic community, and humanity as a whole. We must diligently pursue individual human revolution while working with others to actualize creatively the ideal of overcoming suffering and securing peace wherever possible.

What Dewey calls "creative democracy" resembles the path of creative social amelioration that you, President Ikeda, call the "third path." Of course, there are many different ways to walk this path—we must sometimes create the path ourselves, and we often need help along the way from others different from ourselves, even when we would rather avoid them. Accepting this help is the wisdom of creative, pluralistic, democracy—and is the task before us.

It is also why creative dialogue is so immensely important. Reading this Harvard lecture greatly advanced my understanding of democratic humanism in our times.

CONVERSATION SIXTEEN

Many Kinds of Democracy

IKEDA: Educational exchanges transcend nations and epochs to broaden our connections. In Tokyo, in November 2010, I enjoyed an unforgettable meeting with Chancellor J. Keith Motley of the University of Massachusetts Boston and a group of his associates.

William Smith Clark of the Massachusetts Agricultural College, one of the original institutions of the University of Massachusetts, traveled to Japan, where he made an important contribution to the dawning stage of Japanese modernization. As the first vice principal of the Sapporo Agricultural College in Hokkaido, he built a brilliant educational tradition that produced many outstanding people, among them Inazo Nitobe, well known for his international activities. Nitobe also had a deep connection with Makiguchi.

Thus, from an early phase in our modernization, U.S. educators were sources of inspiration for Japanese society, introducing the wisdom and free spirit of democracy—a role they played in many parts of the world.

What do you, Professor Hickman and Professor Garrison, regard as the fundamental strength and appeal of American democracy?

HICKMAN: I would say that one of the most important components of American democracy is the concept of a second chance. It is said that when a traveler arrived in a town in the American frontier, the first question put to him would be not "Where are you coming from?" but "Where are you headed? What are your plans?" A large part of the very idea of the frontier was a chance to start over, to redeem past mistakes.

Americans seem to have a strong sense of looking to the future for new opportunities. That idea introduces a measure of flexibility into American social and political life.

IKEDA: This is one of the great appeals of America, a spirit still alive in American society today. Moreover, the United States is a conglomeration of many diverse ethnic, linguistic, cultural, and religious groups. The dynamism and innovation engendered by the democratic spirit of freedom and diversity are sources of tremendous energy for growth and vitality.

HICKMAN: As you suggest, another important component is the ability of most Americans to welcome peoples from many nations and cultures to the quest for democracy. Of course, there are inevitable cultural clashes when new immigrants arrive. But I think there is a deep understanding among the American people that our democracy will be refreshed and nourished by the ideas and practices of our immigrants.

Dewey rejected the idea of America as a melting pot. He preferred the metaphor of the symphony orchestra, in which each person contributes something of value to the whole enterprise. You get both of these ideas in his concept of democracy, and you also get both ideas in the work of Walt Whitman, whom we discussed before (see Conversation Fifteen).

Democracy and the Arts

Ikeda: The world-renowned violinist Yehudi Menuhin shared with me his evaluation of American dynamism from a musical standpoint:

> Many of the immigrants brought with them little more than their memories and the clothes they could carry, but they could all bring their music, a possession of the heart and mind. It took root in a new and distinctive way, flowering in music of extraordinary diversity and color, from which were to spring ragtime and jazz.[1]

As Dewey pointed out, the American people's diversity contributed greatly to the creation of new music and art, and was the source of American cultural dynamism. Something similar can be said about American democracy.

Garrison: Democracy is an organic, living, evolving thing. As is true in all living organisms, every function, like every individual, that sustains life, no matter how humble, is necessary and important. Dialogue, however, is like the lifeblood of American democracy or any other democracy.

At the same time, education and democracy have an intimate connection. The arts and literature are not luxuries in a democracy. Dewey says art is the best form of criticism because it "fixes those standards of enjoyment and appreciation with which other things are compared; it selects the objects of future desires; it stimulates effort."[2]

The arts release the possibilities hidden within the actual and provide visions of ideal, moral values never before seen or heard. Such ideals may take control of our desires. Today, many peoples' imaginations remain captured by ideals of political, military, and economic competition. It is here that art may not only provide the best tools for social criticism but also create ideals that we may pursue through humanistic competition.

IKEDA: In his celebrated *The Lonely Crowd*, the American sociologist David Riesman described true education as training people to feel the poetry in science and the beauty and elegance in mathematics. A society that doesn't prize poetry or art would be an arid, desolate world. It would be a society characterized by low regard for life and nature, dominated by egoism, and incapable of presenting anything but the most feeble resistance to evil. In this sense, we must reexamine and rediscover in education, too, the value and meaning of art in elevating human life.

Value-creating education supports democracy and helps reinforce its foundation. At the same time, development of a wholesome democracy based on open dialogue and free communication steadily fosters a social and educational environment that makes true education possible.

New Democracies

GARRISON: But I fear that the modern dialogue is being confused by mass media owned and operated by the rich and powerful, who are more intent on marketing material goods and defending their elite status than on informing public discourse. Today, commercial advertising and mass media are the arts that control our desires and tell us what we want. They sell us our politicians and wars, while they sell us our soap and automobiles.

So, perhaps, the most important form of reflective, critical, and creative education must emphasize media literacy. We need the kind of education that allows us to distinguish between what we impulsively value and the truly valuable, between objects of immediate desire and the truly desirable.

IKEDA: In a Japan awash in information, it is important to acquire the ability to tell truth from falsehood and to grasp the reality beneath the torrent of data presented to us. Each individual citizen needs to become wiser and stronger.

More than twenty years ago (in 1989), at the conclusion of the Cold War, when one communist state after another adopted democracy, many people said that history had reached its culmination with the triumph of liberal democracy. It was frequently claimed that American and Western democracy were the ultimate ideal among all the political systems humanity had experienced, and that we were drawing close to a general realization of this ideal.

But this version of democracy was by no means perfect, nor could it be said to be the sole, ideal form of human government. Ultimately, we human beings are responsible for the true worth of any system we create.

GARRISON: Dewey begins the last paragraph of "From Absolutism to Experimentalism" by stating:

> I think it shows a deplorable deadness of imagination to suppose that philosophy will indefinitely revolve within the scope of the problems and systems that two thousand years of European history have bequeathed to us. Seen in the long perspective of the future, the whole of western European history is a provincial episode.[3]

If the aim of education for Dewey is growth, the meaning of life for Dewey is to continue to make more meaning. Different cultures are bound to have different ideals of what democracy means. We need them all.

Dewey thought individuals only have potentiality insofar as there are other individuals with whom we are yet to interact. He points out that we should encourage the expression of difference not only as a right of other people but also as a way of enriching the democratic experience.[4]

The interaction among different cultures will likewise allow each to actualize its potential in unique ways that are bound to alter the meaning of democracy. However, to achieve this growth, we must first have greater tolerance and the extension of human rights.

IKEDA: Arnold Toynbee expressed to me his own moderate evaluation of democracy as the "least bad of the political systems that man has yet hit upon."[5] To cultivate and perfect democracy, we need to have a thorough understanding of what it is and, based on that, persevere in enhancing its good points and compensating for its shortcomings.

GARRISON: In truth, we have only secured the conditions of democracy, which we are in the process of achieving. True democracy is an ever-evolving ideal that should guide our social-political actions.

Democracy cannot mean the same thing for different people with different cultural traditions and customs. What Dewey said about women in his essay "Philosophy and Democracy" could also be applied to different cultures and democracy:

> When women who are not mere students of other persons' philosophy set out to write it, we cannot conceive that it will be the same in viewpoint or tenor as that composed from the standpoint of the different masculine experience

> of things. Institutions, customs of life, breed certain systematized predilections and aversions.[6]

When other cultures cease being mere students of Western democracy and come to write their own constitutions, we cannot conceive it will be from the same viewpoint or tenor of Western experience. These cultures have different institutions and social customs that result in different predilections and aversions.

While a Westerner might be unable to imagine such novel democracies, those such as yourself surely can. Indeed, because you have perhaps participated in more dialogues across differences than anyone else in the world, you might be able to imagine different democracies in India, the Middle East, South America, Africa, and elsewhere.

The Buddhist precept of "adapting to local customs"[7] allows the Soka Gakkai to propagate around the world. I wish the United States would apply a similar principle to the propagation of democracy.

IKEDA: I appreciate your understanding of our work and agree that there are as many kinds of democracy as there are cultures. Indeed, such diversity is the spiritual mainstay and the foundation of democracy. One of the sources of democracy's dynamism is its emphasis on learning from and incorporating the best from others as fuel for further growth and development.

The Soka Gakkai is in communication with the Nobel laureate in economics Amartya Sen, who has lectured at the Ikeda Center for Peace, Learning, and Dialogue in Boston. He has written that India today is a democratic state as the result not of the influence of British colonialism but of a longstanding indigenous democratic tradition. His assertion made a great impression on me. Many other Asian nations also have developed their own form of democracy in keeping with their rich spiritual and cultural traditions.

HICKMAN: This is a very interesting and important subject, especially given attempts by the administration of President George W. Bush to export American-style democracy. Dewey did not think that American democracy could be exported, nor did he think that American democracy was the ultimate ideal among the political systems of humanity.

Jessica Ching-Sze Wang underscores that point. She argues that, "Dewey hoped that China would not imitate the West blindly, but would rely on its own cultural strengths to transform itself from within."[8]

In that vein, Daniel A. Bell, in his 2006 book *Beyond Liberal Democracy: Political Thinking for an East Asian Context*, argued that the Confucian tradition of China will produce forms of democracy that are quite unlike Western forms of liberal democracy but that he nevertheless regards both as legitimate and appropriate for their context. He views China at this moment in its history as a laboratory, where some of the most interesting experiments in democracy in the entire world are being conducted. It will be interesting to see whether his assessment of the situation in China holds true.

Dewey thought that democracy is a process that grows from the bottom up rather than one imposed from the top down. He thought that, as long as there is change and novelty in the world, democracy will never have a fixed and finished form.

POPULAR SOLIDARITY

IKEDA: The idea of a process that grows from the bottom up is so important in considering democracy's foundations. As you have both pointed out, when Dewey visited Japan in 1919, he was disturbed by the lack of any mediating systems or institutions standing between the family and the militarist state authority, which he recognized as a sign of the society's weakness. He saw a society generally devoid of what we would today call NPOs (nonprofit organizations) and ideologically free and open, diverse local communities; even though they might have existed in some form, all policies and organizations served the totalitarian state. Later history substantiated Dewey's concern as state militarism ran out of control and led Japan down a path of complete self-destruction.

I discussed this in a speech some years ago at the University of East Asia in Macau. I pointed out lessons to be learned from the twentieth century, engulfed in runaway nationalism and totalitarianism, and the necessity of creating a network of human beings built from the bonds of a new awareness of our shared humanity.[9]

As President Makiguchi wrote in *The System of Value-Creating Pedagogy*:

> Driven by their instinct for self-preservation, evil-minded people band together, increasing the force with which they persecute the good. In contrast, people of goodwill always seem to be isolated and weak. When the former expands, the latter will shrink, inevitably resulting in an extremely evil society.[10]

The people must be wise and strong enough to build a network of awakened, concerned individuals to prevent abuses of power and build a society in which democracy is vigorous. What do you consider necessary to build such a network?

HICKMAN: You have once again raised a difficult issue. One of the important lessons to be learned from efforts by the Obama administration to reform health care in the United States is that solidarity can cut a number of ways. There is the solidarity of the sympathetic and informed, but there is also the solidarity of the self-centered, uninformed, and highly vocal—the solidarity of those who act, vote, and sometimes even commit violence against their own interests and those of their neighbors because of their adherence to authoritarian ideas and movements.

As an educator, I think the solution to this problem begins in kindergarten, or even earlier, where the basics of dialogue and civility can be taught and nurtured. Even though it might not be the case that to know good is to do good, as Socrates suggested, it does seem clear that it is difficult to do what is good without knowing what is good. One of the ways we come to know about the good is learning to listen to others and educating ourselves about issues of common interest.

IKEDA: You raise an essential educational issue. Individualism has the negative aspect of overstressing individual rights to the point of weakening communal bodies, in which people should cooperate and collaborate. This tendency is becoming increasingly conspicuous in society today. And this is what makes education so important—when it fosters an open mind and thus enables us to humbly learn from one another's differences and create new value.

HICKMAN: In my keynote address to the 2008 meeting of the International Network of Philosophers of Education, held in Kyoto, I argued that it is possible to evaluate the claims of institutions of all sorts—political, religious, commercial—in evolutionary terms.[11] The fact is that we are moving toward a world—if we are not indeed already there—in which cooperation and understanding must replace violence and distrust if we are to survive as a human race. I suggested that the test of a religious institution, for example, is the contribution it makes to a common faith, a faith that unites rather than divides, a faith that is flexible in the face of changing circumstances.

After more than a decade of research into the ideals and activities of the Soka Gakkai, I have found just that sort of faith at work in your life and commitments, and the lives and commitments of the two presidents, Makiguchi and Toda, who preceded you. I have found outlooks, proposals, and programs that I am convinced are much more evolved than most of their alternatives, if we understand the term *evolved* as I just characterized it.

GARRISON: We must *create* popular solidarity of the good for the sake of social reform. I am thinking about neither government nor social expediency but about a metaphysic of the relation of human experience to nature. This is a strong expression of religious humanism.

Instead of mis-education of the people, it is imperative that the mass media—radio and newspapers in Dewey's time, the Internet, cell phones, and so on in ours—help educate the people, so that they can identify their true interests and form publics of shared concern, interests that effectively petition and transform government.

Soka Gakkai discussion meetings, which we have already mentioned (see Conversation Twelve), are a wonderful example of such grass-roots democracy that can bypass manipulation by the mass media controlled by capitalists and the politicians who do their work. They justify Dewey's belief.

IKEDA: Thank you for the depth of your understanding. As you say, only dialogue among equals allows us to speak the truth and engage in real communication. SGI members in 192 countries and territories are leading lives as good citizens in their local communities, making positive contributions to society. Discussion meetings give them opportunities to encourage one another, share their joy in this Buddhist faith and practice, and study and grow together. Naturally, of course, non-members from the community are also welcome to participate.

Discussion meetings are held on a monthly basis around the world, as occasions where joyous dialogue flourishes. From Iceland to the southernmost city on the tip of Argentina to the islands of the Pacific and Atlantic, members enjoy lively exchange and interaction and expand a spiritual oasis for the people.

As I have said before (see Conversation Four), from the early days of our movement, President Makiguchi and President Toda focused on and stressed discussion meetings, which are the starting point of our people's movement. This remains unchanged today.

GARRISON: Whitman, Makiguchi, and Toda provide profound examples of how poetry—what the ancient Greeks called *poiesis*, or making, creating, calling into existence—becomes religion by courageously intervening in the world to prevail over injustice. Such involvement requires participating in the messiness of everyday power politics in which honest, as well as dishonest, mistakes do occur.

I staunchly defend the separation of church and state as systems, by which I mean that no particular religious dogma should control government. However, to engage in politics in defense of the weak and in pursuit of peace, freedom, and equality constitutes an appropriate expression of religiosity in Dewey's sense of natural piety and faith in ideals.

To overcome suffering and discord is a political act, which the Soka Gakkai has practiced for its entire history. The ideas and actions of President Makiguchi, President Toda, and yourself, like those of Nichiren, are necessarily and appropriately political, which is not to say you may not make mistakes. To remain aloof from the active pursuit of peace just because one does not wish to become sullied by the material world means one is really only selfishly concerned with one's own salvation and self-righteousness rather than with the amelioration of suffering. Nichiren Buddhism and the Soka Gakkai do not seem to be like that to me.

For Dewey, moral conviction meant being conquered by our

highest ideals and acknowledging that they have a rightful claim over our desires and purposes. In *A Common Faith,* he asserted that "any activity pursued in behalf of an ideal end against obstacles and in spite of threats of personal loss because of conviction of its general and enduring value is religious in quality."[12]

Tsunesaburo Makiguchi and Josei Toda showed the greatest courage and conviction in pursuit of peace while sustaining great personal loss—even death in Makiguchi's case—in overcoming the obstacle of militarism. They deserve mention among the greatest heroes for peace, freedom, and social justice in the twentieth century, including Mohandas Gandhi and Martin Luther King Jr.

CONVERSATION SEVENTEEN

Science and Technology

IKEDA: I want to discuss education and scientific progress. In 1855, in the preface to *Leaves of Grass*, Walt Whitman wrote, "Exact science and its practical movements are no checks on the greatest poet but always his encouragement and support."[1] Affirming the benefits bestowed on humankind by a society built on science and technology, he also said, "In the beauty of poems are the tuft and final applause of science."[2]

At the beginning of the twentieth century, as we can see in the journalism of those days, many people believed that progress in scientific technology promised a rosy future. But in 1930, more than seventy-five years after Whitman wrote that preface, Dewey wrote in his *Individualism, Old and New*: "They [science and technology] are not controlled now in any fundamental sense. Rather do they control us."[3] "We are not even approaching a climax of control; we are hardly at its feeble beginnings. . . . We hardly have commenced to dream of managing."[4]

GARRISON: In *Individualism, Old and New,* Dewey stated, "Quantification, mechanization and standardization: these are then the marks of the Americanization that is conquering the world."[5] Written in 1929, this statement is even truer today, when Americanization is the idea steering the global economy, although it has little to do with nationality. What I mean is that the American worship of quantification, mechanization, and standardization has become integrated into the global economy.

IKEDA: Dewey, as if anticipating the problems that society would run up against, warned that human beings might be reduced from the masters of scientific technology to the tools of it. The tendencies toward quantification and mechanization that he warned against led to a society in which people were forced into a standardized mold and treated as a uniform "product"—one of our world's great problems today.

The establishment of a sound ethical system is an urgent issue in today's science-based society.

In our dialogue, Arnold J. Toynbee vigorously insisted that the "disparity between our technology and our ethics is greater today than it has ever been,"[6] and he lamented that

> human technology, misused to serve the diabolic purposes of human egoism and wickedness, is a more deadly danger than earthquakes, volcanic eruptions, storms, floods, droughts, viruses, microbes, sharks, and sabre-toothed tigers.[7]

I believe this point is important to university education as well.

GARRISON: At the Virginia Polytechnic Institute and State University, my appointments are in the School of Education, Department of Philosophy, and Science and Technology Studies. I primarily teach courses in education for teachers from all disciplines, and I have noticed a disturbing pattern. Students with degrees in science or engineering are confident in the powers of these disciplines but rarely have exposure to courses in the philosophy or ethics of science. Meanwhile, those without a background in the techno-sciences are much more likely to distrust science and technology and may even see it as a definite evil.

Many of the nonscientists among my students often participate in the contemporary rage against reason. What they are rightly rebelling against is scientism: the narrow, dogmatic use of scientific results rather than the tentative methods of hypothesis, testing, and revision that are never absolutely certain. Dewey, too, rejected "The Quest for Certainty," which is the title of his most extensive work on the theory of knowledge (epistemology).

Generally, few students, regardless of background, have been exposed to ethics or philosophy of any kind. There are now more offerings in the curriculum at Virginia Tech, and I am starting to see positive results in my classes.

IKEDA: Professor Hickman, what is the situation at Southern Illinois University Carbondale? Students of science and technology at Soka University are strongly aware of ethics and philosophy in relation to science. What advice can you give in connection with cultivating humane scientists?

HICKMAN: In 1959, British physicist and novelist C. P. Snow published a very important book titled *The Two Cultures*. In it he lamented the split, or one might almost say the gulf, between the culture of science and the culture of the humanities. Our situation today has not significantly improved.

I once taught at a very large technical university, where engineering students were allowed only one free elective course during their four-year program. On the other hand, liberal-arts students are often quite ignorant of the history of the natural sciences and current work in those fields.

IKEDA: You have been striving to improve the situation?

HICKMAN: Yes, as a part of my effort to bridge the gap between the two cultures, I have for many years taught courses with titles such as "Technology and Human Values" and "Science and Technology in Western Society." My courses have been attended by students in the humanities, education, the natural sciences, and engineering.

Southern Illinois University Carbondale has a well-designed and continually updated program of so-called core courses that seek to educate science and engineering students in the humanities and to inform humanities students about the sciences and engineering. I advise students of science and engineering to study the histories of their own disciplines and acquaint themselves with the work being done by philosophers that addresses the ethical dimensions of scientific and technical change. Their professional lives will be greatly enriched, I advise them, by the study of philosophy, and courses in the humanities will prepare them for the ethical decisions their professions will demand.

Of course, there is also much we could discuss about the relation between the sciences and the arts and between the arts and the humanities. Dewey thought that philosophy at its best is a kind of liaison officer helping the various disciplines to communicate with one another.

THE LOTUS FLOWER

IKEDA: Dewey insisted that development of a wholesome society must rest on the formation of a new individualism:

> It is through employing them [science and technology] with understanding of their possible import that a new individualism, constant with the realities of the present age, may be brought into operative being.[8]

He also wrote, "The greatest obstacle to that vision is, I repeat, the perpetuation of the older individualism now reduced, as I have said, to the utilization of science and technology for ends of private pecuniary gain."[9]

Dewey warned here that the old individualism played "into the hands of those who would keep it alive in order to serve their own ends."[10] In contrast, in the new individualism that he sought, one is constantly aware of the existence of others, faces the challenge of social reform, and strives to create oneself anew.

GARRISON: Wisdom demands we be constantly disposed to helping and caring for others. It involves moral perception of the unique, one-time-only character of individuals, so that we may respond appropriately to their needs, desires, and abilities. It also acquires moral imagination to see beyond the actual to grasp the best possibility of every individual in any given situation.

Dewey insisted on the essential unity of the individual self and its acts. In expressing the present self, we form the future self. From Francis Bacon, Auguste Comte, and others, Dewey took the notion that the sciences can allow humankind to take control of its destiny intelligently by engineering a better future, but only if we are caring, careful, and fully reflective.

Dewey wrote that for him humanism means an "expansion, not a contraction of human life, an expansion in which nature and the science of nature are made the willing servants of human good."[11] The problem, which, unfortunately, can actually be traced to Bacon, is that thus far the science of nature in the hands of global capital has tended to make nature the unwilling servant. Worse still, it has turned science on human nature and made human individuals themselves unwilling servants of techno-science.

Dewey often made the classical Greek observation that anyone who takes the purposes of his conduct from another is a slave. Thus far, the power of science has been used by the rich and powerful to enslave the minds of the masses.

IKEDA: How to open enslaved minds to the possibilities of freedom, independence, and humanity—this is the challenge of humanistic education. In light of Dewey's ideas on this, Professor Garrison, how do you think modern education should be reformed?

GARRISON: Following Emerson, Dewey believed we must accept the place in history into which we are born and then strive to transform its muddy waters into beautiful blossoms. So, we must accept the capitalist economy along with the techno-sciences we have inherited. However, if we can realize the promise of pluralistic democracy, we can put science and capitalism to new purposes for the good of the people.

Instead of education as molding human resources into interchangeable parts for the global production function, we must reaffirm moral equality and educate every individual to actualize his or her unique potential to make unique contributions to the democratic community. This is largely the difference between Soka education and most state-run educational institutions.

IKEDA: Working with the faculty and students, I am resolved to expend every effort to see that our schools live up to the high expectations you have for them.

You have explained Dewey's view of education with a wonderful metaphor. As you know, the Lotus Sutra, the quintessence of Mahayana Buddhism, also employs the simile of the lotus flower blooming out of muddy waters. It rises above them and blooms immaculately, unstained by their impurities.

The Lotus Sutra teaches a way of life in which, though we exist within the difficult reality of our world, as it swirls with greed and hatred, we can shine radiantly with the noblest humanity and contribute to society—just as the lotus rises to flower in purity from the muddy waters.

Courageously striving to create value based on a sound ethical and moral foundation—in this society enriched by scientific and technological developments and awash in material goods—is how we can embody the Lotus Sutra in the present.

Starting Where We Are

Hickman: Dewey was born the year that Americans drilled their first oil well. He died the year that the hydrogen bomb was tested, and that laboratory tests proved the success of the birth-control pill. He took it as a part of his challenge as a philosopher to understand the human impact of the many scientific and technical changes that occurred during his lifetime.

It is important to remember that he understood the sciences from the inside, as it were. During his years at the University of Chicago, for example, he and his colleagues conducted experiments on the psychology of perception. Late in his life, he collaborated with medical researcher Myrtle McGraw, whose research involved the physiological development of twins. His daughter Jane was a pioneer in physics, who worked in the laboratory of Niels Bohr and later for universities and the U.S. government.

The quotation that you, President Ikeda, referenced from *Individualism, Old and New* is a wonderful example of Dewey's idea that we must start where we are, in a world that is messy and uncertain, and build up value from there in piecemeal fashion, always striving to do and be our very best. I think he would have loved the metaphor of the lotus, rising from muddy waters to produce a pure bloom, since it was so close to his own ideas about taking things as we find them and reconstructing them so as to create value.

Ikeda: The key is to become strong, wise, and good, and make what life presents to us into opportunities for creating value. The Greek word *techne,* from which *technique* and *technology* derive, means the method or means for creating something, not necessarily the use of objects such as tools or machines. As in the case of a furniture maker creating a table or chair from wood, *techne* suggests bringing forth something hidden and making it a reality—creating something new through the use of the human mind.

Professor Garrison, you have elsewhere said that the word *techne* means to create an object or to create meaning. You pointed out its similarity to the Greek *poiesis,* from which *poetry* derives, which means to make something manifest as reality or, in other words, create value. Dewey, you said, saw this as pragmatism—real action for the sake of changing the world.

Regarding technology today, short-term profit is the driving force, and there is fierce competition to make new discoveries and findings without sufficient examination of their effects on either human beings or the natural world. As a result, technological and scientific advancement is destroying the natural world, the very foundation of human life, and threatening our ecosystem.

To confront and resolve this danger, we must heed Dewey's words:

> There is of course an extrinsic limit of science. But that limitation lies in the ineptitude of those who put it to use; its removal lies in rectification of its use, not in abuse of the thing used.[12]

This reminds me of something President Toda said:

> One cause of people's misfortune today is that they confuse knowledge and wisdom. . . . Knowledge may serve as a door that opens the way to wisdom, but knowledge itself is definitely not wisdom.[13]

In the modern age, we have learned the hard way that scientific knowledge, which can be used for good or bad, is indeed a double-edged sword. Humanistic wisdom dictates that knowledge be put to use for true progress and happiness.

GARRISON: The disaster of techno-science in the contemporary social context of global capitalism is that we apply knowledge without wisdom. The old individualism places knowledge before wisdom, because it wishes to use knowledge to exploit nature and other human beings. The new individualism seeks to use knowledge wisely to alleviate suffering and liberate human creativity and self-expression.

The problem is not the techno-sciences but the purposes to which they are put. First, I believe that we must avoid the excesses of scientism, so that we can properly understand the power of science as a cultural phenomenon. We must avoid harnessing the power of science to traditional purposes, which often tend to oppress individuals and groups.

We must release critical, creative intelligence, as refined by modern science into all cultural domains, including religion, the economy, philosophy, the family, and individual life. Humanistic education emphasizing cultural criticism, creative imagination, and social responsibility cultivates such new individualism, which resembles what you, President Ikeda, call the human revolution in a single life.

Rotblat and Pauling

HICKMAN: A split between *poiesis* and *techne*, observable as early as Plato and Aristotle, was exacerbated at about the time of the Industrial Revolution. Dewey tried to heal it by building the ethical and the human back into the notion of technology. He tried to point out that in technology, there is an intelligence that is humanistic in its outlook.

When there are deviations in this intelligence, it is due not to technology but to self-centeredness, greed, laziness, clannishness, or any number of other factors. It is not the fault of technology, which is basically a humanistic enterprise.

IKEDA: Joseph Rotblat, whom I mentioned earlier (see Conversation Ten), was a man of the highest moral conscience striving to introduce humanism into science. As a nuclear physicist, he participated in the Manhattan Project during World War II, helping to develop atomic weapons, but when he learned that the Nazis were unable to produce nuclear weapons, he quit the project—the only scientist to do so—and returned to his home in England. Later, he was horrified to learn of the bombings of Hiroshima and Nagasaki.

It was then Dr. Rotblat resolved to strive for the elimination of nuclear weapons, leading to his long-term efforts for peace through the Pugwash Conferences. He refocused his research on radiology, making his results available to medical science. The radioactive element cobalt 60, which he developed, is still used to treat malignant tumors.

He has described his decision to make this change:

> I consider myself a scientist who strives for the benefit of humankind, not for its destruction. . . . I felt that if my scientific research was going to be used, I would want to decide how it could be used and to see with my own eyes it being used in beneficial ways. One way that I thought that this could happen was in the field of medicine . . . so I decided to abandon my ambitions in the field of nuclear physics and specialize in the medical application of physics.[14]

Many scientists are so focused on the products of scientific technology that they fail to pay attention to the ways new technologies are used.

I can't help but think that Rotblat's career, based on sound, moral convictions, stands as a model for all scientists.

Linus Pauling was another scientist who gave the most serious consideration to the path science ought to pursue. In the preface of *General Chemistry*, a college text he wrote in 1947, he stressed the importance of morality in science. Reflecting on his decision to do so, he recalled: "I formulated a scientific derivation of the basic moral principle of human behavior and considered it a good thing to mention it in my book on chemistry."[15]

Dr. Pauling expressed his interest in cooperating with our SGI peace movement in any way he could. When I last met him—he was ninety-two at the time—he told me that he had just come back from encouraging three sick people. He was a person of great character.

In considering the nature and future of scientific technology, and to avoid lapsing into mere abstraction and theoretical musings, I believe we must base our discussions on the beliefs and lives of scientists like Rotblat and Pauling, individuals of sound, moral character. I engaged in dialogues with them to share the wisdom and lessons of their lives with the young people who will shoulder the future.

HICKMAN: Your account of the work of Drs. Rotblat and Pauling provides a wonderful example of how it is possible to begin to heal the split between the "two cultures" that C. P. Snow deplored.

Like Rotblat and Pauling, Dewey was greatly concerned with the moral consequences of decisions made in the techno-scientific sphere. Unlike most of the European philosophers who were his contemporaries, however, including Martin Heidegger, Max Horkheimer, and Karl Jaspers, he never regarded technology as the "problem."

In 1929, in a remarkable statement, he wrote:

> Technology signifies all the intelligent techniques by which the energies of nature and man are directed and used in satisfaction of human needs; it cannot be limited to a few outer and comparatively mechanical forms. In the face of its possibilities, the traditional conception of experience is obsolete.[16]

After the humanitarian disasters of World Wars I and II, Hiroshima and Nagasaki, Bhopal, and Chernobyl, is it still possible to accept Dewey's identification of technology with intelligent techniques? I believe it is.

I would add that even though the way we humans have used our tools and techniques has sometimes led to disasters, it has also led to great good. Who could have imagined in 1939, for example, that the age-old enemies Germany and France could become partners in forming a community of European nations? And who, during the Cold War era, could have imagined the degree of cooperation that now exists between China and the United States? I believe that much of the basis for these successes involves technology—the intelligent use of tools and techniques. Dewey recognized that the problems we face are not due to technology but to overemphasis on private interest, ignorance, or the lack of what Jane Addams termed *sympathetic knowledge*.

GARRISON: After witnessing the horrors of World War I, Dewey made a deep commitment to peace and used his status as a world-renowned philosopher to advocate for it at home and abroad. Whether famous or not, all of us should strive to live such a life. Within the larger wheel of fortune, no one can say whose acts will matter most across generations. Many of the best, most socially meaningful lives go unheralded.

Museums and exhibitions are powerful means for educating the public about the authentic nature of science and its socially responsible use. Often employing the same technologies, such modes of education can counter the mis-education broadcast by state- and business-controlled media.

I am aware that the Soka Gakkai International engages in many such activities, including exchanges in the arts and sciences. These are powerful forms of political action, since they inform the public dialogue on international peace and cooperation.

CONVERSATION EIGHTEEN

A Responsive Philosophy

IKEDA: Dewey was pleasantly surprised by the eagerness of his audiences in Japan. In March 1919, he wrote from Japan to his children in the United States describing the lectures he was delivering at Tokyo Imperial University with his typical self-deprecating humor and wit:

> I have now given three lectures. They are a patient race; there is still a good-sized audience, probably five hundred. We are gradually getting a superficial acquaintance with a good many people.[1]

Consisting of eight talks, the series was published in 1920 under the title *Reconstruction in Philosophy*. As the preface reveals, his lectures aimed to "exhibit the general contrasts between older and newer types of philosophic problems,"[2] casting traditional philosophy in a new light and attempting to reconstruct it.

HICKMAN: In *Reconstruction in Philosophy*, the famously mild-mannered Dewey vigorously criticized the long tradition of

Western philosophy for its failure to address real human problems. He and his colleagues William James and F. C. S. Schiller were attempting a revolution in philosophy, and their efforts were being met with stubborn opposition by philosophers who wanted their discipline to remain in an ivory tower.

IKEDA: He was trying to revive the wisdom of an insular world and make it widely available. In *Reconstruction in Philosophy,* he rebuked the long-held misperception that intelligence has a static nature:

> Intelligence is not something possessed once for all. It is in constant process of forming, and its retention requires constant alertness in observing consequences, an open-minded will to learn and courage in re-adjustment. In contrast with this experimental and re-adjusting intelligence, it must be said that Reason as employed by historic rationalism has tended to carelessness, conceit, irresponsibility, and rigidity—in short absolutism.[3]

This is a splendid insight into the essence of the learning process. To me, it is a starting point to which all engaged in intellectual pursuits should return.

He went on to say, "The modern world has suffered because in so many matters philosophy has offered it only an arbitrary choice between hard and fast opposites: Disintegrating analysis *or* rigid synthesis."[4]

Dewey considered freeing philosophy from this dualistic reasoning extremely important to a philosophical reconstruction.

GARRISON: Dewey much preferred the word *intelligence* to *rationality* precisely because it expressed the creative character of the human mind that has to carry out constant reconstruction to adapt to an ever-changing world. Unlike the static concept of rationality with its fixed concepts and categories, individual and collective intelligence itself also undergoes continuous reconstruction within the world it strives to shape.

The Latin word *intellectus*, from which we derive words like *intellect* and *intelligent*, translates as "chosen among" or "understood." It derives from the compound *inter* (among) and *legere* (to choose). Intelligence involves many things rationality not only ignores but also denigrates. For Dewey, all inquiry begins with the intuition of a qualitative situation that presents an obstacle to proper functioning.

In his essay "Qualitative Thought," he shared Henri Bergson's view that "intuition precedes conception and goes deeper."[5] Further, we must intelligently choose from among the many different things present in any given situation if we are to determine the correct data for eventually defining a situation as a cognitive problem.

When we attend to a situation, we always rely on selective attention driven by our needs, interests, desires, concepts, and values. If we are a corrupt person, we will almost never intuit the situation properly or make the correct selections, so we will almost never be able to overcome the situation properly, however correct our thought.

IKEDA: Though we speak of intelligence, it is essential to cultivate the qualities that form our foundation as human beings—our system of values and ethics, and our creativity and sensibility.

GARRISON: For Dewey, imagination and emotions are also important parts of intelligence. In *Art as Experience*, he wrote:

> No "reasoning" as reasoning, that is, as excluding imagination . . . can reach truth. . . . He [the inquirer] selects and puts aside as his imaginative sentiments move. "Reason" at

> its height cannot attain complete grasp and a self-contained assurance. It must fall back upon imagination—upon the embodiment of ideas in emotionally charged sense.[6]

Elsewhere, he goes so far as to insist that rationality is a "working harmony among diverse desires."[7] Hence, rationality, or rather intelligence, is never a fixed thing; it is an evolving life function.

THE POISONED ARROW

IKEDA: Dewey issued a stern warning against the folly of being led astray by abstract concepts and ideologies, and losing sight of the realities of life and society.

His cautionary attitude calls to mind the Buddhist parable of the poisoned arrow:

> One of Shakyamuni's disciples had a penchant for posing abstract philosophical questions, such as "Is the world infinite or finite?" or "Are the spirit and the physical body one or separate?"
>
> Shakyamuni would not heed such questions, knowing only too well that life's problems could not be solved by abstract philosophical speculation divorced from the realities of living. This attitude irritated the disciple, who was fond of such intellectual discussion. One day, he rose and voiced his dissatisfaction, saying, "World Honored One, if you persist in refusing to answer my questions, I shall leave the order."
>
> At this, Shakyamuni said reprovingly: "There once was a man who was hit by a poisoned arrow and lay writhing in agony. His friends and loved ones rushed to his side and tried to remove the arrow and treat his wound. But the man wouldn't let them. Who was it that had fired the arrow? What was his name and what did he look like, he

> wanted to know. He insisted that no one remove the arrow and administer medicine until these questions had been answered. He then proceeded to ask what kind of arrow it was, what it was made of and so on, until finally, he died.
>
> "You, too, will no doubt die without attaining anything, still exclaiming until your last breath that you will not persevere in your practice unless you know whether the world is infinite or finite."[8]

With this parable, Shakyamuni teaches that absorption in empty speculation solves none of the problems encountered in life. What matters is tapping the wisdom to achieve happiness and to take concrete action for others' welfare.

This is the purpose of philosophy. I believe that Dewey's philosophy resonates with what Shakyamuni teaches here.

HICKMAN: That is a wonderful story and an eloquent reminder of the importance of engaging real world problems with all of the intelligence we can muster.

Dewey was particularly critical of idle speculation or what he termed *pure intellectualism* because he thought that it tended to separate thinking from doing. I believe that Dewey would have been pleased to hear of the contributions that philosophers are now making to disciplines that address difficult questions that affect us all—disciplines such as environmental sciences, food biotechnology, medical research and practice, and especially education. *Pure intellectualism* doesn't get one very far in addressing the problems faced by twenty-first-century men and women.

PROCRUSTES' BED

IKEDA: What happens when human beings become imprisoned in ideologies and fixed conceptual frameworks?

In lectures in China, Dewey spoke of how William James

abhorred the concept of the universe as a closed system, which James compared to Procrustes' bed in Greek mythology. As you know, Procrustes had a bed on which he forced all the travelers he encountered to lay. If they were too tall to fit it, he lopped off their legs. If they were too short, he stretched them. Employing this parable, James sharply criticized dogmatic philosophies for judging things by pre-existing criteria.

All things are in a state of continual flux, and our value criteria and actions must respond in a flexible fashion to these changes. Dewey expressed it this way: "Since changes are going on anyway, the great thing is to learn enough about them so that we be able to lay hold of them and turn them in the direction of our desires."[9]

HICKMAN: Once again, you go to the heart of Dewey's philosophy. He continually argued against basing inquiry on what is outside of what has been developed in the course of human experience. That would include ideologies and authoritarian systems of all types.

Dewey even criticized the logic of Aristotle as being Procrustean, to use your example. He thought that, whereas Aristotle had attempted to make experience fit his logical forms, real productive inquiry should develop logical forms as tools to generate further experience.[10] In this regard, he was not against abstractions, but he was against treating them as absolutes. In his view, abstractions are tools that are properly understood as tools of inquiry.

There are many ways to avoid disciplined inquiry. One is to acquiesce to ready-made ideology, to repeat slogans and prepackaged claims that have not been examined and tested. This is a type of intellectual laziness. In this regard, given the current explosion of information, I think it is important to teach our students to use the Internet critically.

GARRISON: Using authoritarian, Procrustean, preset standards preserves feudal beliefs and values, even after the emergence of modern science and democratic institutions. Such unreflective rules, norms, and laws hold the old order in place and make it easy to reduce science to scientism before placing it in the service of the military-industrial-academic complex.

In the essay "Construction and Criticism," which we may read as a coda to *Individualism, Old and New,* Dewey wrote:

> We do not know what we really want and we make no great effort to find out. We, too, allow our purposes and desires to be foisted upon us from without. We, too, are bored by doing what we want to do, because the want has no deep roots in our own judgment of values.[11]

Mindless, unreflective, and unintelligent living is not only morally corrupt, it is aesthetically dull, boring, and repetitive. As an educator, I am sadly aware of how the tendency (of politicians, media, the mavens of industry, and such) to judge others greatly affects education. Most forms of education are little more than subtle indoctrination into the established political, economic, and social order.

In the United States, standards of learning, standardized curricula, and standardized tests that emphasize quantitative measurement and statistical averages dominate and control the field of public education and increasingly higher education, as well. Dewey despised such standardization as destructive of the very idea of qualitative democratic individualism. He thought it the task of democratic educators and educational institutions to educate for the individual's potential that each may make his or her own unique contribution.

James and Darwin

IKEDA: You bring up an important theme and perspective that educators must always address. I believe that, in addition to educators, our politicians, religious leaders, philosophers, and scientists must all work together to create an educational environment that promotes such human development.

Do you agree that the influence of William James is a vital key to understanding Dewey's thought?

GARRISON: Dewey was immensely impressed by James's biological concept of the mind and greatly admired his profound sense for life and the wisdom of thinking of life in terms of action. Dewey pointed out how important this emphasis on life was for the appreciation of novelty, freedom, and individuality in James's philosophy. Dewey added that James's biological approach to psychology helped him see the "importance of distinctive social categories, especially communication and participation."[12]

IKEDA: What is the nature of life? Dewey wrote: "Wherever there is life, there is behavior, activity. In order that life may persist, this activity has to be both continuous and adapted to the environment."[13]

In addition to the word *activity*, Dewey uses the term *adapted* but most definitely not in a passive sense. He means not simply adapting to the environment but interacting and communicating with it.

Living beings constantly grow and change through a give-and-take of energy and matter with the surrounding world. They take in oxygen and nourishment from the outside world to build their bodies, then act on the outside world, expending energy.

In other words, change and communication are major characteristics of life. Dewey devoted considerable attention to this point.

GARRISON: The things he appreciated in Charles Darwin, as well as James, help us understand Dewey's own thoughts. In his essay "The Influence of Darwinism on Philosophy," Dewey declared:

> The conceptions that had reigned in the philosophy of nature and knowledge for two thousand years, the conceptions that had become the familiar furniture of the mind, rested on the assumption of the superiority of the fixed and final. . . . In laying hands upon the sacred ark of absolute permanency . . . the *Origin of Species* introduced a mode of thinking that . . . was bound to transform the logic of knowledge, and hence the treatment of morals, politics and religion.[14]

IKEDA: Darwin famously employed the phrase "the struggle for existence" in articulating his theory of evolution, but he was referring primarily not to a struggle to dominate other living beings so much as the struggle to survive—in other words, the energetic actions of each individual being necessary to live.

Darwin was critical of the traditional philosophical approach that comprehended life based on assumptions of fixed and final essences. He constructed a "logic of knowledge" that sought to view the actuality of life in its ever-changing mutability. This is why, as Dewey perceived it, Darwin's "logic of knowledge" transcended the field of biology and transformed our ways of thinking about society, history, and politics as well.

GARRISON: Dewey realized that Darwinism would have a dramatic impact on Western philosophy. First, he understood that the rejection of fixed and final essences (i.e., substance) had deep implications for the essence of humankind or an individual human being. Second, he comprehended that we could no longer speak of absolute origins or absolute ends in an ever-evolving universe. Further, there are no absolute foundations, only relatively stable structures. Even mountains someday fall into the sea. And one of the things Darwinism was sure to affect was the very idea of good and evil.

Good and Evil

Ikeda: Regarding the issue of good and evil, a major theme for traditional philosophy and theology, Dewey rejected a rigid dualism in favor of a pragmatic approach. He wrote:

> No individual or group will be judged by whether they come up to or fall short of some fixed result, but by the direction in which they are moving. The bad man is the man who no matter how good he *has* been is beginning to deteriorate, to grow less good. The good man is the man who no matter how morally unworthy he *has* been is moving to become better. Such a conception makes one severe in judging himself and humane in judging others.[15]

Even the worst person is not unconnected to good, nor is the best person unconnected to evil. Accepting this as a premise makes it impossible to claim that one side is always good, and everything opposed to it is always bad.

This approach corresponds closely to Mahayana Buddhist thought. Nichiren wrote:

> The opposite of good we call bad, the opposite of bad we call good. Hence we know that outside of the mind there is no good and there is no bad. What is apart from this good and this bad is called the unlabeled. The good, the bad, and the unlabeled—outside of these there is no mind, and outside of the mind there are no concepts.[16]

The "unlabeled" is that which can be designated as neither good nor bad.

Anger, for instance, works for good if directed against whatever threatens human worth and dignity. If it is purely ego-driven, however, it works for evil. Thus good and evil are not fixed substances but are constantly changing and manifesting themselves in relation to the environment and one's mental attitude.

In my 2010 peace proposal, I discussed the danger of reification manifest in the simplistic categorization of people and things into good or bad, ally or enemy. The Buddhist philosophy of the contingent nature—or good, evil, and the unlabeled—enables us to avoid the trap of reification, clearly see the phenomena before us, and confront reality in its ceaseless process of growth and flux.[17]

HICKMAN: The more I read of the central works of Buddhism, the more impressed I am by their similarities to the work of Dewey. He was above all a proponent of the idea that context must always be taken into account if we are to understand a situation. This did not mean, however, that he was a relativist, in the sense that everything is as good as everything else.

I should note that Dewey *did* think that there are many ethical ideals that are warranted and assertible in ways that are highly unlikely ever to require reconstruction. It is inconceivable, for example, that there will ever be a time when slavery will again be considered good by educated people, as it was in the South until the Civil War. Dewey called this type of ethical judgment a platform; it is a relatively stable basis from which we can engage in further ethical inquiry.

It is important to note that a platform is not the same as a foundation. Philosophers such as Descartes who have sought the certainty of a foundation for their ideas have invariably failed. Dewey's idea was quite different. He thought that the quest for foundational certainty is doomed.

Nevertheless, we can operate from platforms—operating areas that we stand on to build the next level of understanding and knowledge. It makes little sense to ask where the original platform is, since it is shrouded in the misty past of our pre-human ancestors. So Dewey took his cue from Darwin instead of Descartes.

IKEDA: The platforms you speak of are the ethical views and morality—the "Golden Rules," as it were—that humanity has learned and acquired from long history and experience.

Shakyamuni said: "'Just as I am so are they, just as they are so am I.' He should neither kill nor cause others to kill."[18] This passage contains two important perspectives: First, the statement "just as I am so are they" tells us that moral laws are derived from inner reflection motivated by looking at others in the same way we look at ourselves, as fellow beings, not from externally imposed rules. Second, "nor cause others to kill" asserts that we should apply the philosophy of the worth and dignity of life not only to our own actions, preventing us from killing, but to others as well.

The reciprocal dynamic that is both inner and outer, self and other directed, calls upon us to continually reflect on ourselves, believe in and reinforce the goodness of others, and aim for the mutual elevation of both self and others.

GARRISON: I have read your *Wisdom of the Lotus Sutra: A Discussion* several times. It was while reading this dialogue that I first fully realized how much self-awareness and moral growth depend on finding the means for surmounting obstacles and overcoming evil.

The following passage made an especially lasting impression:

> Good and evil in themselves have no substance. In other words, they are not in themselves absolute but reflective distinctions. It is important, therefore, to ceaselessly direct one's heart, and take action, toward good.[19]

As soon as I read this comment, my understanding of good and evil was profoundly and permanently transformed. I then began to reread Dewey on the topic and found a passage where he insists that

> there exists a *mixture* of good and evil, and that reconstruction in the direction of the good which is indicated by ideal ends, must take place, if at all, through continued cooperative efforts.[20]

Amazing! Allow me to thank you for this insight, even as I acknowledge my understanding of it remains incomplete.

IKEDA: Thank you for your generous words. I am grateful for the many things I have learned from this dialogue with you both.

The widely practiced Buddhist discipline known as the four right efforts sets forth what is required to attain enlightenment: (1) to put an end to existing evil; (2) to prevent evil from arising; (3) to bring good into existence; and (4) to encourage existing good.

Good is the force leading both self and others in the direction of happiness. Evil is what works to plunge the self and the other into unhappiness and destruction. Therefore, while explaining this method of practice, Shakyamuni told his disciples that all compounded things are impermanent, exhorting them to strive earnestly.

Existing in a world of ceaselessly changing phenomena, we must choose the best path to build happiness for self and others alike and, constantly renewing ourselves, take courageous action and keep pressing ahead. Through such ceaseless effort, we can realize the full, unlimited potential of our lives, grow, and follow the path of value creation—in other words, bring a life of great value creation into full bloom.

CONVERSATION NINETEEN

Religious Humanism

IKEDA: The goal of religion must always be human happiness. Religion exists for the sake of people, never the other way around. This conviction is the fundamental starting point and guiding principle for the SGI in our continuing efforts to make the twenty-first century a century of life.

With this in mind, I hope in this conversation to focus on *A Common Faith*, in which Dewey expressed his view of religion, and discuss various aspects of the revival of the religious spirit and the role of religion in modern society that he advocated. *A Common Faith* and *Art as Experience*, both published in the same period, represent the philosophy of his later phase when, directing his attention to experience and imaginative powers, he explored ways for people to manifest their inherent goodness.

In his considerations, Dewey made a rigorous distinction between established religion and its doctrines, which he called *religion*, and what he called *the religious*, which each individual possesses within. He argued that the task of the present is to liberate the religious from religion.

HICKMAN: In particular, I think it is important to emphasize Dewey's suggestion that religious institutions should not attempt to monopolize spiritual values. As you note, he thought that there is a natural tendency among humans toward the religious, or the spiritual, broadly defined, and was eager to see that tendency reconstructed in ways that continually promoted the creation of new meanings and newly enriched values. It is important that religious institutions offer support for the creation of new meanings but not attempt to force those energies into narrowly defined theological channels.

IKEDA: He described *the religious* as the "common faith," not delimited by sect, class, or ethnic group, and argued that the task left to us is to "make it [the common faith of mankind] explicit and militant."[1] Dewey held that the established religions were afflicted by the notion of the supernatural existing in a realm separate from daily life and by the ways of thinking emerging from that belief, which he called "irrelevant encumbrances."[2] He also perceived that traditional religions were heavily burdened with beliefs, systems, and customs accrued over the ages that bore no direct relation to the basic ideals of religion.

Buddhism distinguishes between formalities (i.e., ceremonies and systems) on the one hand and the doctrine or teaching to be expounded on the other. Ceremonies change from period to period and region to region but are always only methods or means and never the true aims of religion.

Arnold J. Toynbee, too, stressed the importance of winnowing out and discarding nonessential accretions and extraneous trappings from religions. This is very much in keeping with Dewey's ideas.

GARRISON: Dewey and his wife decided not to join a church when they moved to Chicago. In the decades to follow, Dewey developed his own religious humanism in which ideal possibilities are imaginative projections of human values requiring collective human struggle supported only by the natural forces of the universe. By courageously identifying ourselves with the good in the universe and using it to combat evil, all of us can live a magnificently meaningful life, cooperating with others in our community to create ideal values that ameliorate suffering. In this way, every individual may unify herself or himself while expanding human happiness.

IKEDA: This can be called the core of Dewey's religious humanism. In our dialogue, Professor Toynbee expressed his view of the mission and ideal of religion consonant with Dewey's religious humanism:

> A future religion that is to bring into being, and to keep in being, a new civilization will have to be one that will enable mankind to contend with, and to overcome, the evils that are serious present threats to human survival.[3]

In 1934, when *A Common Faith* was published, the Great Depression was ravaging society, and the world was taking its first steps on the destructive path toward global war. It is noteworthy that, in these circumstances, Dewey criticized established religion as divorced from reality and proposed a religious humanism that would engender good actions conducive to social reform.

Religious humanism, whatever form it may take, demonstrates its true worth and is tempered through actions for the sake of human happiness and growth. This resonates deeply with Mahayana Buddhist thought, which stresses social practice as part of the pursuit of truth.

Essentially, the very term *Buddha* means an enlightened, wise person, in the sense of one who has been awakened. In other words, the Buddha is one who sees constantly changing reality as it is, embodies the truth in his or her own being, and has the wisdom and open mind to lead others and society in the directions of goodness and value.

What people and ideas influenced the formation of Dewey's concept of religious humanism, rooted in reality and focused on action?

GARRISON: Dewey's religious humanism relies on Samuel Taylor Coleridge's theory of imagination and William Wordsworth's notion of "natural piety." Dewey acknowledged the enduring influence of first reading Samuel Taylor Coleridge's *Aids to Reflection* as a young student. In this book, Coleridge urges each individual to seek Christian wisdom within himself or herself and to use it to alleviate suffering in worldly affairs.

Dewey came to believe in the power of practical wisdom to unify the ideal and real and, thereby, to unify the self. His subsequent study of Hegel broadened this way of thinking about religious issues. In Hegelian idealism, unlike conventional Christianity, the unification of ideal and real is a necessary process that actualizes the ideal through human effort (but only at the end of history).

IKEDA: I understand that his wife also influenced the formation of Dewey's religious humanism.

GARRISON: Alice contributed a great deal to John's religious humanism.

I know you consulted with Steven C. Rockefeller during the drafting of the Earth Charter. He is a highly regarded scholar of Dewey's philosophy of religion. Rockefeller believes that the deep love between Alice and John helped Dewey to realize concretely the idea that religiosity resides in all our relationships.

On the evidence of Dewey's children as adults, it appears the

Dewey household was a loving and caring environment. It included Dewey, Alice, and the children, as well as his parents.

IKEDA: This point is important to understand Dewey's philosophy. Professor Toynbee told me that he considered the ideal to be the three-generation family, in which children, parents, and grandparents together lead the kind of life illustrative of the best of humanity. Dewey's family was precisely this. Such an arrangement is only what is to be expected from a man like Dewey, who strove to develop ideas and a philosophy for the sake of building a good life, a good home, and a good society.

HICKMAN: Dewey developed a strong sense that religious belief must be comfortable with the sciences; it must be comfortable with what we are intellectually entitled to believe. But he didn't come to these conclusions entirely on his own. His wife was an important influence, as was his teacher George S. Morris, when he was a graduate student at Johns Hopkins University, and his reading of the works of Charles Darwin.

Jane Addams, too, as we have mentioned before, strongly influenced Dewey's thinking. Addams viewed her efforts at Hull House as a part of a revival of the humanitarian aspects of early Christianity. She thought that a reconstructed Christianity would "seek a simple and natural expression of the social organism." She shared with Dewey the idea that Jesus did not have any special truths that could be labeled religious, and that "action is the only medium [humanity] has for receiving and appropriating truth."[4]

Inner Transformation

IKEDA: I believe that Addams's work at Hull House proved to be a great source of inspiration for Dewey's views on religion—it should be for the sake of humanity, inspiring a sense of solidarity and the formation of a new community. This is the kind of religion most urgently needed in modern society, with its oft-cited lack of humanity and connections linking people together.

HICKMAN: Reading your work, I see that you and Dewey agree that appeals to supernatural forces and deities should be rejected on at least two grounds. First, such forces and entities have no place in a conceptual order that is consistent with a scientific worldview. Second, appeals to such forces and entities tend to subvert the type of candid and rigorous inquiry that has proven to be, and continues to prove to be, successful within human affairs.

IKEDA: I am deeply grateful to you for your profound understanding of my views. In *A Common Faith*, Dewey criticized the concept of the supernatural because relying on and resigning one's fate entirely to unseen forces leads people to cease making efforts. He wrote:

> If I have said anything about religions and religion that seems harsh, I have said those things because of a firm belief that the claim on the part of religions to possess a monopoly of ideals and of the supernatural means by which alone, it is alleged, they can be furthered, stands in the way of the realization of distinctively religious values inherent in natural experience. . . .[5]
>
> There are values, goods, actually realized upon a natural basis. . . . They are had, they exist as good, and out of them we frame our ideal ends.[6]

In other words, the ideal exists in reality but remains unattained. Consequently, there is value in the struggle to strive to give form to the ideal within the real.

Dewey stressed that some remote heavenly realm is not the

source of human value. He had profound faith in human beings and keenly perceived humanity's boundless possibilities.

I likewise expressed the main theme of my novel *The Human Revolution* in this statement: "A great human revolution in just a single individual will help achieve a change in the destiny of a nation and further, will enable a change in the destiny of all humankind."[7] Because the individual is the protagonist who creates his or her own destiny, a religion of the human revolution that can develop the human being's infinite possibilities is most needed.

HICKMAN: I see a fundamental connection between Dewey's belief that the ideals we ought to pursue exist as good within us and the SGI humanistic movement, which addresses the challenge of value creation based on a revolution of the internal human spirit.

Dewey arrived at the idea that the key to the religious spirit is inner human reform, as you put it. He was thus moving away from his earlier commitment to the workings of a Hegelian ideal absolute to the idea that ameliorative change in the social organism must come through the reconstruction and renewal of individual consciousness and action, not by reliance on the movement of an abstract or absolute ideal. As I said earlier, this movement was fostered by his wife, Alice, his teacher George S. Morris, Jane Addams, and also by his friend William James.

IKEDA: Dewey criticized established religions based on a sense of responsibility to bequeath something positive to all humanity, present and future. It was not the criticism of an irresponsible bystander who had placed himself in some kind of safety zone. The sharpness of his criticism was motivated by a powerful sense of responsibility. Many of the world leaders I have met have spoken of the need for a new religious view, based on a similar deep sense of responsibility.

If we ask the aim of Dewey's severe criticism of religion, I think it was to urge people to return to the true origins of religion, to make them aware of the religiosity that is the common foundation of us all.

HICKMAN: In this sense, he was critical of people who identified as being stridently antireligious as well.

IKEDA: For instance, about the bad practices people are likely to fall into, he wrote,

> I believe that many persons are so repelled from what exists as a religion by its intellectual and moral implications, that they are not even aware of attitudes in themselves that if they came to fruition would be genuinely religious.[8]

He sounded the alarm that, repelled by the all-too-apparent close-mindedness and negativity of organized religion, people had lost sight of the dormant inner goodness that motivated them to lead a better life and had become incapable of manifesting it.

Arguing that, in a turbulent age, a revival of religiosity is an urgent necessity to bring to flower and spread humanity's inherent potential for goodness throughout society, Dewey wrote, "It [religious experience] can unify interests and energies now dispersed; it can direct action and generate the heat of emotion and the light of intelligence."[9]

Theologians and others representing established religions have directed various criticisms at Dewey's religious theory. Nonetheless, I find it offers much food for thought in reexamining the role of religion in the global age. What are your thoughts on this?

INTERFAITH DIALOGUE

HICKMAN: Your question regarding the role of religion in our globalizing environment is highly pertinent: Mere tolerance will not be enough. There must also be active engagement among the world's religions with a view to mutual understanding that transcends mere tolerance.

IKEDA: Though our powers are limited, we of the SGI are working to build bridges among the world religions, including Islam and Christianity. For instance, in February 2011, the Toda Institute for Global Peace and Policy Research and the Muhammadan League of Scholars cooperated in holding an international conference on the theme "Global Visioning for a Common Future: Hopes, Challenges, and Solutions" in the Moroccan capital of Rabat.

Dialogue among religions was a major theme of discussion, and all the participants were of one accord in reaffirming the importance of dialogue. We hope to continue to promote this kind of dialogue.

I believe the mission of religious people becomes increasingly important in the present globalizing world. In today's society, in which diverse value systems and cultures come into contact with great momentum, the spirit of mutual respect, learning from one another, and helping one another is important.

Though taking different forms, each religion teaches the spirit of respect for others and the caring attitude of mutual help, which can also be found in the wisdom of the traditional cultures and tales of every land and people. What's important is to ensure that this insight is widely communicated, especially to the young generations.

HICKMAN: It is important to promote progressive and generous interpretations of one's own sacred texts. Increased interfaith dialogues, too, are important, as well as exchanges of students, especially those enrolled in religious schools. To this, I should add a call for enhanced cooperation between religious humanists and secular humanists on matters of mutual interest and concern.

The good news here is that there appears to be a diminishing emphasis on theology and religious dogma among Americans affiliated with religious institutions. A sense of religious venues as places of community and educational opportunities and social services is increasing.

IKEDA: I have been hearing about this trend lately. In Japan, especially in reaction to the earthquake and tsunami that struck eastern Japan in March 2011, people have become newly aware of the importance of volunteer work in the local community, and various organizations and groups are actively engaged in noble service to others. I think it is urgent for religious people to act together with them and broadcast the dignity of life and the significance of each individual.

THE LOTUS SUTRA TEACHING

GARRISON: Although I am not a Buddhist believer, my experience reading the Lotus Sutra, which was motivated by your philosophy and behavior, has been splendid. Indeed, I have now read it twice. The poignant message of moral equality expressed by the notion of Dharma rain in the "Parable of the Medicinal Herbs" greatly impressed me.

For me, the greatest moment of insight, the most expedient means for realizing my unique potential at that particular moment in my life, came when I read about the instantaneous enlightenment of the eight-year-old daughter of the dragon king at the end of the "Devadatta" chapter. It sent chills down my spine.

I instantly understood many things and still return to it for new insights. What I immediately comprehended was the profound sense of moral equality among not only men and women but all living things.

IKEDA: "The Parable of the Medicinal Herbs" was introduced to American society in an English-language translation in *The Dial*, the journal published by the Transcendentalists, a group which included Emerson and Thoreau. The story of the Dharma rain refers to the parable of the three kinds of medicinal herbs and two kinds of trees, and metaphorically explains how, just as the rain falls equally on all plants and trees large and small, so the Buddha's compassion falls equally on all living things. Everyone and everything receives the Buddha's compassionate rain equally and has the equal potential to grow and flourish.

Of the story in the "Devadatta" chapter, Nichiren wrote,

> This chapter, the "Devadatta" chapter, tells us that, while there are the different realms of human beings and of animals, if even the dragon king's daughter, who belongs to the realm of animals, can become a Buddha, then we . . . cannot fail to become Buddhas.[10]

The dragon king's daughter, not only a child with a reptile's body but also a female, attains enlightenment sooner than some of the Buddha's prominent disciples.

Shakyamuni's eminent disciple Shariputra could not believe this. In response, the daughter said, "Employ your supernatural powers and watch me attain Buddhahood."[11]

Nichiren Buddhism interprets this passage in the following way:

> When the dragon girl says, "Watch me attain Buddhahood," Shariputra thinks she is referring only to her own attainment of Buddhahood, but this is an error. She is rebuking him by saying, "Watch how one attains Buddhahood."[12]

The passage is a castigation against the arrogance and egoism of the intellectual class. It is further expounded in this chapter that Buddhahood is possible for all living beings throughout the ten realms of life, including evil people, represented by Devadatta.

From this discussion, we see that, in terms of pursuing goodness and living a good life, there is no distinction between the sexes or between adults and children. This is a powerful proclamation of the equality and dignity of all living things. We could say that the Lotus Sutra demonstrates a spirit compatible with Dewey's "common faith."

GARRISON: Every living being contributes something valuable to the functioning of the universe. Anyone, at any time, in any form of life, even Devadatta, can suddenly awaken to goodness and the greater self, and begin to perform good works. There are always grounds for hope in the universe.

The thing that impresses me most about the SGI is the people I have met. The true test of any religion is what it does for those who practice it. SGI members are always eager to tell me about the difference it has made in their lives.

Pondering President Toda's revelation in prison that the Buddha is life itself helped me understand that the SGI's global commitment to peace, culture, and education for the happiness and welfare of all humanity arises out of the depths of Buddhist respect for the sanctity of life in its ordinary, daily manifestations. The SGI is still young and flowering. As long as it remains open, flexible, and willing to learn as well as teach, it will continue to grow.

CONVERSATION TWENTY

Expanding Opportunity, Expanding Democracy

IKEDA: One interesting fact about Dewey, as the Japanese philosopher Shunsuke Tsurumi pointed out, was his acknowledgment of the influence of women and young people on his work. He was an open-minded, modest individual who learned good things from others, absorbed them, and used them to nourish his further development in the pursuit of truth. We have already discussed how women, including Alice Dewey and Jane Addams, influenced him and deepened his philosophy.

In this, I find a resemblance to Josei Toda, who had supreme respect for the great strengths of women and boundless expectations for the future of children.

Incidentally, Mr. Tsurumi recalled having studied as a youth *Suirishiki shido sanjutsu* (A Deductive Guide to Arithmetic) by Mr. Toda. The contents, he said, were skillfully designed to guide the reader from life experience into learning, and he remembers the book inspiring in him a sudden desire to study.

GARRISON: Dewey's participation in the progressive reform

movement brought him into close contact with many women who no doubt affected his thinking. These include social activist Emma Goldman, who was imprisoned more than once for such things as inciting people not to register for the military draft in World War I, and Ellen Gates Starr, cofounder of Hull House with Jane Addams, who was active in union organizing and the reform of child labor laws.

Few notice that he acknowledges the "many criticisms and suggestions" of a graduate student, Elsie Ripley Clapp, in the preface to his famous *Democracy and Education*. Clapp went on to do important work in progressive education and wrote an influential book for which Dewey contributed a foreword.

IKEDA: At the time, Dewey was one of the leading American philosophers. For him to express in one of his books his gratitude for the numerous criticisms and suggestions he received from a student is refreshing. He continued to watch over this student's development and encourage her in her academic career, revealing his warmth as a person and his modesty and sincerity as a scholar.

Based on my wish that students always come first at Soka University, I have often shared Dewey's exemplary behavior with our faculty. Cultivating outstanding students and successors—even at the cost of self-sacrifice—is the spirit of Soka education and the educational method of presidents Makiguchi and Toda. I can well understand how both of them valued Dewey.

Ella Flagg Young, too, greatly influenced Dewey. She was the first woman to head the school system of a major American city, serving as Chicago school superintendent, and the first woman president of the influential National Education Association.

HICKMAN: I am pleased that you mentioned Ella Flagg Young. Dewey praised her in an undated 1915 letter to John T. McManis, who was writing a book about her life and work. Dewey wrote:

> It was from her that I learned that freedom and respect for freedom mean regard for the inquiring or reflective processes of individuals, and that what ordinarily passes for freedom—freedom from external restraint, spontaneity in expression, etc.—are of significance only in their connection with thinking operations.[1]

IKEDA: In addition to candidly thanking her, Dewey clearly expressed his thoughts about the nature of true freedom as something never bestowed by others but internally generated and acquired during the process of one's development.

When she was already past fifty, while carrying out her duties as Chicago school superintendent, Ella Flagg Young studied philosophy under Dewey and participated in the University of Chicago Laboratory Schools. For his part, Dewey learned much from this woman who had many years' teaching experience and enjoyed the warm trust of many Chicago public-school teachers. This unwavering devotion to self-improvement, flexibility of thought, and openhearted personality are important keys to the development that Dewey himself demonstrated.

HICKMAN: Yes, that is certainly an accurate characterization of Dewey's personality.

There is a wonderful ambiguity in the phrase *Dewey's teachers*. Teachers, usually female, studied with him and in that sense were his *teachers*—women who looked up to and learned from him, and whom he supported and nurtured as professional educators. But in another sense of the phrase, they were also *his* teachers. They were the classroom teachers from whom he learned a great deal, whose experiences encouraged him to continually check, rethink, and revise his ideas about education. During a time when women were widely considered the intellectual inferiors of men, Dewey sought them out as sources of insight and intelligent practice.

Women's Education

Ikeda: Your description of the dual significance of *Dewey's teachers* is impressive. When teaching and learning are deeply intertwined and both parties play the roles of teacher and student, the relationship is profoundly enriched and strengthened.

At a time when men and women usually attended separate colleges, Dewey strongly advocated coeducation, insisting that women were equal to men in learning ability. He wrote, "Today the objection is more likely to read that women do so much better than young men as to discourage the latter."[2]

The constitutional scholar Thomas R. Powell, who was from Dewey's hometown and was a colleague at Columbia, candidly said that, though he had been opposed to coeducation and women's suffrage and their participation in labor unions, talking with John Dewey opened his eyes.

As I mentioned earlier, over a century ago, in still-feudalistic Japan, President Makiguchi highlighted the outstanding potential of women and stressed the importance of educating them. In 1905, he took a pioneering step in correspondence-course education for ordinary women by instituting the Women's Higher-school Lectures. The correspondence-course education, which was focused on liberal arts, aimed for women's independence. Entrance fees were waived for students in difficult financial situations, and monthly tuition was either halved or eliminated.

President Makiguchi also published a monthly journal for women, *Daikatei* (The Great Family). In it, he declared that surely no one felt education for women was unnecessary, and that the time for suppressing women's love of learning as useless or dangerous had already passed.

He was proclaiming a new age. It is important to appreciate the valiant efforts of these pioneering figures, who paved the way for women's education.

HICKMAN: With respect to the matter of full participation of girls and women in American society, studies indicate that from 1900 to 1930, the ratio of male to female university students was about equal. The percentage of male students rose dramatically after World War II, but by the 1980s, the ratio was again about equal. At the current time, university students are about 60 percent women and 40 percent men.

Some colleges and universities are now concerned that the gender balance among their students has shifted too far toward women. Of course, fields of study such as engineering and the sciences do not reflect that gender ratio, since in those areas men far outnumber women.[3]

IKEDA: In recent years, excellent female students have been brilliantly active in universities throughout the world. René Simard, an authority in cancer research and former rector of the University of Montreal, once told me:

> Many of the students who complete the very demanding course of studies at our medical school are women. A higher percentage of women complete their courses and receive their diplomas. . . . Women doctors are better communicators than their male counterparts. With an increase in their numbers, I think the patient-doctor relationship will improve.[4]

Soka Girls Gakuen (now coeducational as Kansai Soka Junior and Senior High Schools) and Soka Women's College sprang from President Makiguchi's vision. Women are also vibrantly active at Soka University and Soka University of America.

When they take up their noble mission of social contribution and fully manifest their abilities in diverse areas, women are a powerful force for the creation of a world of peace and symbiosis.

This is why I believe that Japanese society must evolve to let women develop their outstanding abilities and put them to good use.

GARRISON: Women are increasingly present in the public domain, including politics, in the United States. Men and women need not find exactly the same representation in all cultural roles, domestic or public. Indeed, it is likely that representation will evolve over time in all spheres, public and private. Only a generation ago, few would have ever thought that women would outnumber men in higher education in the United States, but it has happened.

What matters most is that we equally honor everyone's contribution to human happiness, wherever it occurs. For the sake of all humanity, the ultimate goal is that every human being, regardless of gender, carries out cultural functions that actualize his or her potential to make unique contributions to society.

HICKMAN: Regarding women's social progress, there is an interesting story, perhaps apocryphal, that Dewey once stepped out of his building into the street to find a women's suffrage parade in progress. He picked up a sign, held it high, and joined the crowd. It was not until he noticed the laughter of the onlookers that he read his sign, which said, "Men Can Vote, Why Can't I?" As I said, the story may not be entirely true, but it does reflect Dewey's commitment to the rights of women as the moral and intellectual equals of men.

IKEDA: The person who honors and listens to women and who loves and is the ally of young people, desiring to enable them to surpass their teacher, is a true, wise leader with a sense of responsibility for the future.

Dewey prized many young people, not just his own students, and, while at Columbia, was caring toward overseas students.

Similarly, Mr. Makiguchi taught at the Kobun Gakuin (Kobun Institute), where he prized his visiting Chinese students, for whom the school had been established. Many young Chinese who would later take part in the Chinese revolution are known to have studied there, including the celebrated author Lu Xun.

Makiguchi's Chinese students, inspired by his lectures on *A Geography of Human Life*, translated them into Chinese and published them in magazine and book form. Today, the existence of these materials has been confirmed in many Chinese universities and libraries, including Beijing Normal University, Fudan University, and Soochow University. I have received numerous reports on this from Chinese faculty members and students visiting Soka University and from Soka University students studying in China.

I am moved by the care Mr. Makiguchi showed his Chinese students, at how the seeds he sowed helped deepen ties of friendship between the two nations, and the enduring record of his efforts that remains in China.

Young people have sharp minds and a keen sense of justice. Their critical spirit is strong. They can tell the genuine from the spurious. This is why relating to them with truth and sincerity is most important.

The Root of Evils

Garrison: In his talks and speeches, Dewey often urged the young to dedicate themselves to ameliorating suffering by reconstructing the world.

Following Dewey's December 19, 1929, lecture at New York University, the *New York Times* reported that he urged young people to

> adopt a philosophy that would go to the root of evils rather than remedy them in their individual manifestations. . . . The philosophy of the new generation, he held, must find

> a way of bringing about that "the right of every individual to work will be recognized morally and legally. The social philosophy must be a general public hygiene or sanitation. In other words, we need a politics and an economy that will prevent these evils instead of taking care of their victims after they have fallen by the wayside." . . . Vital requirements in shaping such a philosophy, he said, were sympathy for others and independence of thought.

This advice to the young is as sound today as it was in 1929.

IKEDA: In his admonition to youth to adopt a philosophy that goes to the "root of evils," I perceive a sense of mission and responsibility, which is as passionate and genuine as that of young people.

This reminds me of how the economist John Kenneth Galbraith, having also witnessed the misery of the Great Depression, chose economics as his field in hopes of helping people improve their daily lives. He once told me that if his sons, no matter how high a position in society they might achieve, did not help others less fortunate, he would be disappointed in them. The prime requirement, he said, for civilized existence is for people to have consideration for others and society at large.

He also stressed that he expected young people to have caring hearts and a strong sense of right and wrong, and to fight the injustice of poverty and inequality. Similarly, Dewey's words convey a deep trust and affection for the younger generations and the upright idea for joint action with them.

HICKMAN: There are many stories about Dewey's concern for his students. He was known to listen—not just in an absent-minded way but really to listen to his students. After his death, one of his younger colleagues shared that his first impression of Dewey was his "impulse to think of the young people coming on, to take seriously anything they said, and to reply, no matter how wild the person was who wrote to him and how silly it seemed."[6]

I should add that Dewey's correspondence with young people provides researchers with important insights into his private life and into the background and motivation for his published works. As mentioned before, in one letter, written in response to a question posed by a private in the U.S. Army, he explained his motivation for writing *A Common Faith*.

Can We Change?

IKEDA: The story eloquently reveals Dewey as an individual who placed being a good human being above being a scholar. Though busy with his research, he extended himself fully for each young person he met. This is what it means to be a great humanistic educator. Each of his letters attests to his noble actions.

Like him, President Makiguchi was an educator who believed in and cared about young people. A few days before being arrested on suspicion of lèse-majesté under the militarist government's infamous Peace Preservation Law, he held friendly, encouraging discussions with students from Tokyo Shoka University (now Hitotsubashi University).

Also, immediately before his arrest, he lectured for young people on Nichiren's "On Establishing the Correct Teaching for the Peace of the Land." He did this at a time when young Japanese were indoctrinated to think that life's primary goal was to die for the sake of the nation.

Even in the dark, militarist society of the day, until the very last, he strove to teach young people the correct human philosophy, to illuminate all with the light of hope and courage. This was because of his immense faith in human beings' goodness and his belief in their limitless possibilities.

In the chapter in *Problems of Men* titled "Does Human Nature Change?" Dewey comes to the conclusion that it can indeed change, thus demonstrating his great faith in human development and growth. I am also convinced that we can change ourselves, that we can change our lives for the better. The reason that I have, inheriting my mentor's intent, continued writing my novels *The Human Revolution* and *The New Human Revolution* for nearly half a century is that I believe human revolution is the fundamental key for solving the various problems facing humankind.

Our SGI movement of peace, culture, and education takes the concept of human revolution as its starting point, which is why I hope to go on studying in greater depth the thought of John Dewey, a vigorous proponent of improving human nature.

In this dialogue, I have had the opportunity to discuss Dewey's superb philosophy, a shining treasure in the legacy of human thought, with the two of you, for whom I have the greatest respect.

How do you think we can transmit Dewey's thought to the youth who will lead the twenty-first century?

HICKMAN: Your observation that Dewey's philosophy is permeated with trust in humanity goes directly to the heart of what his spiritual heritage can mean for the twenty-first century.

Dewey's educational experiments with children in Chicago convinced him that human beings have an enormous capacity for change, and especially for what he termed *growth*, or, in other words, *value creation*. In Dewey's view, it is only by means of attention to, and learning from, our experiences, both personal and collective, that "further experience can grow in ordered richness."[7]

Dewey's faith in the possibilities of human experience is expressed in his view that democracy and education are inter-definable. We can do nothing better to honor this vision than to promote and expand educational opportunities and, consequently, democratic forms of life.

Your life's work as founder of two great universities, as well as numerous secondary and elementary schools and other educational institutions, provides an excellent example of how Dewey's spiritual heritage can be conveyed to the young men and women who will be the leaders of the twenty-first century. Your trust in humanity and the improvement of human nature binds your life's work to that of John Dewey.

GARRISON: Human nature does change. More generally, we must not only recognize that what it means to be truly human may evolve over the generations but that, while less dramatically than the dragon king's daughter in the Lotus Sutra, every human being may achieve a revolution in his or her individual lifetime. As a Deweyan pragmatist, I strongly endorse your trust in the future of humanity and the improvement of human nature.

The SGI is committed to many of the same principles that appeal to people attracted to Deweyan pragmatism. Both understand that any sense of religiosity that does not make a difference in the daily lives of its adherents fails to appreciate the sanctity of life. Neither of them attempts to escape the reality of life. They only seek to unify the real with the ideal.

The SGI and Deweyan pragmatism share a commitment to the intrinsic potential inherent in the life of each of the individuals who comprise all of humanity. While acknowledging and appreciating human plurality, the SGI and Deweyan pragmatism strive to overcome such dualisms as those of organism and environment, knower and known, self and other, and individual and community.

Both seek to overcome obstacles and ameliorate suffering by creating value in such a way as to benefit ourselves and our community simultaneously.

Our Greatest Hope

IKEDA: Thank you again for the warmth and depth with which you accurately understand and generously laud the meaning of Soka education and the SGI movement. I can only imagine how happy presidents Makiguchi and Toda would be to hear these words from such outstanding specialists in Dewey's philosophy.

Your thought-provoking statements serve as a model for future society and human action. And your ideas to promote and expand "educational opportunities and, consequently, democratic forms of life," to overcome dualisms while acknowledging and appreciating human plurality, have much in common with our Buddhist movement.

GARRISON: This surprising compatibility between Nichiren Buddhism and Deweyan pragmatism has made an enduring impression on me, as have the differences in their expression. The idea of dependent origination finds its concomitant in Dewey's transactionalism, while his anti-dualism is readily recognized in such basic Buddhist principles as the oneness of life and its environment and the oneness of body and mind. President Ikeda, you explicitly identify Dewey as a follower of the Middle Way and an exponent of religious humanism.

These and many other ideas support the shared ideal of context-dependent, value-creating, ameliorative action in an endlessly evolving universe to create beauty and bring benefit to oneself while helping others in the community of humankind. I believe these ideas and ideals will have tremendous appeal in the twenty-first century, as people begin to perceive the limits of every political ideology and dogmatic religion along with the excessive belief in the unaided power of human reason.

The SGI commitment to peace, culture, education, and dialogue, seen in the trialogue we have now completed, will push the Soka spirit forward. These commitments are the best hope for preserving and revitalizing the spirit of Deweyan pragmatism.

IKEDA: Thank you yet again for your understanding. We are resolved to redouble our efforts to improve and to live up to the expectations of you two fine educators. Dewey's philosophy greatly illumines and strengthens not only educational and social development but also human progress in general.

Religion's important task is contributing to people's welfare in the real world and imparting hope and courage to future generations. Its focus must be on the needs of the people, sharply perceiving their future dreams. In this connection, Deweyan pragmatism has inexhaustible value for us.

In concluding, let me express my enormous gratitude to you both.

HICKMAN: I very much appreciate the opportunity that this extended dialogue with you and Dr. Garrison has afforded. Our exchange of ideas has stimulated my deeper appreciation of the many points of contact between the ideas of you and your predecessors, Tsunesaburo Makiguchi and Josei Toda, and John Dewey's vision of a world in which the ideals of democracy and education are honored. I am happy to report that I have learned a great deal from you and Dr. Garrison as a result of these exchanges, and that our conversation has been a wonderful opportunity for personal growth.

Our dialogue has addressed some of the most important issues now faced by our human community. We have discussed educational issues such as the problem of bullying in schools, the role of the university in creating global citizens, the home learning environment, and the importance of life-long learning. We have considered how scientific technology can serve human happiness, how religious experiences can be expressed as a "common faith," and how conflict can be resolved through dialogue. Our thoughts have also turned to how people with diverse customs and interests can live together in democratic communities.

The world has changed in significant ways since we began our dialogue. The people of Japan are now recovering from a great natural disaster. The people of North Africa and the Middle East are experiencing great political upheavals. The United States and Europe continue to be caught up in crises of economic confidence.

The test of the ideas and ideals that we have discussed will be their ability to be of service in times such as these. I know that you and Dr. Garrison share my hope that our dialogue will be a source of comfort and encouragement to many, and that it will be a stimulus to further growth and value creation.

APPENDIX 1

Selected Works

Daisaku Ikeda

A Forum for Peace: Daisaku Ikeda's Proposals to the UN. London: I. B. Tauris & Co. Ltd, 2014.

A New Humanism: The University Addresses of Daisaku Ikeda. London: I. B. Tauris & Co. Ltd, 2010.

A Lifelong Quest for Peace: A Dialogue with Linus Pauling. London: I. B. Tauris & Co. Ltd, 2009.

Choose Life with Arnold Toynbee. New York: I. B. Tauris & Co. Ltd, 2007.

A Quest for Global Peace with Joseph Rotblat. London: I. B. Tauris & Co. Ltd, 2007.

Moral Lessons of the Twentieth Century with Mikhail Gorbachev. London: I. B. Tauris & Co. Ltd, 2005.

The New Human Revolution, vols. 1–26 (ongoing series). Santa Monica, Calif.: World Tribune Press, 2001–2014.

The Wisdom of the Lotus Sutra: A Discussion, vols. I–VI, with Katsuji Saito, Takanori Endo, and Haruo Suda. Santa Monica, Calif.: World Tribune Press, 2001–2003.

AVAILABLE IN JAPANESE:

Heiwa no kakehashi, ningen kyoiku o kataru (Humanistic Education, a Bridge to Peace) with Gu Mingyuan. Tokyo: Institute of Oriental Philosophy, 2012.

Heiwa e no Taiwa: Waitsuzekka-shi Rainichi Zenhatsugen (Dialogues for Peace: Collected Statements Made by Richard von Weizsäcker during His Visits to Japan). Tokyo: Mainichi Shimbunsha Shochi Osaka Jikko Iinkai, 1999.

APPENDIX 2

Selected Works

Jim Garrison

John Dewey's Philosophy of Education: An Introduction and Recontextualization for Our Times with Stefan Neubert and Kersten Reich. New York: Palgrave Macmillan, 2012.

Teaching with Reverence: Reviving an Ancient Virtue for Today's Schools. Edited and with an introduction (with A. G. Rud). New York: Palgrave Macmillan, 2012.

John Dewey at 150: Reflections for a New Century. Edited and with an introduction (with A. G. Rud and Lynda Stone). West Lafayette, Indiana: Purdue University Press, 2009.

Reconstructing Democracy, Recontextualizing Dewey: Pragmatism and Interactive Constructivism in the Twenty-first Century. Editor. Albany, New York: State University of New York Press, 2009.

Dewey and Eros: Wisdom and Desire in the Art of Teaching. New York: Teachers College Press, 1997.

APPENDIX 3

Selected Works

Larry Hickman

Pragmatism as Post-Postmodernism. New York: Fordham University Press, 2007.

Philosophical Tools for Technical Culture: Putting Pragmatism to Work. Bloomington, Indiana: Indiana University Press, 2001.

The Correspondence of John Dewey. Vol. 1: 1871 – 1918, Vol.2: 1919–1939, Vol. 3: 1939 – 1952, Vol. 4: 1953–2007. General Editor. Charlottesville, Virginia: InteLex Corporation, 1999, 2001, 2005, 2008.

The Essential Dewey; vol. I: *Pragmatism, Education, and Democracy*, vol. II: *Ethics, Logic, Psychology*. Edited and with introductions (with Thomas Alexander). Bloomington, Indiana: Indiana University Press, 1998.

John Dewey's Pragmatic Technology. Bloomington, Indiana: Indiana University Press, 1990.

APPENDIX 4

Selected Works

John Dewey

The Early Works of John Dewey, 1882–1898, vols. 1–5, Jo Ann Boydston, ed. Carbondale, Illinois: Southern Illinois University Press, 2008. These volumes include:

"Evolution and Ethics" (vol. 5)
"The Late Professor Morris" (vol. 3)
"A College Course: What Should I Expect From It?" (vol. 3)
"My Pedagogic Creed" (vol. 5)

The Middle Works of John Dewey, 1899–1924, vols. 1–15, Jo Ann Boydston, ed. Carbondale, Illinois: Southern Illinois University Press, 2008. These volumes include:

Studies in Logical Theory (vol. 2)
The School and Society (vol. 1)
Democracy and Education (vol. 9)
The Child and the Curriculum (vol. 2)

The Later Works of John Dewey, 1925–1953, vols. 1–17, Jo Ann Boydston, ed. Carbondale, Illinois: Southern Illinois University Press, 2008. These volumes include:

"From Absolutism to Experimentalism" (vol. 5)
"Creative Democracy—The Task Before Us" (vol. 14)
A Common Faith (vol. 9)
Ethics (vol. 7)
Individualism, Old and New (vol. 5)

The Correspondence of John Dewey, 1871–1952, vols. 1–3. Carbondale, Illinois: Southern Illinois University Press, 2004.

The Essential Dewey, vols. 1–2. Bloomington, Indiana: Indiana University Press, 1998.

The Poems of John Dewey, Jo Ann Boydston, ed. and intro. Carbondale, Illinois: Southern Illinois University Press, 1977.

APPENDIX 5

Selected Works

Tsunesaburo Makiguchi

Geography of Human Life, A, Dayle M. Bethel, ed. San Francisco, California: Caddo Gap Press, 2002.

Education for Creative Living: Ideas and Proposals of Tsunesaburo Makiguchi, Dayle M. Bethel, ed., Alfred Birnbaum, trans. Ames, Iowa: Iowa State University Press, 1989.

Available in Japanese:

Makiguchi Tsunesaburo zenshu (The Complete Works of Tsunesaburo Makiguchi), vols. 1–9. Tokyo: Daisan Bunmei-sha, 1981–88.

Soka kyoikugaku taikei (The System of Value-Creating Pedagogy), vols. 1–4, Josei Toda, ed. Tokyo: Soka Kyoiku Gakkai, Nov. 18, 1930.

About Makiguchi:

Jason Goulah and Andrew Gebert, "Tsunesaburo Makiguchi: Introduction to the Man, His Ideas, and the Special Issue" in

Educational Studies: A Journal of the American Educational Studies Association, vol. 45, issue 2, 2009.

Dayle M. Bethel, *Makiguchi: The Value Creator: Revolutionary Japanese Educator and Founder of Soka Gakkai*. New York: Weatherhill, Inc., 1973.

Notes

Conversation One
What Dewey Stood For

1. Quoted in Corliss Lamont, ed., *Dialogue on John Dewey* (New York: Horizon, 1959), pp. 58, 88, 162.
2. Soon after Japan's devastating defeat in World War II, Josei Toda (later inaugurated as the Soka Gakkai's second president) attended a Soka Gakkai discussion meeting in Kamata, Tokyo. Among the twenty or so participants was the nineteen-year-old Daisaku Ikeda, who was attending his first Soka Gakkai meeting. After the lecture, Ikeda asked several questions, which Toda answered from the standpoint of Buddhism. Ikeda was moved by Toda's response. Ten days later, on August 24, 1947, Ikeda joined the Soka Gakkai. Ikeda went on to become Toda's greatest support and eventually was inaugurated as the Soka Gakkai's third president.
3. Soka schools: The Soka Junior and Senior High Schools—established by Daisaku Ikeda in Kodaira, Tokyo, in 1968—were the beginning of the Soka school system, which today includes kindergartens, elementary, junior, and senior high schools, a university in Tokyo, and a university in Aliso Viejo, Calif. Kindergartens have also been established in Hong Kong, Singapore, Malaysia, South Korea, and Brazil. The schools are based on Soka education.
4. In their entirety, as couched by the university's founder, Daisaku Ikeda, the mottos are: Be philosophers of a renaissance of life; Be

world citizens in solidarity for peace; Be the pioneers of a global civilization.

5. Dewey described the "difference between an experience which is *mere existence* or occurrence, and one which has to do with worth, truth, right relationship." *See* John Dewey, *Studies in Logical Theory* in *The Middle Works of John Dewey, 1899–1924*, vol. 2: 1902–1903, p. 331.
6. Tsunesaburo Makiguchi (1871–1944) was a forward-thinking educational theorist and religious reformer in Japan. His opposition to Japan's militarism and nationalism led to his imprisonment and death during World War II. Makiguchi is best known for two major works, *A Geography of Human Life* and *The System of Value-Creating Pedagogy*, and as founder, with Josei Toda in 1930, of the Soka Gakkai, which is today the largest lay Buddhist organization in Japan. Through the Soka Gakkai International, it has 12 million members worldwide. Consistent throughout his writing and in his work as a classroom teacher and school principal is his belief in the centrality of the happiness of the individual. This same commitment can be seen in his role as a religious reformer: He rejected the attempts of authorities to subvert the essence of the Buddhist teachings, insisting that religion always exists to serve human needs.
7. The Outlawry of War movement: Credited with initiating this movement, Chicago attorney Salmon Oliver Levinson argued that violence by nation-states should be declared illegal. He assisted in drafting the international General Treaty for Renunciation of War as an Instrument of National Policy (also known as the Kellogg-Briand Pact) in 1928, which outlawed war.
8. Japan's Peace Constitution (properly called the Constitution of Japan) was enacted on May 3, 1947, and is well known for Article 9, which renounces Japan's right to wage war.
9. *See* John Dewey, "Evolution and Ethics" in *The Early Works of John Dewey, 1882–1898*; vol. 5, 1895–1898, Jo Ann Boydston, ed., William R. McKenzie, intro. (Carbondale, Illinois: Southern Illinois University Press, 2008), pp. 34–53.
10. *See* Thomas H. Huxley and William Jay Youmans, *The Elements of Physiology and Hygiene; A Text-book for Educational Institutions* (New York: D. Appleton and Company, 1868).
11. John Dewey, *Logic: The Theory of Inquiry* in *The Later Works of John Dewey, 1925–1953*; vol. 12, 1938, Jo Ann Boydston, ed., Ernest Nagel,

intro. (Carbondale, Ill.: Southern Illinois University Press, 2008), p. 32.

12. *See* John Dewey, "Public Opinion in Japan" in *The Middle Works of John Dewey, 1899–1924*; vol. 13, 1938–1939, Jo Ann Boydston, ed., Steven M. Cahn, intro. (Carbondale, Ill.: Southern Illinois University Press, 2008), p. 257.
13. *See* Kaneko Ikeda, *Kaneko's Story* (Santa Monica, Calif.: World Tribune Press, 2008).

Conversation Two
Learning Together

1. *See* Larry A. Hickman, *John Dewey's Pragmatic Technology* (Bloomington, Ind.: Indiana University Press, 1990).
2. The Dewey Decimal System, a library classification system, was formulated in 1876 by Melville Dewey.
3. "Value-Creating Society" is the English translation of "Soka Gakkai."
4. John Dewey, *The Poems of John Dewey*, Jo Ann Boydston, ed. and intro. (Carbondale, Ill.: Southern Illinois University Press, 1977), pp. 64–65.
5. This dialogue was originally serialized in *Todai*, a Japanese magazine published monthly by Daisan Bunmei-sha. It ran from December 2009 through July 2011.

Conversation Three
From Mentor to Disciple

1. Arnold Toynbee, *Civilization on Trial* (New York: Oxford University Press, 1948), p. 213.
2. The Ikeda Center for Peace, Learning, and Dialogue was founded by Daisaku Ikeda as the Boston Research Center for the 21st Century in Cambridge, Massachusetts, in 1993. Through a variety of books, seminars, and events, created in collaboration with leading scholars, the Ikeda Center promotes the ideas and convictions that will lead to a peaceful and flourishing twenty-first century. The Institute for Oriental Philosophy, founded by Daisaku Ikeda in 1962, is dedicated to advancing scholarly inquiry on Buddhism and other world religions to clarify their universal value and make them a part of humanity's rich spiritual heritage in the modern age.

3. As of publication, centers are located in Germany, Italy, Hungary, Poland, Japan, Turkey, and China. The Center for Dewey Studies at Southern Illinois University partners with these sister centers for conferences and other scholarly forums for discussion and investigation of Dewey's works and ideas, and also partners with some centers in other activities, such as, in the case of the Chinese center, translating and publishing.
4. John Dewey, "From Absolutism to Experimentalism" in *The Later Works of John Dewey, 1925–1953*; vol. 5, 1929–1930, Jo Ann Boydston, ed., Paul Kurtz, intro. (Carbondale, Ill.: Southern Illinois University, 2008), p. 154.
5. Ibid., p. 155.
6. Ibid.
7. Richard Rorty, *Contingency and Solidarity* (Cambridge and New York: Cambridge University Press, 1989), p. 130, n24.
8. James Webster and Georg Feder, *The New Grove Haydn* (New York: Oxford University Press, 2003), p. 29.
9 Daisaku Ikeda, *The Human Revolution*, Book Two (Santa Monica, Calif.: World Tribune Press, 2004), p. 1967.
10. "Three thousand realms" refers to the entire phenomenal world.
11. Nichiren, *The Record of the Orally Transmitted Teachings* (Tokyo: Soka Gakkai, 2004), pp. 81–82.
12. For decades following the establishment of the Soka Gakkai (1930), it wholeheartedly supported the Nichiren Shoshu priesthood, building hundreds of temples and restoring the head temple. The crux of the priesthood's motives, however, lay in its view that priests are necessary intermediaries between lay believers and the teachings of Nichiren Buddhism. The priests sought to make veneration and obedience to themselves the keys to a practitioner's faith. It taught, for example, that the high priest is absolute; without unquestioningly following the high priest, practitioners cannot attain enlightenment. In contrast, the Soka Gakkai bases itself directly on the spirit and intent of Nichiren as set forth in his writings. *See* "Soka Spirit: Three Key Errors of the Nichiren Shoshu Priesthood," http://sgi-usa.org/introstudy/2013_intro/Pdf/IntroToBuddhism_15Soka_Spirit.pdf (accessed on July 7, 2014).
13. John Dewey, "Creative Democracy—The Task Before Us" in *The Later Works of John Dewey, 1925–1953*; vol. 14, 1931–1941, Jo Ann Boydston,

ed., R. W. Sleeper, intro. (Carbondale, Ill.: Southern Illinois University, 2008), p. 229.

14. John Dewey, *A Common Faith* in *The Later Works of John Dewey, 1925–1953*; vol. 9, 1933–1934, Jo Ann Boydston, ed., Milton R. Konvitz, intro. (Carbondale, Ill.: Southern Illinois University, 2008), p. 34.
15. Ibid., pp. 57–58.

Conversation Four
Growth Is the Goal

1. John Dewey, "Ends, the Good and Wisdom" in *The Later Works of John Dewey, 1925–1953*; vol. 7, 1932, Jo Ann Boydston, ed., Abraham Edel and Elizabeth Flower, intro. (Carbondale, Ill.: Southern Illinois University Press, 2008), p. 198.
2. *See* Charles Sanders Peirce, *Collected Papers of Charles Sanders Peirce*, vol. 5: *Pragmatism and Pragmaticism*, Charles Hartshorne and Paul Weiss, eds. (Cambridge, Mass: Harvard University Press, 1934), paragraph 412.
3. Daisaku Ikeda, *The Human Revolution*, Book One (Santa Monica, Calif.: World Tribune Press, 2004), p. 229.
4. John Dewey, "The Need for a Recovery of Philosophy" in *The Middle Works of John Dewey, 1899–1924*; vol. 10, 1916–1917, Jo Ann Boydston, ed., Lewis E. Hahn, intro. (Carbondale, Ill.: Southern Illinois University Press, 2008), p. 46.
5. George Dykhuizen, *The Life and Mind of John Dewey* (Carbondale, Ill.: Southern Illinois University Press, 1973), p. 299.
6. *See* Dewey, "From Absolutism to Experimentalism" in *The Later Works*, vol. 5, p. 148.
7. *See* John Dewey, "The Late Professor Morris" in *The Early Works of John Dewey, 1882–1898*; vol. 3, 1889–1892, Jo Ann Boydston, ed., S. Morris Eames, intro. (Carbondale, Ill.: Southern Illinois University, 2008), pp. 3–13.
8. By the time Dewey completed his doctorate in 1884, Morris had moved on to the University of Michigan.
9. Ralph Waldo Emerson, *The Conduct of Life* in *Essays and Lectures*, Joel Porte, ed. (New York: Library of America, 1983), p. 1094.
10. Linus Pauling and Daisaku Ikeda, *A Lifelong Quest for Peace: A Dialogue* (London: I. B. Tauris & Co. Ltd, 2009), p. 66.

11. This phrase appears throughout the Lotus Sutra. The ceremony referenced here is the Ceremony in the Air, which begins in chapter 11, "The Emergence of the Treasure Tower," and ends in chapter 22, "Entrustment." Shakyamuni, *The Lotus Sutra and Its Opening and Closing Sutras*, Burton Watson, trans. (Tokyo: Soka Gakkai, 2009), pp. 109–322.
12. Translated from the Japanese. Tsunesaburo Makiguchi, *Makiguchi Tsunesaburo zenshu* (The Complete Works of Tsunesaburo Makiguchi), vol. 6 (Tokyo: Daisan Bunmei-sha, 1983), p. 289.
13. Ikeda, *The Human Revolution*, Book Two, p. 1021.

CONVERSATION FIVE
THE COST OF WAR

1. In 1939, the year that World War II began and a time when most religious organizations in Japan supported state Shinto (Japan's indigenous religion, which centers on the worship of nature and ancestors), Makiguchi took a strong stand against what he recognized as the Japanese militarist government's strategy to deprive people of the freedoms of conscience and religion. Despite surveillance by police and the government's constant demand that the Soka Kyoiku Gakkai members worship the Shinto talisman, Makiguchi attended more than 240 Buddhist discussion meetings over two years, where he openly expressed his convictions. In July 1943, Makiguchi and Toda were arrested and charged with violations of Japan's notorious Peace Preservation Act. Makiguchi was 72 and spent the next 16 months in prison, where he died on Nov. 18, 1944, never compromising his beliefs. *See* Daisaku Ikeda, *A New Humanism: The University Addresses of Daisaku Ikeda* (London: I. B. Tauris & Co. Ltd, 2010), pp. 246–47.
2. John Dewey, *The School and Society* in *The Middle Works of John Dewey, 1899–1924*; vol. 1, 1899–1901, Jo Ann Boydston, ed., Joe R. Burnett, intro. (Carbondale, Ill.: Southern Illinois University, 2008), p. 24.
3. John Dewey, "Democracy and Education in the World of Today" in *The Later Works of John Dewey, 1925–1953*; vol. 13, 1938–1939, Jo Ann Boydston, ed., Steven M. Cahn, intro. (Carbondale, Ill.: Southern Illinois University Press, 1988), p. 301.
4. *See Human Events*, May 31, 2005, http://humanevents.com/2005/05/31/ten-most-harmful-books-of-the-19th-and-20th-centuries/ (accessed on July 4, 2014).

5. In December 2013, John Podesta stepped down from his role as chair of the Center for American Progress to join the Obama administration as counselor to the president.
6. Nichiren, *The Writings of Nichiren Daishonin*, vol. I (Tokyo: Soka Gakkai, 1999), p. 303.
7. Ibid., p. 287.
8. John Dewey, *Democracy and Education* in *The Middle Works of John Dewey, 1899–1924*; vol. 9, 1916, Jo Ann Boydston, ed., Sidney Hook, intro. (Carbondale, Ill.: Southern Illinois University Press, 2008), p. 314.
9. Mohandas K. Gandhi, *The Words of Gandhi*, Richard Attenborough and Johanna McGeary, eds. (New York: Newmarket Press, 2008), p. 89.

Conversation Six
All Children Unique

1. John Dewey, *The Child and the Curriculum* in *The Middle Works of John Dewey, 1899–1924*; vol. 2, 1902–1903, Jo Ann Boydston, ed., Sydney Hook, intro. (Carbondale, Ill.: Southern Illinois University Press, 2008), p. 276.
2. Tsunesaburo Makiguchi, *Education for Creative Living: Ideas and Proposals of Tsunesaburo Makiguchi*, Dayle M. Bethel, ed., Alfred Birnbaum, trans. (Ames, Iowa: Iowa State University Press, 1989), p. 17.
3. Dewey, *The School and Society* in *The Middle Works*, vol. 1, pp. 12–13.
4. *See What We Know from Shokuiku, the Japanese Spirit—Food and Nutrition Education in Japan* (Tokyo: Office for Shokuiku Promotion, Cabinet Office, Government of Japan); http://www8.cao.go.jp/syokuiku/data/english/eng_pamph/index.html (accessed January 14, 2014).
5. Nichiren, *The Writings of Nichiren Daishonin*, vol. II (Tokyo: Soka Gakkai, 2006), p. 1060.
6. *See* John Dewey, "Reality as Experience" in *The Middle Works of John Dewey, 1899–1924*; vol. 3, 1903–1906, Jo Ann Boydston, ed., Darnell Rucker, intro. (Carbondale, Ill.: Southern Illinois University Press, 2008), p. 96.
7. For more on testing, the work of Gerald W. Bracey is a good resource, as well as Rethinking Schools: http://www.rethinkingschools.org.
8. Starting in the 1970s, President Ikeda has made substantial proposals based on his commitment to improve education everywhere.

His proposals have included a world charter on education, an international Conference of University Presidents, and a World Federation of Student Associations. He also proposed the establishment of the United Nations Decade of Education for Sustainable Development, which was adopted and began in 2005. *See* Daisaku Ikeda, *Soka Education: For the Happiness of the Individual* (Santa Monica, Calif.: Middleway Press, 2010).

9. Dewey, *The School and Society* in *The Middle Works*, vol. 1, p. 22.
10. Jason Goulah and Andrew Gebert, "Tsunesaburo Makiguchi: Introduction to the Man, His Ideas, and the Special Issue" in *Educational Studies: A Journal of the American Educational Studies Association*, vol. 45, issue 2, 2009, pp. 115–132.
11. Arnold Toynbee and Daisaku Ikeda, *Choose Life* (New York: I. B. Tauris & Co. Ltd, 2007), pp. 99–100.

CONVERSATION SEVEN
EDUCATIONAL WISDOM

1. Quoted in Michael Eldridge, *Transforming Experience: John Dewey's Cultural Instrumentalism* (Nashville, Tenn.: Vanderbilt University Press, 1998), p. 5.
2. Dewey, *Experience and Education* in *The Later Works*, vol. 13, p. 48.
3. Dewey, *The School and Society* in *The Middle Works*, vol. 1, p. 36.
4. Translated from Japanese. Tsunesaburo Makiguchi, *Makiguchi Tsunesaburo zenshu* (The Complete Works of Tsunesaburo Makiguchi), vol. 9 (Tokyo: Daisan Bunmei-sha, 1988), p. 18.
5. James Alan Fox, Delbert S. Elliott, R. Gil Kerlikowski, and Sanford A. Newman, *Bullying Prevention Is Crime Prevention* (Washington, D. C.: Fight Crime: Invest in Kids, 2003). This report is available free of charge at www.fightcrime.org.
6. Quoted in Daisaku Ikeda, *The New Human Revolution*, vol. 7 (Santa Monica, Calif.: World Tribune Press, 2001), p. 11.
7. Quoted in Ikeda, *Soka Education*, p. 124.

CONVERSATION EIGHT
CREATIVE FAMILIES

1. Dewey, *The School and Society* in *The Middle Works*, vol. 1, p. 5.
2. Felix Unger and Daisaku Ikeda, *Ningenshugi no hata wo* (The Ban-

ner of Humanism) (Tokyo: Institute of Oriental Philosophy, 2007), p. 190.

3. Nichiren, *The Writings*, vol. II, p. 1060.
4. Nichiren, *The Writings*, vol. I, p. 24.
5. Dewey, *Ethics* in *The Later Works*, vol. 7, p. 302.
6. Quoted in Ikeda, *Soka Education*, p. 14.
7. Mark Mather, "U.S. Children in Single-Mother Families," a brief published by the Population Reference Bureau, May 2010, http://www.prb.org/pdf10/single-motherfamilies.pdf (accessed January 20, 2014).

Conversation Nine
The University Experience

1. Dewey, "A College Course: What Should I Expect From It?" in *The Early Works*, vol. 3, p. 54.
2. John Dewey, *The Public and Its Problems* in *The Later Works of John Dewey, 1925–1953*; vol. 2, 1925–1927, Jo Ann Boydston, ed., James Gouinlock, intro. (Carbondale, Ill.: Southern Illinois University, 2008), p. 330.
3. Ibid., p. 367.
4. Ibid., p. 368.

Conversation Ten
The Twenty-First Century University

1. Ikeda and Toynbee, *Choose Life*, p. 51.
2. The Hippocratic Oath is widely believed to have been written by Hippocrates in the late fifth century BCE, although no one knows for sure. It has been rewritten several times and also varies among countries. The version referenced here is a later English translation. *See* http://www.princeton.edu/~achaney/tmve/wiki100k/docs/Hippocratic_Oath.html (accessed November 3, 2013).
3. *See*, for example, *Social Forces*, December 2010, pp. 389–415.
4. Makiguchi, *Education for Creative Living*, p. 168.
5. *Conversations of Goethe with Johann Peter Eckermann*, J. K. Moorhead, ed., John Oxenford, trans. (London: Da Capo Press, 1998), p. 286.
6. Dewey, "A College Course: What Should I Expect From It?" in *The Early Works*, vol. 3, p. 53.

7. Dewey, *Democracy and Education* in *The Middle Works*, vol. 9, p. 221.
8. Ibid., p. 226.
9. George Santayana, *The Life of Reason or Phases of Human Progress*, vol. 1: *Introduction and Reason in Common Sense* (New York: Charles Scribner's Sons, 1920), p. 284.
10. For example, Dewey wrote: "Geography and history supply subject matter which gives background and outlook, intellectual perspective, to what might otherwise be narrow personal actions or mere forms of technical skill. With every increase of ability to place our own doings in their time and space connections, our doings gain in significant content.... To 'learn geography' is to gain in power to perceive the spatial, the natural, connections of an ordinary act; to 'learn history' is essentially to gain in power to recognize its human connections. *See* Dewey, *Democracy and Education* in *The Middle Works*, vol. 9, p. 217.
11. Erasmus Mundus (European Community Action Scheme for the Mobility of University Students): This European Union program provides scholarships for higher education and also supports academic cooperation between Europe and the rest of the world.
12. The Aspen Institute's Socrates Program in Washington, D. C. provides a forum for emerging leaders from various professions to convene and explore contemporary issues through expert-moderated dialogue.
13. *U.S. News and World Report* has placed Soka University among the top 50 liberal arts colleges in the United States since 2012. In 2014, SUA was ranked #41 (up from its original position of #49). *See* http://colleges.usnews.rankingsandreviews.com/best-colleges/soka-university-of-america-38144 (accessed on July 13, 2014).

CONVERSATION ELEVEN
EDUCATION FOR WORLD CITIZENS

1. *Seikyo Shimbun* is the daily Japanese-language newspaper of the Soka Gakkai.
2. *See* Ikeda, "Thoughts on Education for Global Citizenship" in *A New Humanism*, p. 55.
3. Ikeda, "Mahayana Buddhism and Twenty-first-Century Civilization" in *A New Humanism*, p. 171.

4. Ibid.
5. Translated from Japanese. Tsunesaburo Makiguchi, *Makiguchi Tsunesaburo shingen-shu* (An Anthology of Tsunesaburo Makiguchi's Works), Takehisa Tsuji, ed. (Tokyo: Daisan Bunmei-sha, 1994), p. 40.
6. William Blake, "Auguries of Innocence" in *The Complete Poetry and Prose of William Blake*, David V. Erdman, ed., Harold Bloom, commentary (New York: Anchor Books, 1997), p. 490.
7. Nichiren, *The Writings*, vol. I, p. 629.
8. The Universal Declaration of Human Rights was adopted by the UN General Assembly on Dec. 10, 1948. For the full text, *see* http://www.un.org/en/documents/udhr/ (accessed January 29, 2014).
9. Dewey, *Democracy and Education* in *The Middle Works*, vol. 9, p. 107.

Conversation Twelve
Ongoing Education

1. Dewey, "My Pedagogic Creed" in *The Early Works*, vol. 5, p. 93.
2. Dewey, *The Public and Its Problems* in *The Later Works*, vol. 2, p. 360.
3. Ibid., p. 372.
4. Dewey, "Creative Democracy" in *The Later Works*, vol. 14, p. 227.
5. Quoted in Daisaku Ikeda, "Discussion Meetings: An SGI Tradition" in the Feb. 17, 2006, *World Tribune*, p. 2.
6. Quoted in Daisaku Ikeda, *The New Human Revolution*, vol. 7 (Santa Monica, Calif.: World Tribune Press, 2001), p. 10.
7. Quoted in Daisaku Ikeda, *The New Human Revolution*, vol. 14 (Santa Monica, Calif.: World Tribune Press, 2007), p. 72.

Conversation Thirteen
Dialogue and Transformation

1. Lamont, *Dialogue on John Dewey*, p. 21.
2. John Dewey, *Art As Experience* in *The Later Works of John Dewey, 1925–1953*; vol. 10, 1934, Jo Ann Boydston, ed., Abraham Kaplan, intro. (Carbondale, Ill.: Southern Illinois University Press, 2008), p. 111.
3. In a letter to U. S. Army Private Charles E. Witzell, Dewey wrote: "I have taught many years and I don't think that any of my students would say that I set out to undermine anyone's faith.... The lectures

making up [*A Common Faith*] were meant for those whose religious beliefs had been abandoned, and who were given the impression that their abandonment left them without any religious beliefs whatever. I wanted to show them that religious values are not a monopoly of any one class or sect and are still open to them." Quoted in A. G. Rud, Jim Garrison, Lynda Stone, *John Dewey at 150: Reflections for a New Century* (West Lafayette, Ind.: Purdue University Press, 2009), p. 25.

4. Nichiren, *The Writings*, vol. I, p. 1086.
5. Dewey, "From Absolutism to Experimentalism" in *The Later Works*, vol. 5, p. 153.
6. *See* Huxley and Youmans, *The Elements of Physiology and Hygiene*.
7. Dewey, "From Absolutism to Experimentalism" in *The Later Works*, vol. 5, p. 147.
8. Dewey, *Democracy and Education* in *The Middle Works*, vol. 9, p. 338.
9. John Dewey, *Experience and Nature* in *The Later Works of John Dewey, 1925–1953*; vol. 1, 1925, Jo Ann Boydston, ed., Sidney Hook, intro. (Carbondale, Ill.: Southern Illinois University Press, 2008), p. 132.
10. Ibid.
11. Ibid.
12. Dewey, *Ethics* in *The Later Works*, vol. 7, p. 323. In this same section of the chapter "Morals and Social Problems," Dewey makes further observations about Western scientific thinking that resonate strongly with the Buddhist concept of dependent origination: "Nothing in the universe, not even physical things, exist apart from some form of association; there is nothing from the atom to man which is not involved in conjoint action."
13. Walt Whitman, "Miracles" in *Poetry and Prose*, Justin Kaplan, ed. (New York: Library of America, 1982) p. 514.
14. Daisaku Ikeda met with former president Richard von Weizsäcker on June 12, 1991. Translated from Japanese: Richard von Weizsäcker, *Heiwa e no Taiwa: Waitsuzekka-shi Rainichi Zenhatsugen* (Dialogues for Peace: Collected Statements Made by Richard von Weizsäcker during His Visits to Japan) (Tokyo: Mainichi Shimbunsha Shochi Osaka Jikko Iinkai, 1999). *Also see* SGI Newsletter No. 663.
15. *See* Ikeda, "Mahayana Buddhism and Twenty-first-Century Civilization" in *A New Humanism*, pp. 165–75.
16. Dewey, "Creative Democracy" in *The Later Works*, vol. 14, p. 229.

Conversation Fourteen
Breaking the Cycle of Violence

1. Quoted in Daisaku Ikeda, "The Century of Health and Long Life" in the Feb. 6, 2004, *World Tribune*, p. 2. *Also see* SGI Newsletter No. 5838 (December 25, 2003).
2. Jane Addams, *Twenty Years at Hull House: With Autobiographical Notes* (New York: The Macmillan Company, 1911), p. 60.
3. John Dewey, *The Correspondence of John Dewey, 1871–1952*, vol. I: 1871–1918 (Charlottesville, Va.: InteLex Corp.), 1894.10.10 (00206): John Dewey to Alice Chipman Dewey.
4. *See* Marilyn Fischer, "Jane Addams's Critique of Capitalism as Patriarchal" in *Feminist Interpretations of John Dewey*, Charlene Haddock Seigfried, ed. (University Park, Penn.: Pennsylvania State University Press, 2002), p. 281.
5. Jane Addams, *A New Conscience and an Ancient Evil* (New York: The Macmillan Company, 1912), p. 11.
6. Dewey, *Ethics* in *The Later Works*, vol. 7, p. 270.
7. Jane Addams, *Peace and Bread in Time of War* (New York: The Macmillan Company, 1922), p. 4.
8. *See* "Queen's University Honors SGI President" in *World Tribune*, June 12, 2009, pp. 1, 8. *Also see* SGI Newsletter No. 7872 (October 13, 2009).
9. In 1983, Daisaku Ikeda began writing peace proposals and since then has sent them annually to the United Nations. The publication date each year is January 26, the anniversary of the founding of the Soka Gakkai International. These proposals offer perspectives on critical issues facing humanity, suggesting solutions and responses grounded in Buddhist humanism. They also put forth specific agendas for strengthening the United Nations, including avenues for the involvement of civil society.
10. "SGI President Meets with Betty Williams" in *World Tribune*, Jan. 26, 2007, p. 1. *Also see* SGI Newsletter No. 7035 (November 28, 2006).
11. Ibid.
12. Ibid.
13. Ibid.
14. Dewey, *The Public and Its Problems* in *The Later Works*, vol. 2, p. 371.

Conversation Fifteen
Creative Democracy

1. The Marco Polo Bridge Incident, also known in China as the Lugouqiao Incident, was a battle between the Republic of China's National Revolutionary Army and the Imperial Japanese Army. It is considered the start of the Second Sino-Japanese War (1937–45).
2. Quoted in Jessica Ching-Sze Wang, *John Dewey in China: To Teach and to Learn* (Albany, N. Y.: State University of New York Press, 2007), p. 80 (quotes from Dewey, *The Middle Works*, vol. 13, p. 222).
3. In 1927, just a few years after the Deweys returned to the United States, China entered into a long period of civil war (interrupted by the Sino-Japanese War from 1937 to 1945) that concluded with Mao Zedong's establishment of the People's Republic of China in late 1949. Dewey's philosophy is explicitly non-revolutionary, which made it a poor fit with Mao's ruling philosophy, which advocated active suppression of what the Communist Party identified as counter-revolutionary thinking. This suppression culminated with the Cultural Revolution, which began in 1966 and ended with Mao's death in 1976. In recent decades, China has moved toward renewed engagement with Western philosophy, including that of Dewey.
4. Dewey, "Creative Democracy" in *The Later Works*, vol. 14, p. 226.
5. Ibid., p. 230.
6. Dewey, *The Public and Its Problems* in *The Later Works*, vol. 2, p. 350.
7. Walt Whitman, preface to *Leaves of Grass* in *Poetry and Prose*, pp. 5–6.
8. John Dewey, "Maeterlinck's Philosophy of Life" in *The Middle Works of John Dewey, 1899–1924*; vol. 6, 1910–1911, Jo Ann Boydston, ed., H. S. Thayer and V. T. Thayer, intro. (Carbondale, Ill.: Southern Illinois University Press, 2008), p. 135.
9. Whitman, *Democratic Vistas* in *Poetry and Prose*, p. 948.
10. In October 2012, the Walt Whitman Birthplace Association presented Daisaku Ikeda with a lifelong honorary membership.
11. Dewey, *The Correspondence of John Dewey*, vol. I. 1887.04.16, 17 (00057), John Dewey to Alice Chipman Dewey.
12. Whitman, *Leaves of Grass* in *Poetry and Prose*, p. 357.
13. Horace Traubel, *With Walt Whitman in Camden*, vol. 3 (New York: Mitchell Kennerley, 1914), p. 410.

14. Whitman, *Democratic Vistas* in *Poetry and Prose*, p. 949.
15. Dewey, "The Live Creature and 'Ethereal Things'" in *The Later Works*, vol. 10, p. 30.
16. Dewey, "Maeterlinck's Philosophy of Life" in *The Middle Works*, vol. 6, p. 135.
17. Ikeda, "Mahayana Buddhism and Twenty-first-Century Civilization" in *A New Humanism*, p. 171.
18. Ibid.

Conversation Sixteen
Many Kinds of Democracy

1. Yehudi Menuhin and Curtis W. Davis, *The Music of Man* (York, U.K.: Methuen Publications, 1979), p. 206.
2. Dewey, *Experience and Nature* in *The Later Works*, vol. 1, p. 159.
3. Dewey, "From Absolutism to Experimentalism" in *The Later Works*, vol. 5, p. 159.
4. *See* Dewey, "Creative Democracy" in *The Later Works*, vol. 14, p. 228.
5. Toynbee and Ikeda, *Choose Life*, p. 216.
6. John Dewey, "Philosophy and Democracy" in *The Middle Works of John Dewey, 1899–1924*; vol. 11, 1918–1919, Jo Ann Boydston, ed., Oscar Handlin and Lilian Handlin, intro. (Carbondale, Ill.: Southern Illinois University Press, 2008), p. 45.
7. Buddhism teaches a principle called, in Japanese, *zuiho bini*, or adapting the rules to match the place. *Zuiho* means "according to the place," and *bini* is part of the word for the Buddhist rules of self-discipline—or, by extension, the rules of correct behavior to be observed in life. In other words, one may act in accordance with local customs (e.g., different cultures, traditions, and manners and customs) so long as the fundamental principles of Buddhism are not violated.
8. Ching-Sze Wang, *John Dewey in China*, p. 10.
9. *See* Ikeda, "A New Global Awareness" in *A New Humanism*, pp. 101–09.
10. Translated from Japanese. Tsunesaburo Makiguchi, *Makiguchi Tsunesaburo zenshu*, vol. 6, p. 69.
11. *See* Larry A. Hickman, "Teaching Religion in a Global Culture," presentation for meeting of the Eleventh Biennial Conference of the

International Network of Philosophers of Education, Kyoto University, August 9–12, 2008, http://www.educ.kyoto-u.ac.jp/~bambi/InpePlenary072508.pdf (accessed February 5, 2014).

12. Dewey, *A Common Faith* in *The Later Works*, vol. 9, p. 19.

Conversation Seventeen
Science and Technology

1. Whitman, preface to *Leaves of Grass*, p. 15.
2. Ibid.
3. Dewey, *Individualism, Old and New* in *The Later Works*, vol. 5, p. 86.
4. Ibid.
5. Ibid., p. 52.
6. Toynbee and Ikeda, *Choose Life*, p. 342.
7. Ibid., p. 306.
8. Dewey, *Individualism, Old and New* in *The Later Works*, vol. 5, p. 88.
9. Ibid., p. 89.
10. Ibid., p. 80.
11. Dewey, "What Humanism Means to Me" in *The Later Works*, vol. 5, p. 266.
12. Dewey, *Individualism, Old and New* in *The Later Works*, vol. 5, p. 88.
13. Quoted in Daisaku Ikeda, *The Heart of the Lotus Sutra* (Santa Monica, Calif.: World Tribune Press, 2014), p. 72.
14. Joseph Rotblat and Daisaku Ikeda, *A Quest for Global Peace* (London: I. B. Tauris & Co. Ltd, 2007), p. 23.
15. Pauling and Ikeda, *A Lifelong Quest for Peace*, p. 41.
16. Dewey, "What I Believe" in *The Later Works*, vol. 5, p. 270.

Conversation Eighteen
A Responsive Philosophy

1. John Dewey and Alice Chipman Dewey, "March 5" in *Letters from China and Japan*, Evelyn Dewey, ed. (New York: E.P. Dutton & Company, 1920), p. 52.
2. John Dewey, *Reconstruction in Philosophy* in *The Middle Works of John Dewey, 1899–1924*; vol. 12, 1920, Jo Ann Boydston, ed., Ralph Ross, intro. (Carbondale, Ill.: Southern Illinois University Press, 1988), p. 79.

3. Ibid., p. 135.
4. Ibid., pp. 136–37.
5. Dewey, "Qualitative Thought" in *The Later Works*, vol. 5, p. 249.
6. Dewey, *Art as Experience* in *The Later Works*, vol. 10, p. 40.
7. John Dewey, *Human Conduct and Nature* in *The Middle Works of John Dewey, 1899–1924*; vol. 14, 1922, Jo Ann Boydston, ed., Murray G. Murphy, intro. (Carbondale, Ill.: Southern Illinois University Press, 2008), p. 136.
8. Daisaku Ikeda, *The New Human Revolution*, vol. 3 (Santa Monica, Calif.: World Tribune Press, 1996), pp. 169–70.
9. Dewey, *Reconstruction in Philosophy* in *The Middle Works*, vol. 12, p. 146.
10. *See* John Dewey, "Logical Method and Law" in *The Middle Works of John Dewey, 1899–1924*; vol. 15, 1923–1924, Jo Ann Boydston, ed., Carl Cohen, intro. (Carbondale, Ill.: Southern Illinois University Press, 2008), pp. 70–71. *See also* Dewey, "Some Stages of Logical Thought" in *The Middle Works*, vol. 1, p. 164.
11. Dewey, *Construction and Criticism* in *The Later Works*, vol. 5, p. 134.
12. Dewey, "From Absolutism to Experimentalism" in *The Later Works*, vol. 5, p. 159.
13. Dewey, *Reconstruction in Philosophy* in *The Middle Works*, vol. 12, p. 128.
14. John Dewey, "The Influence of Darwinism on Philosophy" in *The Middle Works of John Dewey, 1899–1924*; vol. 4, 1907–1909, Jo Ann Boydston, ed., Lewis E. Hahn, intro. (Carbondale, Ill.: Southern Illinois University Press, 2008), p. 3.
15. Dewey, *Reconstruction in Philosophy* in *The Middle Works*, vol. 12, pp. 180–81.
16. Nichiren, *The Writings*, vol. II, p. 843.
17. Daisaku Ikeda, "Toward a New Era of Value Creation," 2010 peace proposal, http://www.sgi.org/assets/pdf/peace2010(2).pdf (accessed February 4, 2014).
18. *Sutta-Nipata*, Hammalawa Saddhatissa, trans. (London: Curzon Press, 1994), pp. 81–82.
19. Daisaku Ikeda, Katsuji Saito, Takanori Endo, Haruo Suda, *The Wisdom of the Lotus Sutra: A Discussion*, vol. III (Santa Monica, Calif.: World Tribune Press, 2001), p. 81.
20. Dewey, *A Common Faith* in *The Later Works*, vol. 9, p. 32.

CONVERSATION NINETEEN
RELIGIOUS HUMANISM

1. Dewey, *A Common Faith* in *The Later Works*, vol. 9, p. 58.
2. Ibid., p. 19.
3. Toynbee and Ikeda, *Choose Life*, p. 293.
4. Quoted in Steven Rockefeller, *John Dewey: Religious Faith and Democratic Humanism* (New York: Columbia University Press, 1991), pp. 208, 592.
5. Dewey, *A Common Faith* in *The Later Works*, vol. 9, pp. 19–20.
6. Ibid., p. 33.
7. Ikeda, *The Human Revolution*, Book One, p. viii.
8. Dewey, *A Common Faith* in *The Later Works*, vol. 9, p. 8.
9. Ibid., p. 35.
10. Nichiren, *The Writings*, vol. II, p. 39.
11. *The Lotus Sutra and Its Opening and Closing Sutras*, p. 227.
12. Nichiren, *The Record of the Orally Transmitted Teachings*, p. 109.

CONVERSATION TWENTY
EXPANDING OPPORTUNITY, EXPANDING DEMOCRACY

1. Quoted in *John Dewey at 150: Reflections for a New Century*, A. G. Rud, Jim Garrison, and Lynda Stone, eds. (West Lafayette, Ind.: Purdue University Press, 2009), p. 77.
2. Dewey, "Is Co-Education Injurious to Girls?" in *The Middle Works*, vol. 6, p. 159.
3. *See* Jerry A. Jacobs, "Gender Inequality and Higher Education," *Annual Review of Sociology*, 1996, 22: 153–85.
4. Daisaku Ikeda, René Simard, and Guy Bourgeault, *On Being Human* (Montreal: Les Presses de I'Université de Montréal, 2002), p. 21.
5. "Prof. Dewey Urges New Social Policy," Dec. 20, 1929, *New York Times*.
6. Lamont, *Dialogue on John Dewey*, p. 22.
7. Dewey, "Creative Democracy" in *The Later Works*, vol. 14, p. 229.

Index

About the Authors

JIM GARRISON is a professor of philosophy of education at Virginia Tech in Blacksburg, Virginia, where he also holds appointments in the department of philosophy, the science, technology, and society program, and the alliance for social, political, ethical, and cultural thought, as well as in the School of Education. His work concentrates on philosophical pragmatism, especially that of John Dewey. Awards include the John Dewey Society Outstanding Achievement Award and the Medal of Highest Honor from Soka University (Japan). He is a past president of the Philosophy of Education Society as well as the John Dewey Society and the Society of Professors of Education. Author of over 230 publications, his books include *Dewey and Eros: Wisdom and Desire in the Art of Teaching* (1997). He most recently co-edited with A. G. Rud the book *Reverence in Teaching* (2012), and co-authored, with Stefan Neubert and Kersten Reich, *John Dewey's Philosophy of Education – An Introduction and Recontextualization for Our Times* (2012).

LARRY A. HICKMAN is director of the Center for Dewey Studies and professor of philosophy at Southern Illinois University Carbondale. With 180 presentations in the United States and 18 foreign countries, his work as an ambassador for the Center has contributed to the global renaissance of Dewey studies. A past president of the John Dewey Society, Dr. Hickman has published influential studies on Dewey's philosophy of technology. At SIUC, Dr. Hickman teaches courses on the philosophy of technology, classical American philosophy, and the philosophy of education. His monographs include *John Dewey's Pragmatic Technology* (1990) and *Pragmatism as Post-Postmodernism: Lessons from John Dewey* (2007). He edited *The Essential Dewey* (1998) with Thomas Alexander and *The Correspondence of John Dewey* (1999, 2001, 2005, 2008). In addition, he has published articles on technology, environmental philosophy, critical theory, pragmatism, education, film studies, and the philosophy of religion.

Daisaku Ikeda is president of the Soka Gakkai International, a lay Buddhist organization with more than twelve million members worldwide. He has written and lectured widely on Buddhism, humanism, and global ethics. More than fifty of his dialogues have been published, including conversations with figures such as Mikhail Gorbachev, Hazel Henderson, Elise Boulding, Joseph Rotblat, Linus Pauling, and Arnold Toynbee. Dedicated to education that promotes humanistic ideals, President Ikeda founded Soka University in Tokyo in 1971 and, in 2001, Soka University of America in Aliso Viejo, California.